WILLIAM PALMER OF RUGELEY
An enlargement of a picture originally used in the *Illustrated times* 2nd February 1856. It also appeared in George Fletcher's book, *"The Life & Career of Dr. William Palmer of Rugeley"* (published 1925) when it was entitled WILLIAM PALMER AT THE OAKS (1854).

Contents

A photograph of the Palmer Family grave taken around 1925
Picture from *Life and Career of Dr William Palmer* published in 1925.
Palmer's body was buried within the grounds of Stafford Gaol.

Introduction

Few people entering the quiet Staffordshire churchyard of St.Augustine's Parish Church in Rugeley would give a second glance at the old grave of John Parsons Cook that lies beneath the yew tree.

Photograph of the grave of John Parsons Cook taken in March 2003 (D. Lewis).

However, the agonizingly painful death, in 1855, of Palmer's friend and racing companion, John Parsons Cook, led to a major scandal that made headline news throughout the civilized world. It led to Dr. William Palmer being publicly hanged for murder outside Stafford Gaol at 8.00 a.m. on 14th June1856. By then, so great was the interest in the case that, at a time when Stafford's population was only about twelve and a half thousand, a crowd in excess of thirty thousand turned up to see Palmer's final moments at the end of a hangman's rope.

After Palmer had been arrested and accused of poisoning Cook, reporters descended upon Rugeley and interviewed any and all of the potential witnesses. Newspapers printed every damning story that the local gossips could come up with and, in the months leading up to his trial, people throughout England were devouring each new sordid and scandalous revelation. Effectively Palmer was tried and convicted by the national press in a manner that hopefully, since the Contempt of Court Act 1981, would not be permitted today. Amongst his many "alleged victims" were his outrageous mother-in-law, four of his five children, Annie his lovely wife, and Walter his drunken brother, to name but a few.

Murder amongst the lower classes could be expected once in a while. Even an occasional dastardly deed perpetrated by a member of the aristocracy might hit the headlines. The public were, however, genuinely shocked by the possibility that a member of the medical profession, one who you should be able to trust with your life, could be linked to such a hideous series of murders, made all the

4

more shocking by the fact that most victims had been a close relative or friend.

In the end Palmer was only actually tried and convicted of one murder, that of John Parsons Cook, but with all the gossip and bad press surrounding the case he soon stood accused of at least a dozen other suspicious deaths. So infamous did he become that Palmer's waxwork effigy stood for 127 years in Madame Tussaud's Chamber of Horrors (London). He was branded as a cold, callous serial killer and commonly given the title of "The Rugeley Poisoner" or "The Prince of Poisoners".

Two Acts of Parliament were made law as a direct result of the case, including the one often referred to as the "Palmer Act". This Act allowed the case to be tried at London's Old Bailey, rather than in Staffordshire where the crime was committed, in the hope of finding an unbiased jury. The other Act served to limit people so that they could not insure a person unless there was proof that they would directly suffer financially as a result of that person's death. There also needed to be proof of a 'money interest' up to the value of the insurance sum proposed.

The two post mortems on John Parsons Cook were conducted in a most unprofessional manner with no strychnine ever being found in the body. Top medical experts of their day, in this the first case of strychnine poisoning to be brought before a British court, failed to agree that strychnine poisoning had been the cause of death. His trial is still widely regarded as the most memorable trial of the Nineteenth Century, with the Attorney General himself, one of the finest orators of his generation, personally leading the prosecution for the Crown, seemingly desperate to get a conviction. Many aspects of the case might have been considered farcical had the crime not been so monstrous and had not the life of the accused man depended upon the verdict. This book relates the tales of witnesses going missing, a Defence lawyer's last-minute defection to the Prosecution and the victim's stepfather having regular meetings with a Prosecution witness. Unfortunately for Palmer, his main Defence witness, who was to provide him with an alibi, was totally discredited in court because of his alleged affair with Palmer's widowed mother.

To the very end **Palmer always maintained that Cook did not die from strychnine** in contradiction of the Prosecution's allegation. Even when the hangman's rope awaited him he did not confess to murder, in spite of the many opportunities afforded him.

That he was a rogue, a gambler, a womaniser, heavily in debt, guilty of attempted bribery, fraud and forgery, is beyond doubt, but was he actually a serial killer? Read all the rumours, the gossip and the evidence then make up your own mind: -

"Just how many, if any, did Dr. William Palmer poison?"

THE TALBOT ARMS, RUGELEY, THE SCENE OF COOK'S DEATH

Taken from a print in
THE TIMES
REPORT
OF THE
TRIAL OF WILLIAM PALMER,
FOR POISONING JOHN PARSONS COOK,
AT RUGELEY.

Published by Ward Locke 1856

Chapter 1: The Death of John Parsons Cook

The crime for which William Palmer was hanged

William Palmer, a ruddy-faced, some would say handsome, solidly built country doctor and racehorse owner in his early thirties was, by 1855, heavily in debt with his debts rapidly mounting. His expensive string of racehorses was costing far in excess of the meagre winnings that they brought in. An insurance company, with whom he had insured his brother Walter's life, was refusing to pay up. A girlfriend called Jane was blackmailing him. Moneylenders charging exorbitant rates were hounding him for their money. He was also concerned because he had forged his mother's signature on loan guarantees for which offences he could face fraud charges. His answer was to continue desperately gambling in the hope of winning enough money to pay back what he owed.

John Parsons Cook, who was born in Catthorpe and lived in Lutterworth, Leicestershire, had been a very close friend of Dr. William Palmer for around two years. Originally Cook was articled to a solicitor in Watling; however, having inherited £12,000, he retired from being a solicitor to spend a great deal of time and money on horse racing. After gaining his inheritance Cook "ran wild", leading a riotous life. He had never had good health and his new style of living did nothing to improve the situation. He was described as "a pale weak-looking young man" and it was even rumoured that Palmer was treating him for syphilis.

When 28 year old Cook died, in the early hours of the 21st November 1855, there began a chain of events that brought to the public a tale that scandalised the whole country. The build up to Cook's death is chronicled below.

Tuesday 13th November 1855: Palmer and Samuel Cheshire, the Rugeley postmaster, went with their friend John Parson Cook, to Shrewsbury Races. Cook won around £3,000 when his horse, *Polestar*, came first in the Shrewsbury Handicap Race. An hour later Palmer left Cook and returned to Rugeley. Cook meantime threw a celebratory meal, at the Raven Hotel in Shrewsbury, for some of his friends, treating his guests to "foaming beakers of provincial champagne".

Wednesday 14th November 1855: Palmer received a threatening letter from Thomas Pratt, a solicitor and moneylender, demanding his money. Palmer, in the company of George Myatt (a saddler from Rugeley), returned to Shrewsbury Races. That evening Palmer dined at the Raven Inn in Shrewsbury with Cook, Cheshire, Ishmael Fisher (a wine merchant), George Herring (an independent gentleman), George Myatt and George Read (who "kept a house frequented by sporting gentlemen").

At one stage in the evening Palmer went out to the housemaid's pantry. Here he was visited by Mrs. Ann Brookes from Manchester, who was later described in court as "a lady who attends races". She had come to ask him about a jockey. When she first saw him she observed Palmer pouring some fluid from a small bottle into a tumbler and then watched him shake it up and down before holding it up to the gaslight.

Palmer did not seem distressed by her seeing him do this and told her that he would be with her in a minute. He returned to the room and a tray of brandy was brought in. When Cook drank his brandy he jumped up and complained that it burnt his throat. At this Palmer took the tumbler and drank from it then handed the glass to Read saying, "Taste it; there's nothing in it. Cook says it's drugged".

Read replied, "What is the good of giving it to me when you have drunk the very dregs?"

Cook was not feeling well and retired to his bedroom taking Herring and Fisher with him. He gave Fisher his money belt to keep safe for him. A doctor was sent for and again in the early morning they sent for help.

Thursday 15th November 1855: Cook was a little better in the morning and was able to get up and eat some breakfast. That day Palmer lost heavily when his horse, *Nettle*, failed to win his race. Had *Nettle* won Palmer stood to win around £5,000. In the evening Cook and Palmer returned to Rugeley where Cook booked into Room 10 at the Talbot Arms, the hotel which stood opposite Palmer's house. Cook went straight to bed.

From the '*Times Report of the Trial of William Palmer, for Poisoning John Parsons Cook, at Rugeley'. Published 1856*
It was labelled High Street but was in fact Market Street and shows to the left the Talbot Arms where Cook died and to the right, behind the railings, Palmer's house.

Friday 16ᵗʰ November 1855: Cook got up in the afternoon and dined with Palmer.

Saturday 17ᵗʰ November 1855: Palmer visited Cook early in the morning and ordered some coffee for him. Palmer called in the rather elderly Dr. Bamford, an old family friend, to treat Cook. Unfortunately Cook was very ill and was constantly being violently sick. Palmer was in and out all day to visit his sick friend.

Sunday 18ᵗʰ November 1855: Dr. Bamford, together with Palmer, again visited Cook. The chambermaid Elizabeth Mills later claimed that she had been sick after tasting some broth that Palmer had sent for Cook to eat.

Monday 19ᵗʰ November 1855: Palmer went to London with Cook's betting books and managed to "obtain" most of Cook's winnings before returning to Rugeley where he found Cook to be slightly recovered. This was the night that Newton, later to be a prosecution witness, claimed Palmer bought three grains of strychnine from him at 9.00 p.m. However Jere Smith gave Palmer an alibi stating that he could not have bought poison at the time Newton claimed, as Palmer had not returned from London by that time. When the case came to court another witness, the driver of the "fly" who had brought Palmer from Stafford Railway Station to Rugeley, *"went missing"* and could not be called by the Defence.

Tuesday 20ᵗʰ November 1855: Cook was very ill in the early hours but rallied. Dr. Jones, Cook's long-time friend and doctor, arrived at 2.00 p.m. Palmer had written to Dr. Jones because of Cook's poor state of health.

Wednesday 21ˢᵗ November 1855: Cook, aged 28, died in agony at 1.00 a.m. *The Illustrated Times* of 2ⁿᵈ February 1856, under the heading DEATH BED SCENE, gave the following account of the gruesome scene:

> *...........Old Dr. Bamford, aged 82, had been called in before, and had prescribed two opiate pills, which Mr. Palmer himself had from him. Mr. Jones slept in the same room with his friend; the foot of the beds were opposite to each other, the room being sufficiently large, and Mr. Cook lying between the door and the window. A little after eleven Mr. Palmer went across and gave the sick man two pills supposed to be morphine vomiting ensued but the pills remained on the stomach. About midnight Mr. Jones undressed himself and turned in. He had not lain down above twenty minutes, when his friend called to him in alarm, and begged that Mr. Palmer might be sent for immediately. That gentleman was by his bedside within three minutes, foolishly volunteering the remark that he had never dressed so quickly in his life before. He then gave him two pills which he brought with him, saying that they were ammonia pills - a preparation never kept ready made up, because of evaporation. A terrible*

scene now ensued. Wildly shrieking, the patient tossed about in fearful convulsions; his limbs were so rigid that it was impossible to raise him, though he entreated that they would do so, as he felt that he was suffocating. Every muscle was convulsed; his body bent upwards like a bow; they turned him over on his left side; the action of the heart gradually ceased; and he was dead.

As soon as Cook had died Mary Keeley, a widow from Rugeley, was sent for by Palmer to "lay out the body". She came immediately with her sister-in-law. Mary was later called to give evidence at Palmer's trial in London. She stated that she had laid out many corpses before but had never found a body as stiff as Cook's.

Cook was dead, but, at this stage, no one suspected that he had been murdered.

✝ ✝ ✝

Cook's nearest relative was his stepfather, Mr. William Stevens, a retired merchant. On the same day that Cook died Dr. Jones left Rugeley and took the train to London to inform Mr. Stevens of Cook's death. On the Thursday Stevens, accompanied by Dr. Jones, went to Lutterworth to search for Cook's will. Then on the Friday they travelled to Rugeley arriving in the middle of the morning and proceeded straight to the Talbot Arms where they met Palmer and went to view Cook's body.

It appears that Stevens took an instant dislike to Palmer. Stevens had often lectured Cook on the dangers of wasting his time and money on gambling and horse racing and had associated Palmer with his stepson's wayward lifestyle. He was surprised and a little annoyed to find that Palmer had already ordered a coffin without first asking him.

Was the ordering of the coffin the action of a thoughtful friend or the action of someone trying to quickly dispose of any evidence?

After viewing the body Stevens asked Palmer if he knew about Cook's business affairs. Stevens was alarmed when Palmer told him that he held legal papers which showed that there were outstanding bills totalling £4,000 that Cook alone had been responsible for paying. Stevens replied that there wouldn't be even 4,000 shillings in Cook's estate with which to pay the bills. Later Stevens ordered lunch for Doctors Bamford and Jones and, finding Palmer still loitering, felt obliged to extend an invitation for him to join them.

After the meal Stevens asked Dr. Jones to go to Cook's room and bring down Cook's papers and his betting book. Palmer accompanied Jones but they returned after ten minutes without the betting book. Palmer said that it did not matter as all bets were void when someone died, but Stevens was suspicious and insisted

Cook's stepfather Mr. Stevens:
From a book of the Palmer story,
found in the William Salt Library,
Stafford, written in Greek,
published in 1860.

that the betting book should be found. Palmer replied in an off-hand manner, "Oh I dare say they will turn up". Stevens ordered Cook's room to be locked and that no one be given access until he returned from London.

It is safe to say that, without the intervention of Mr. Stevens, Palmer would not have been brought to trial for the murder of John Parsons Cook. Mr. Stevens wrote to the Stafford Coroner urgently requesting that an inquest needed to be held into Cook's death. At the same time he also wrote to Dr. Harland, a consulting physician from Stafford, requesting him to conduct the post-mortem.

Stevens then travelled to London where he sought advice from a solicitor. By chance, when returning from London the next day, he met Palmer who had been to London to see the moneylender Thomas Pratt. They were both returning to Rugeley on the same train.

On the train Stevens informed him that he intended to insist upon a post-mortem but it was reported that Palmer did not seem upset by the news but asked who would be conducting the post-mortem. Stevens also appointed a solicitor to investigate Cook's financial affairs and arranged for the specimens, taken at the post-mortem, to be sent for analysis by Dr. Alfred Swaine Taylor (Fellow of the College of Physicians) at Guy's hospital who considered himself to be an expert in poisons.

On Sunday 25th November 1855 Palmer obtained a death certificate from the elderly Dr. Bamford which stated that Cook had died from apoplexy. Later in the day Palmer tried to persuade Cheshire, the postmaster, to sign a form to say that he was witness to Cook having signed, shortly before his death, the bills for £4,000 that Palmer claimed Cook had been responsible for. Cheshire refused to do this and Palmer is reputed to have responded, "Oh, it doesn't matter, as Cook's friends will never think of disputing it".

Mr. Stevens became very active before the trial and wrote several letters concerning the case that were printed in the Times newspaper suggesting that Palmer should be brought to justice for murdering his stepson. He also had many meetings with one particular prosecution witnesses, namely the chambermaid Elizabeth Mills who, after Cook's death, had moved to live in London. He later claimed in his evidence to the court that Mills and he had not discussed evidence that she was to later give in court.

The original earth covered grave of John Parsons Cook.
From the Times Report of the Trial of William Palmer, *published 1856.*

John Parsons Cook was buried in Rugeley but for several years his grave was merely covered with an earth mound. In 1859 or 1860 the Reverend Atkinson had a stone placed upon his grave where it lies to this day. The gravestone was made of limestone but the inscription inaccurately stated that Cook died 22nd November 1855, when in fact he died on at around 1.00 a.m. on 21st November 1855. Later the date was scratched out.

In all accounts written in 1856 they referred to Cook and his stepfather as having a close relationship. If they were so close why then did his stepfather permit Cook to be buried in Rugeley rather than in the family vault in London? Also why did the stepfather himself not purchase a headstone for Cook's grave?

What was the cause of John Parsons Cook's death?   Did Palmer poison Cook or was Palmer merely treating Cook for syphilis? If Palmer poisoned Cook was it strychnine that he used as they later claimed in court?

Chapter 2: The Inquest

The post-mortems and inquest verdict on Cook:

The first post-mortem on Cook was held in the Assembly Room at the Talbot Arms on 26th November 1855, and was conducted in a most shambolic way. Surprisingly, several townsfolk were allowed to attend and watch the opening of the body, including the landlord Mr. Masters, Jere. Smith a solicitor and friend of the Palmer Family, Cheshire the Rugeley postmaster and many others, although why such a motley crowd were allowed to attend remains a mystery. The proceedings were conducted by Dr. John Harland, a Stafford physician, who also happened to be an acquaintance of Palmer. In fact Dr. Harland was one of the doctors who had passed Palmer's alcoholic brother Walter as being fit to be insured and was rewarded by Palmer for so doing, by being presented with a dozen bottles of port. It was claimed that Harland arrived without his medical equipment and even without a notebook or pencil. Harland had intended to call at the house of Dr. Bamford but was met in the street by Palmer who, Harland claimed, said that he was glad that it was someone he knew who was to conduct the post-mortem.

It is still hard to believe that such a serious exercise as a post-mortem could be conducted so carelessly and so unprofessionally. In spite of the presence of several doctors, Mr. Charles Devonshire and Mr. Charles Newton carried out the actual autopsy on the body. Devonshire was a young inexperienced medical student who was an assistant to Dr. Monkton. Newton was an unqualified assistant to Mr. Salt the Rugeley chemist and was conducting his first ever post-mortem. Before the autopsy Palmer had given Newton a couple of brandies to steady his nerves.

The unqualified Devonshire should have been given guidance and certainly stopped before he went and cut the stomach from end to end, carelessly turning it inside out and throwing it into a jar. As Devonshire was opening the stomach, Palmer was seen to push against Newton who subsequently bumped into Devonshire and some of the contents of the stomach spilled into the body. The stomach contained about three ounces of brownish fluid, which was emptied in to a jar. When Palmer saw this he was heard, by Harland, to say to Dr. Bamford in a loud whisper, "They won't hang us yet." The viscera (stomach organs), with their contents, were removed and placed in a jar, which was then sealed using two bladders. The jar was then placed upon the table near the body but shortly afterwards was found to be missing. Devonshire asked where the jar was and Palmer said straight away that he had moved it, "To make it more convenient for you to take away". He asked Palmer to bring the jar back and noticed that there was a cut in each bladder but that none of the contents had been lost.

Cook's stepfather had arranged for the contents of Cook's stomach to be examined by Professor Taylor a Fellow of the College of Physicians at Guy's Hospital. The famous Dr. Taylor, who considered himself an authority on poisons, had to try to analyse the samples sent to him but was so dissatisfied with what was sent that he immediately telegraphed requesting that new samples be taken. The second post-mortem on the body of Cook was held on 29th November 1855. This time Devonshire removed the liver, kidney, spleen and some blood.

Samuel Cheshire, the postmaster of Rugeley, was a friend of Palmer who was often allowed to borrow Palmer's horse and carriage to take Mrs. Cheshire for rides on Sunday afternoons. Palmer got his friend, to intercept any letters written to the Coroner and, when he read that Professor Taylor could find no traces of strychnine, prussic acid or opium in the post-mortem samples, he wrote to the Coroner a letter accompanied by presents of fish and game. The first present was a splendid hamper sent from London to the Coroner's private address in Stoke-on-Trent and the second delivered by Palmer's groom, George Bates, to the Coroner's house in Stafford.

Finally he sent Bates with a letter (see below) instructing Bates that the letter must be delivered by hand and that he should not let anyone see him deliver it. In the letter Palmer urged the Coroner to bring in a verdict of "death by natural causes" in view of what he had read, and enclosed a £10 note inside the letter.

Dec. 13th, 1855.
RUGELEY.

MY DEAR SIR,
I am sorry to tell you that I am still confined to bed. I don't think it was mentioned at the Inquest yesterday Dec. 12th, that Cook was taken ill on Sunday and Monday night, in the same way as he was on the Tuesday, when he died. The Chambermaid at the Crown Hotel (Master's) can prove this. I also believe that a man by the name of Fisher is coming down to prove he received some money at Shrewsbury. Now, here he could only pay Smith £10 out of £41 he owed him. Had you not better call Smith to prove this? And, again, whatever Professor Taylor may say tomorrow, he wrote from London last Tuesday week to Gardner to say, "We (Dr. Rees and I) have this day finished our analysis, and find no traces of either strychnine, prussic acid, or opium".

What can beat this from a man like Taylor, if he says what he has already said, and Dr. Harland's evidence? Mind you I know and saw it in black and white, what Taylor said to Gardner; but this is strictly private and confidential, but it is true.

As regards his betting-book, I know nothing of it, and it is of no good to anyone. I hope the verdict to-morrow will be that he died from natural causes, and thus end it.

> *Ever yours,*
> *W. P.*

The letter was eventually sent by the Coroner to the Home Secretary and was later produced at Palmer's trial where it was said to have had a damaging effect on the minds of the jury. Cheshire was imprisoned for two years for tampering with the mail and was brought from Newgate Prison to give evidence at Palmer's trial.

The Inquest scheduled for Wednesday 12th December was adjourned until Friday 14th December to allow Professor Taylor a longer time to prepare his report and was held at the Rugeley Borough Court in the Rugeley Town Hall, with William Webb Ward acting as coroner. Dr. Taylor stated that he could not find any trace of strychnine but said that the symptoms led him to believe that Palmer administered strychnine in the pills that he gave to Cook on the Monday and Tuesday. It was commented upon in one newspaper that Dr. Taylor sat by the Coroner and asked more damning questions at the Inquest than the Coroner himself.

Many of Palmer's neighbours crowded into the Town Hall. At almost 11 p.m. on Saturday December 15th 1855, after a 2-day inquest, they heard the foreman of the Coroner's jury, after retiring for six or seven minutes, deliver a verdict that, **"We find that the deceased died of poison wilfully administered to him by William Palmer"**. This in itself was incorrect procedure. The coroner's jury was only supposed to be investigating the cause of death and it would have been normal practice to adjourn any inquest, which might involve a charge of murder, until all criminal proceedings had been finished.

In the *Illustrated Times* dated 14th June 1856 which was, by a bizarre coincidence, the day of Palmer's execution, there was a brief note about Coroner Ward:

> *CORONER WARD.— At the annual general meeting of the Coroners' Society of England and Wales, held last week, it was unanimously resolved, that, "the conduct of Mr. Ward, the coroner for Staffordshire on the occasion of holding the inquest on the body of John Parsons Cook, was discreditable, and if left uncensored by this society, will have the effect of lowering the office of coroner in public opinion; and that, regarding the ancient institution as one of the surest safeguards for the security of life and the detection of crime, we cannot but lament that Mr. Ward should have acted as he appears to have done on the late inquiry, and that he should have laid himself open to the severe censure he received at the hands of the Lord Chief Justice.*

Coroner William Webb Ward from the Times Report of the Trial of William Palmer *published 1856.*

Captain Hatton, Chief of the Staffordshire Constabulary who went from the inquest verdict to Palmer's house to arrest him.

From the Times report of the Trial of William Palmer *published 1856.*

Chapter 3: Palmer's Arrest

Palmer is arrested after the inquest verdict

So it was that late on the Saturday, after the inquest verdict that William Palmer had wilfully murdered John Parsons Cook, the Chief Constable went straight to Palmer's house to arrest him. However Palmer was ill in bed having been too ill to attend the inquest. He was already under house arrest by Sheriff's men because a warrant had been taken out against him by the moneylender, Padwick, on a charge of forgery; a case that was later tried at Westminster on January 20th 1856.

Palmer was still considered too ill to be transferred to gaol, so two police constables were left in charge of him and he remained in his home until late on Sunday night when he was taken by road to Stafford Gaol. They moved him at this time in preference to waiting for daylight because of the strong hostile reaction of some of the public following the inquest verdict. All Sunday a large crowd of people had gathered outside Palmer's house in the hope of catching a glimpse of the prisoner before he was escorted to prison.

A view of the Gateway to Stafford Gaol from The Illustrated Times *dated 14th June 1856 (The view of the gaol is thought to be from before 1856)*

As soon as he arrived at Stafford Gaol Palmer, who was still feeling extremely unwell, went straight to bed, his clothes were taken off him and he was given another suit of clothes. Palmer objected to wearing the new clothes and was very insistent that his own clothes be returned to him. This led to the suspicion that he had some poison secretly hidden in his clothes. The Prison Governor, Captain William Fulford, ordered that the clothes be meticulously searched for any hidden tablets or powder, but when no substances were found, some two weeks later, the clothes were returned to Palmer.

In the article accompanying the print of the prison the Illustrated Times said:

EVEN Stafford Jail itself never contemplated, perhaps, the unhappy interest which surrounds it.

Almost at all hours of the twenty-four groups of earnest gossipers collect before its walls, and discuss the demerits of the convict lying in some mysterious cell. The thoughts of thousands at a greater distance continually revert to this Palmer prison-house; to assist their imagination, we present a faithful portraiture of the building. (See picture on the previous page).

The Gateway to the Gaol was known as the Lodge and contained a room for the turnkeys (later referred to as warders now as officers); a reception room where the prisoners would be first received and examined; a warm and cold bath and an oven in which to fumigate prisoner's clothes. Prisoners were hanged on a gallows erected on the roof of the Lodge until 1817 when the scaffold collapsed with everyone upon it. From then on a portable gallows was used which was erected in front of the Lodge.

Palmer's attempted suicide:

Palmer remained in his bed and went on hunger strike refusing to eat and would only drink small amounts of water. On the sixth day the governor again visited Palmer and gave him an ultimatum. He said that unless he ate his soup he would call several of his turnkeys and they would hold him down and "force-feed" him. Palmer, being a medical man, realised just how painful this process would be, as it involved a tube being forcibly inserted into the mouth down through the throat then, using a "stomach pump", forcing the liquid food into the prisoner's stomach.

Palmer was given five minutes to agree to eat his soup before this dramatic action would be taken. Palmer backed down and ate his bowl of soup and from then on ate his meals normally. The newspapers reported this episode as "*Palmer's Attempted Suicide*" and "*His Voluntary Starvation*".

Almost five months later on Sunday 4th May 1856, ten days before his trial, Mr. Mountford, the Deputy-Governor of Stafford Gaol and one of the turnkeys escorted William Palmer on the 6.26 a.m. train from Stafford to London. There he awaited his trial in a cell at Newgate Prison.

Chapter 4: The Role of the Newspapers

Did the Press convict Palmer before his trial?

It is fascinating to look at the role played by the national newspapers in the five months leading up to Palmer's trial. Most news came from London, even the news printed in local papers. With newspapers in the Mid Nineteenth Century having far more freedom to report on cases before trial than they do today they really did a "hatchet job" on Palmer. They appear to have tried Palmer and found him guilty well before his actual trial. Some examples of articles written months before his trial which commenced in May 1856 are given below:

The Rugeley number of the *Illustrated Times* 2nd January 1856 published a damaging fifteen-page supplement that had statements from most of the key witnesses. It said this of William Palmer:

> *Palmer is spoken of as displaying at this period peculiarly fascinating manners when in the society of women. This is not at all unlikely; for he appears to be one of those individuals who make up for their want of brilliant parts by the assumption of a certain superficial amiability, which causes them to be regarded as universal favourites by their own, as well as by the opposite sex.*
>
> *Later in life, Palmer still preserved his agreeable manners. He was always popular with the poor, and liked by the public generally. Since he has become a betting man he has never shown himself secretive of sporting news of value, and he has seemed always glad to put money in the way of poor men eager for the excitement, sans the risk of betting. These qualities obtained for him considerable influence in his own town, and in the sporting circles of the midland and northern counties. He was, moreover, what has been called a liberal man. Ask the servants at the various hotels he frequented within thirty miles of his native town, and they will invariably speak of him as "a nice, pleasant sort of gentleman." But he was never respected. Latterly, his companions have been of low class, and he only differed from them in his temperate habits and equable tact of manner.*

Even vague compliments were tainted by criticism as eager reporters gathered damning accusations of local gossips. The *Illustrated London Times* 19th January 1856 started with words used a week before but went on to paint the following unflattering picture of, and presumed the guilt of, William Palmer:

> *William Palmer was popular with the poor and with the public generally; for he had a pleasant manner, was never secretive of sporting news of value, and always glad to put money in the way of poor men eager for the excitement sans the risk of betting. He thus obtained considerable influence*

in the town and in the sporting circles of the midland and northern counties. But he was never respected. Although young (about thirty-four), he has lived apparently an indefatigably mischievous life, and his character was tolerably well understood as a man who "would not stick at a trifle." His companions were of a low class, and he only differed from them in his temperate habits and equable tact of manner. His wife was greatly beloved as a gentle, amiable, extremely feminine women; and his notorious unfaithfulness to her, his prolonged absences from her, and the extreme solitude in which she was left in that hideous house in that hideous town, induced dislike of him, originating in pity for her. Now that all the dreadful story is divulged, the daring character of the man is well understood. His attempt to bribe the postboy to smash the jars containing the viscera of Cook, as these jars were being carried to the station for transmission to London - his taking from the telegraph-office the copy of the message - his hint to the weak postmaster to open and read a letter - his reckless misrepresentation to the insurance offices of the social position of Bates, his stable help - his attempt to seduce his maid servant the very night of his wife's death - all these facts are sufficiently suggestive. But stories of that character have been rife for years about him. The day his wife died it was whispered by two or three persons in Rugeley that she had not been properly treated by him. We may infer from Cook's dying hints that sporting men had "queer" ideas about the "Doctor;" and when the insurance-offices began to make inquiries so long ago as September - that is, long before Cook's death - they, of course, were influenced by the common talk about Palmer. If it should be proved in the end that he is one of the greatest of villains, it will also be ascertained that he was one of clumsiest. There is none of the heroic finesse of the historical poisoner about him, His utmost art was to keep out of the way of vulgar arsenic and palpable prussic acid. If he selected refined agents of murder, his process was of the coarsest kind. That he attempted and did so much is accepted as proof of his ability. Of his infamous audacity there can be no question; but what the case proves is the stupidity and timidity of those around him in not sooner dragging him to justice. The utmost that he succeeded in, as a matter of management in his career, was in withholding from the mass of people in Rugeley and Stafford any ground for believing in "motive" for crime. No one knew up to the last moment that he was heavily in debt. When his wife died people said that he must lose money by it, as the annuity left her by her father died with her. He had a large stud of horses; and had among his own neighbours the reputation of being a successful betting man, while it was seen and known that he was not extravagant. It is now perceived that he was from the first, and continuously, in difficulties.

In physique he presented none of the points of a man of finesse, either for a "book" or for a "poison." He was clumsily built, with a course red face. This figure and complexion, with the accompaniments in both cases of thin fair hair and sandy whiskers, have suggested the statement that "Palmer is the image of Manning." In strong, selfish, sensual natures there is probably a general resemblance. But Palmer looks, we are assured, more "gentlemanly" than Manning did. (Frederick Manning was another, earlier, infamous poisoner who along with his wife Maria was hanged on November 13th 1849)

Three months before the trial *"The Rugeley Number of the Illustrated Times"* dated February 2nd 1856 was feeding the county lurid details in words and pictures of the case. Under the heading *THE RUGELEY TRAGEDIES* an article started:

If any readers should think a justification necessary of the course we have this day adopted in making familiar to the public eye the various scenes connected with that fearful series of tragedies which, within the past few weeks, have sent a thrill of horror throughout the land - if they think we are to blame for having transferred to our columns these speaking likenesses of that hitherto obscure circle of individuals, whose names have been on the lips of almost every man, woman and child in the three kingdoms since intelligence of these tragedies became bruited abroad - to them we reply, that we conceive in what we have this day done we have only fulfilled the office that devolves upon us as the conductors of an illustrated journal. We cannot agree with that squeamishness which allows long wordy descriptions of places and individuals to be perfectly admissible and which refuses to tolerate those productions of the pencil, the skillfully indicated lines of which are more suggestive than columns and columns of the best written descriptions. Does even one of our readers believe that "The Times," or any other of the Morning Journals, would not readily avail themselves of the means which we posses and make use of were it only possible to adapt them to the exigencies of a daily newspaper?

The labour that we have been for weeks engaged in, and the results of which are now before the reader, was not entered upon with the idea of pandering to a mere vulgar curiosity. Our object was to lay bare a great social vice, which is gnawing away at the very core of society, and which every day shows to be rapidly on the increase - namely, the fearful amount of gambling in human life for the sake of pecuniary gain. Any one who scans these columns with attention, will approve the spirit in which we have performed our task.

There followed fifteen full pages devoted just to the Palmer case and using such phrases as "*if public rumour be worthy of credit*" and "*rumour goes on to say that ...*" virtually accusing Palmer of being a mass murderer before he was even tried for the one murder with which he was charged. In an earlier edition of *The Illustrated London News* dated January 19th 1856 we find assumptions of his guilt before a trial:

> *The first time that the finger began to be pointed at the house of Wm. Palmer was four or five years ago, when a man of the name of Bladen, a brewer's collector, and a defaulter in his accounts (which is significant in a friend of Palmer's), on a visit to Palmer, fell ill at Rugeley, was treated by Palmer, and died after a few days sufferings. But no one knew a motive, and no one spoke above a whisper.*
> *The whisper was again heard on his wife's death ....*

Later in the same article it said:

> *If one were now to believe all the stories of gentlemen who had drank their liquor in Palmer's company of late years it would be demonstrated that he was hankering after murder day and night.*

And later still the article says:

> *Yet in the assizes* in March, the counsel for the prisoner will doubtless, as a desperate resource, suggest the insanity of Palmer.*
> *Note that Palmer was due to be tried at the Stafford Assizes but the trial was switched to May and to London.

The newspapers controlled from London had decided upon his guilt way before a trial. Were the newspapers politically motivated? Did someone in high office want Palmer found guilty and did the publicity surrounding the trial take publicity and attention away from some near rebellious unrest in the country at the time?

The *Times Report of the Trial of William Palmer* published in 1856 shows that even the Attorney-General who was prosecuting Palmer commented, in his opening speech, upon the fact that the details of the case had been widely reported and discussed. The Attorney-General said:

> *Gentlemen of the jury, the duty you are called upon to discharge is the most solemn which a man can by possibility have to perform - it is to sit in judgment and to decide an issue on which depends the life of a fellow human being who stands charged with the highest crime for which a man can be arraigned before a worldly tribunal. I am sure that I need not ask your most anxious and earnest attention to such a case; but there is one thing I feel it incumbent on me to urge upon you. The peculiar circumstances*

22

of this case have given it a profound and painful interest throughout the whole country.

There is scarcely a man, perhaps, who has not come to some conclusion on the issue which you are now to decide. All the details have been seized on with eager avidity, and there is, perhaps, no one who is not more or less acquainted with those details. Standing here as a minister of justice, with no interest and no desire save that justice shall be done impartially, I feel it incumbent on me to warn you not to allow any preconceived opinion to operate on your judgment this day. Your duty - your bounden duty - is to try this case according to the evidence which shall be brought before you, and according to that alone. You must discard from your minds anything that you may have read or heard, or any opinion that you may have formed.

He was surely asking an impossible task of the jury all of whom must have been aware of much of the sensational publicity surrounding the case. Nowadays, hopefully, the Contempt of Court Act 1981 would restrict journalists preventing articles such as the ones about Palmer from being printed.

Would Palmer have been convicted if it had not been for the unprecedented level of interest shown by the press and the damning articles that they published in advance of the trial?

Rugeley was a quiet, sleepy Staffordshire town that few but the locals even knew existed until the "Rugeley Tragedies" hit the headlines.

The Maypole in Rugeley 1856 from the Illustrated Times 2nd February 1856 also in the Times Report of the Trial of William Palmer *published the same year.*

Chapter 5: Palmer's Childhood

William was born in a large house in Station Road, Rugeley on 21st October 1824, the sixth of seven children born to Sarah and Joseph Palmer.

A print of Mrs. Palmer's house from the *Illustrated Times* February 2nd 1856

His childhood was spent at the "Yard", the house that his father had built for them opposite the recently built St. Augustine's Church. It also stood adjacent to Old Chancel, the partly demolished former Rugeley parish church, where, as a child, William would have undoubtedly played in the ghostly ruins. It reminds one of the proverb of "the nearer to God the further from godliness" or "the nearer the church the farther from God". The house is still there but a road has now been built between the house and the canal, on the land that at one time had been old Mr. Palmer's woodyard before being grassed over to make a lawn gently sloping down to the canal.

When William was still a boy he was playing on the banks of to the canal, beside his home, when he accidentally fell in. A courageous school friend jumped in and rescued him from drowning. Without this act of bravery the story might have been so different.

At the age of ten he enrolled as a day scholar to Rugeley Free Grammar School where the Reverend Thomas Bonney M.A taught him. The school was in the next but one building to Old Mrs. Palmer's house. There is one account that says that in school Palmer was a bully and always had too much money.

Other accounts however, said that he would always fight on the side of the underdog. Another account stated he would rob his sister's pockets and take from his mother's purse, however yet another account says that he was, "the best of Mrs. Palmer's Bunch".

His father had been a strict man but when he died William was twelve years old and it was suggested that from then on his mother just let him run wild. There were stories from Palmer's former school friends that he was, "always up to his tricks", and that he would borrow money from men employed by his father. He would trick them in to giving him money with stories such as his father hadn't any change and needed sixpence or a shilling which would end up in Palmer's own pocket. William left school when he was seventeen and went to work in Liverpool.

Mrs. Palmer remained living in the family home in Station Road until her death in 1861 when she was aged sixty-seven. George Fletcher in his 1925 book remembers meeting Palmer's mother when he visited Rugeley for the first time in 1859. He was a lad of about twelve and had taken a cheap train trip from Birmingham. He walked from the station and came to the Parish Church on the left hand side exactly opposite to the house where Palmer was born and brought up. He wrote:

> *I was staring, with many other trippers, through the bars of a small iron gate into her front garden, when she suddenly came out of the front door and, walking down to the gate, said, "Well! I am Mrs. Palmer the mother of Dr. Palmer. The Judges hanged my saintly Billy, and he was the best of my lot," evidently proud of her notoriety in the case where her saintly son William had forged her name to documents and robbed her of some thirty thousand pounds.*

Chapter 6: Palmer's Family
All the Palmer family scandals unearthed by the press

William Palmer was the son of Joseph and Sarah Palmer. His mother, Sarah, had two boyfriends, one, named Hodson, was a steward for the Marquis of Anglesey but he was a married man so she married Joseph. He was a lowly sawyer but it was claimed that, with help from some of Sarah's "men friends", he made his fortune, partly from stolen timber. Joseph was born in 1777 and died in 1837, when he dropped dead suddenly at home whilst eating bread and cheese. William was then twelve years old and his father, the once penniless sawyer left £75,000 in his will. He left each son £7,000 and the remainder to his wife providing that she did not remarry. She did not remarry remaining in Rugeley even after the infamous trial and hanging.

If, as the stories in the newspapers said, Joseph was "penniless" when he met Sarah, he would have had to steal timber on a colossal scale to have died leaving £75,000 in his will. Was it the case that newspapers always tended to discredit people and their families if they were accused of being murderers? Newspapers in 1856 certainly had a major campaign to discredit Palmer's Family. Palmer's father was damned by *The Illustrated London News* January 19th 1856 in an article from their Special Correspondent:-

> *The founder of the Palmer Family was a sawyer, commencing life as a working man. He was a coarse, unscrupulous, insolent, pushing fellow, who had no friends, and who yet made a fortune. He made the money by going into the timber trade and buying up, from the neighbouring nobility and gentry, " those excrescences of nature grown by Providence to pay the debts of gentlemen"- trees. Stories are rife of his sharp practices with careless sellers and dishonest stewards and agents. It is enough to know that when he died he left (to his widow chiefly, for her life, with portions to each of the sons) a considerable fortune - about £100,000, it is said - and an excessively bad fame. But he died suddenly, and it was said (it is not now said) of apoplexy.*

Another "less criminal" explanation for Joseph making his fortune was provided by the Staffordshire Advertiser 14th June 1856:- "*. . . he commenced business as a timber merchant in Rugeley, at a period when the trade from the great demand for oak for ship building, during the war, was a very lucrative one. For many successive years he purchased large falls of oak timber from Bagot's Woods and Beaudesert.*" Timber was in much demand to build ships for the Napolionic War and prices rocketed. The background was that in the Dutch Wars of the 1660's England had used up much of its oak supplies rebuilding its navy without having a policy of replanting oak trees. As a result they had had to import

German oak, but unlike English oak that hardens in salt water, the German oak rotted more quickly, thus still leaving England short of seasoned oak for ship repairs and rebuilding.

In the *Illustrated Times* February 2nd 1856, a full three months before Palmer's trial, they wrote the following about his grandfather on his mother's side:

> *Mr. Bentley, the father of old Mrs. Palmer, and grandfather of William Palmer (the prisoner), lived, as it is commonly known in Rugeley, with a female who kept a house of ill-fame near Derby. This woman, from time to time, sent Bentley with the proceeds of her house to the bank, where, instead of delivering the money to the receiving-clerk, as the property of his mistress, he entered it on the books as his own. Finally he drew out the amount, and deserting his female companion, became the owner of a farm in the neighbourhood of Lichfield, where Mrs. Palmer was born.*

In another article the lady from Derby who "*kept a house of ill fame*" was named as Peggy Taff. The press also damned Palmer's mother. In the same paper they reported local gossip about Palmer's mother and love letters written by her to a younger man named Duffy:

> *In the Market place, and close to the Town Hall, we find the "Shoulder of Mutton" public-house kept by "Thomas Clewley", as the sign board informs us, where, until seized by the police, you could see love letters which the youthful, fascinating, and unfortunate Duffy received from the giddy, aged, and rich Mrs. Palmer, senior.*

Later in the same newspaper they printed a statement taken from the Landlord of the Shoulder of Mutton concerning an affair between old Mrs. Palmer and Cornelius Duffy a linen-draper from Belfast:

> *"I am the landlord of the Shoulder of Mutton public-house. There was a strapping chap of the name of Duffy - a good-looking fellow - who used to come to lodge with me. He was rather a dull chap in the house, and he'd sit still and drink. He did not run up a very big shot. The first time he came here, Mr. William Palmer paid for him. The second time he came, Mr. William Palmer told me he wouldn't pay, so I gave Duffy the bill, but he did not pay me then; he said he should have some money coming in a day or two. Soon after, he went out of the house without saying anything, and I never set eyes on him again. We gave him three or four years for coming back again; but as he didn't come, and his boxes began to smell very bad, my missus opened them - there was only a lot of dirty shirts and things. He hadn't no clothing only what he had on his back. In the trunks I found some letters, not put by with any care, as if they were particular valuable, but just careless. They were only courting*

letters, and were from Mrs. Palmer (the old lady), written to him. I should think Duffy was about forty years old, and Mrs. Palmer was from about fifty-five to sixty. She has sons now as is above forty. I think Duffy was in the linen drapery line. I never paid no more attention to him than that he was a traveller. The police has been here and got Duffy's traps.

The letters finished off with loving and kissing. They made appointments to meet at a many different places; but I was in no way interested in their loves, and I never troubled my head about it: it was the women as exposed the whole business - nobody would have seen 'em or known anything about the letters if it had not been for them. I should have burn 'em or kept 'em secret. No, I never charged sixpence a-head to see 'em, I only showed 'em for a lark. The way in which they came to be seen was this - My Missus got speaking of 'em and one or two young chaps came here and gammoned the Missus to show 'em. They spent one or two shillings in grog to have a look; then come another and another, and at last I took 'em away: but the Missus got 'em again. There's no keeping the women quiet in these matters. I can't say how many letters there was - they was mixed up with trades-men's bills and that sort of thing."

It should be remembered that Mrs. Palmer Senior was, by then, a widow and in her late husband's will it had stipulated that she kept the money left to her only on the condition that she never remarry. **Why would the police seize these letters? Would newspapers today print such "tittle-tattle"?** There was never any suggestion that Duffy's disappearance was a possible murder as it occurred at a time when Palmer had run away to Walsall with Jane Widnall.

His Brothers and Sisters: Parents Joseph Palmer and his wife Sarah had seven children, five sons and two daughters. The Brothers were damned by *The Illustrated London News* January 19th 1856 (from their Special Correspondent):

The sons were divided, as the sons of the middle class are when there is money enough to start all, into the different professions, one was sent into the church, another to the law, another to trade, another to medicine. It so happened that not one of the sons has, in his own life, purified the name of Palmer, to a proper extent, in the nostrils of Rugeley and its neighbourhood; while, on the other hand it is to be feared that they had not the advantage of a good mother – some of Mrs. Palmer's letters to a man of the name of Duffy, and left by him in a portmanteau at a low public – house, having been unfairly disclosed to the town, and having been considered to justify the accumulated comments of fifteen years of scandal. The marriages of some of the sons were so unlucky as to increase the popular conviction that the family was not amiable. Neglect, drunkenness and separations seem to have been the rule.

The comment ". . not one of the sons has, in his own life purified the name of Palmer." seems unduly harsh when one was a clergyman, one a lawyer and one a timber merchant albeit that one of the brothers was a bankrupt and a drunkard.

Palmer's brothers and sisters were in fact a mixed bunch, some good and some bad. **Joseph Palmer:** In the *Illustrated Life, Career, and Trial of William Palmer of Rugeley* published by Ward and Lock in 1856 we learn that Joseph, the eldest son, started out as an apprentice to the firm of Halhead Fletcher and Company timber merchants in Liverpool. After five or six years he returned to Rugeley and started his own timber merchant business like his father before him. Not long after this he was introduced to the family of Mr. Milcrest, of Liverpool and soon married his eldest daughter "with whom he obtained a considerable fortune". Later he bought a colliery on Cannock Chase where he was an unsuccessful colliery manager before marrying his "rich lady" and retiring from business altogether and going to live with his family in Liverpool. However, Fletcher in his book published in 1925, states that, *"Joseph moved early to Liverpool, where he held a good position and reputation"*, and also stated that Joseph was born in 1819 (this disagrees with the 1818 date found in baptism records). Joseph died, before the scandal, in about 1853. Fletcher tells us that, "Joseph had married a *Miss Milcrest, one of the three daughters of a shipbuilder, and was prosperous in business. Walter persuaded a younger Miss Milcrest to marry him much against the advice of her sister and her husband, his* (Walter's) *brother Joseph"*.

Mary Ann Palmer, born in 1816, the eldest child led a life of "indecent scandal", married a Mr. Heywood from Haywood and drank herself to death, dying in 1853. **George Palmer:** George was one of the twins born in 1821. In the 1856 book, *Illustrated Life and Career of William Palmer of Rugeley* (page 13), it states that George was, "an attorney in Rugeley" and, "He is also, by marriage, connected with a Liverpool family, having married Miss Clarke, a daughter of Mr. Clarke, of Seacombe, formerly an iron merchant in Liverpool." However George Fletcher in his book, *The Life & Career of Dr. William Palmer of Rugeley* published in 1925 (page 31), tells us that George - *was a solicitor, and helped with family matters and had a fair practice at Uttoxeter where he married Miss Flint, daughter of Mr. A. A. Flint, the Coroner. George Palmer died in 1866 aged forty-six and his wife Eliza Catherine died in 1870. Both George and his wife were carried to be buried in the family vault at Rugeley.*

Sarah: Born 1821, the other twin was said to have had a kind heart and devoted herself to good causes. **Walter,** born 1823, was the fourth son was a bankrupt and a drunkard who many believe was poisoned by William in 1855 when he was thirty-two years old. Others believe that he simply drank himself to death (See Chapter 18). Of Palmer's brother Walter one article said: *Walter*

Palmer is spoken of as "the best of the brothers;" and he was a bankrupt in trade, and so confirmed a drunkard that his wife, partial to him, and willing to be his nurse, found it impossible to endure the horror and disgust of living with him.

Fletcher, in his book published in 1925, stated:

Walter had been a corn-merchant, but was always a lazy, indolent drunkard who neglecting his business, had been made bankrupt in 1849. He went to live for a few years in the Isle of Man, but his drinking habits brought on an attack of delirium tremens, and he was again made bankrupt. He returned to Liverpool - for one reason, to be nearer his widowed mother in Rugeley with her £70,000, and near his eldest brother Joseph, who was living in Liverpool, a respectable citizen and a timber-merchant. Joseph married a Miss Milcrest, one of the three daughters of a shipbuilder, and was prosperous in business.

The book goes on to tell us that Walter never supported his wife financially and after his second attack of delirium tremens*, sometimes referred to as "the shakes" she was *"compelled to separate from him, much to her sorrow, for she seems to have had some affection for him, in spite of his dissolute life"*. *Delirium Tremens is the most serious form of acute alcoholism. The tremors or shakes affect the whole body but especially the hands and tongue. The condition is accompanied by horrific hallucinations often referred to as the "blue-devils".

William himself was the next son, born in 1824 with the last son **Thomas** born in October 1827. Thomas became a clergyman and was twenty-eight years old at the time of the trial and living at Coton in the Elms in Derbyshire. For twenty-seven years he was the Rector of Trimley St. Martin, near Felixstowe. He died in 1887 having always maintained that he believed that William had not poisoned John Parsons Cook.

Mrs. Palmer Senior's House in Station Road as it looked in 1980. Photograph taken by D. Lewis

The porch has changed but it is still recognisable as the same house in which William Palmer, his brothers and sisters spent their childhood

Chapter 7: Palmer's Employment
Scandals at all his places of work

When Palmer first left school his mother arranged an apprenticeship with Messrs. Evans and Evans a wholesale chemist in Lord Street, Liverpool. In those days there weren't any bank cheques so cash was sent in sealed envelopes and whilst Palmer was working at Lord Street a considerable amount of money kept disappearing. The General Post-office sent an inspector from London in an attempt to track down the thief, who they thought might be one of their own employees. Numerous traps were set without success until one of the partners followed Palmer and caught him red-handed opening a letter addressed to the company. Palmer was instantly dismissed and was only saved from being sent to prison because his loving mother paid back all the money that he had stolen. To avoid further scandal Palmer's younger brother Thomas was taken on to finish the apprenticeship. Palmer stole the money to spend on his girlfriend called Jane Widnall (his landlady's daughter), who was two years older than him. She, it was said, was trying to trick William in to marrying her by pretending to be pregnant but, when she found out that he wasn't going to inherit (£7,000) if he married before he was twenty-one, her love for him seemed to wane suddenly. The *Illustrated Life and Career of Dr. William Palmer* published by Ward Locke in 1856, claimed he also spent much of his ill-gotten gains betting at Liverpool and Chester Races and, "*Another portion – not by any means an inconsiderable one – went in the society of females of the worst character, with whom, unfortunately, Liverpool, like most large seaport towns, abounds.*"

He next agreed to start a five year apprenticeship as an assistant to Dr. Edward Tylecote at Great Haywood, a village near his hometown of Rugeley. The doctor, who lived opposite William's older sister, was glad to have another live-in assistant especially as William paid for his bed and board. Whilst he was with Dr. Tylecote his former girlfriend, the red-headed Jane Widnall, reappeared on the scene when her mother married Mr. Vickerstaff an assistant gardener who worked at Shugborough Park. They moved in to the house beside the Clifford Arms in Great Haywood. Unlike Dr. Tylecote, Palmer frequently went to church on Sundays, however, he would bribe a local village lad to call him out of church as if he was needed by a patient. He would then visit Jane safe in the knowledge that her mother and step-father were in the church for the next hour or so. Jane, it seems, had not given up on the idea of trying to get her hands on Palmer's inheritance money. To make Palmer jealous she started going out with Peter Smirke who also was apprenticed to Dr. Tylecote. On one occasion Palmer became so jealous that he cut up Smirke's boots and poured acid over his clothes, although he never admitted to doing so.

Again money went missing, this time from Dr. Tylecote's. William and Jane ran off together to Walsall, but when their money ran out Palmer's brothers were forced to go to Walsall to settle his debts although it is claimed that Jane had a hundred pounds in her purse, which was money she had stolen from her stepfather's life savings. William was forced to return home and his mother unsuccessfully begged the doctor to forgive him and to take him back. As for Jane Widnall, she could not return to Haywood and she is said to have written to Peter Smirke claiming that Palmer had deserted her when she told him that it was actually him she loved. Smirke left Dr. Tylecote's, married Jane, and together they set off for a new life in Australia where he set up his practice as a doctor in Sydney.

In the book *Illustrated Life, Career and Trial of William Palmer of Rugeley* published in 1856, there was a claim that:

> *We heard an old man at Haywood count upon his fingers as many as fourteen girls whom Palmer had got in the family-way. He had, by a foolish freak, been concerned in the death of Abley. An illegitimate child, which a woman in Haywood had by him, died suddenly; and he is suspected of foul play.*

Is there any proof of the words of this one old man? Later, on the same page, the book actually had some kind words to say of Palmer supposedly from Mrs. Remington in whose house he lodged when he returned from London:

> *He (Palmer) was a good young man as ever walked; he was with me nearly a twelvemonth; he came to me in October 1846, I think. I remember he asked me when my wedding-day was, and he said, 'Well, then, that shall be mine;' and so it would have been but for the Lord Chancellor. The wedding dinner was provided for forty, at Abbot's Bromley. My husband and I were to go. I never saw him intoxicated but once, and that was one night when he came back from a party.*
>
> *"Mamma," he said - he always used to call me mamma – "Mamma, I am very ill; I have been drunk; it is not what I have had, but I have been drugged". Those were his very words. He told me, when he was going away, without my consent; and, as I felt rather hurt, he said, Never mind, I have let them to a very respectable man, and I have got you 2 shillings a-week rent, for I am sure you deserve it, you are so very kind.*

Forced to leave Dr. Tylecote's, Palmer worked for a short time as a "walking student" at Stafford Infirmary. Minutes from the Weekly Board of the Stafford Infirmary now kept in the County Records Office in Stafford, dated May 24th 1844, show that – *Mr. Wm Palmer of Rugeley having paid the sum of five guineas. Resolved that he be admitted a walking pupil of the Institution according to the 78th and 79th rules of the Infirmary.*

The grave of George Abley and his grandson. Abley was allegedly Palmer's first victim. His grave stands in the churchyard of the Parish Church of St. Michaels and All Angels, Colwich.

Inscribed Sacred to the Memory of George Abley: who died October 24, 1846. Aged 27 years.

Gossips told reporters that there was a suspicious death of a man called Abley whilst Palmer worked at the infirmary (in reality it was probably later, see Chapter 9). It is also thought that it was whilst working at Stafford Infirmary that Palmer first became interested in poisons. It is alleged that he often took books on poison from the hospital library but was stopped, by a new policy introduced by the hospital authorities, from pursuing his habit of taking drugs home with him. It has been said that, in those days, they saw using anesthetic as an unnecessary expenditure, and that they were always short of nurses with some of the ones they did recruit often being drunk or incapable. Many then considered that if you were sent to Stafford Infirmary it was like receiving a death sentence even though Stafford Infirmary gained some praise for its treatment of illness. Fortunately medicine and hygiene have progressed a long way since the first half of the Nineteenth Century.

Palmer did not stay long at Stafford Infirmary but went off to St. Bartholomew's Hospital, London, to train to be a doctor. Whilst he was there it was claimed he wasted his time on women, drinking and singing and did very little studying. Eventually the hospital authorities got in touch with Palmer's mother and told her that there was little chance of her son passing the exams to become a doctor. His mother then hired a Dr. Stegall to help him study for his doctor's exams. In those days they referred to such a tutor as a "grinder". She promised Stegall £100 if he could succeed in getting her son to pass all his exams. Palmer must have worked very hard for the remaining weeks because he managed to qualify as a doctor. Stegall, however, did not receive his money and had to sue Mrs. Palmer. The case was eventually settled out of court although the matter was reported in the London newspapers.

Chapter 8: Palmer the Doctor

Palmer sets up his practice at his house in Rugeley

On 10th August 1846 Palmer qualified as a doctor having obtained his diploma from the College of Surgeons (M.R.C.S.) and he was appointed as a house surgeon at Bart's in September but resigned after a month to return to Rugeley. Later, probably in October 1847 after his marriage to Annie, he started up his doctor's practice by putting up a brass plate outside the house in Market Street that he rented from Lord Lichfield for £25 a year. In this house his mother-in-law, Leonard Bladen, four of his five children and his wife, all died. The house stood opposite the Talbot Arms (later named the Shrewsbury Arms and more recently The Shrew) where John Parsons Cook was later to suffer an agonising death in Room 10.

Palmer must have been well liked as a doctor, at least at first, because he built up his practice to such an extent that he could afford to engage Benjamin Thirlby to be his full time assistant. Thirlby in fact went on to run the practice as Palmer began to spend most of his time occupied with his horses and horseracing.

George Fletcher, in his book *The Life and Career of Dr. William Palmer of Rugeley* published in 1925, told a story of one of his visits to Rugeley. In 1905 the then landlady of the Talbot Arms showed him Palmer's brass plate saying she had been offered £5 for it and asked how she could best dispose of it. Fletcher suggested that Madame Tussaud's Wax Exhibition might want it to put in its Chamber of Horrors. Unfortunately I have been unable to trace what has since happened to the brass plate.

Dr. Palmer's House as it looked in 1856
From the *Illustrated London News, Supplement,* May 24th 1856
The house later became a post office and then a shop.

34

Chapter 9: Suspicious Deaths - First victim?

Natural causes, misadventure, a prank gone wrong or murder?

There were reports in the newspapers before his trial, and in the books published in 1856 after his execution, that there was a suspicious death whilst William Palmer was working, for a short time, as a "walking student" at Stafford Infirmary.

The newspapers and books carry differing versions of the gossip. My investigations of the story suggest that the events actually occurred in October 1846 after Palmer had left Stafford Infirmary and were in fact after he had qualified as a doctor and returned from London.

One published version is that, in spring 1846, Palmer invited a man called George Abley to the Lamb and Flag at Little Haywood and gave him brandy and water to drink but ordered the landlady to give him eight pennyworth of brandy rather than the usual four pennyworth. Abley soon became very intoxicated and refused to drink any more, at which point Palmer offered him a half sovereign if he could down another glass of neat brandy. Abley did so but was immediately sick and went out for a breath of fresh air.

Another version of the story is that Palmer was a regular visitor to the Lamb and Flag. One night he was having a drink with his friend called Timmis when Abley came in. Abley was a thin pale man who suffered indifferent health. As it was cold outside, Palmer offered to buy him a drink of brandy but Abley refused saying that he wasn't much of a brandy drinker. Timmis reckoned that Abley was being modest, as he had seen him "knock back" three large brandies one after the other.

Palmer, always the gambler, offered to bet Timmis three to one in half-sovereigns that Abley could not drink more than one tumbler full of neat brandy. Abley wasn't interested but Timmis took him to one side and offered him ten out of the thirty shillings that he could win if he took on the bet. Eventually Abley agreed to take the bet for fifteen shillings on the condition that Mrs. Bates the landlady kept the winnings until he was sober.

The Lamb and Flag Public House as it looked in January 2001.
Photograph by D. Lewis

Abley drank the first tumbler without flinching whilst Palmer sat quietly holding the next drink. Palmer agreed that he had drunk the first one manfully but would wager that the next one would make him choke. Abley knocked the second drink straight back and everyone had a good laugh at Palmer's expense and Abley even went so far as to suggest that, as times were so hard, for fifteen shillings he would consider drinking another one. Presently however Abley turned a bit green and said that he would go out to the stable for a breath of fresh air. Everyone forgot about him whilst Palmer entertained the bar by telling a funny story which Timmis followed with even ruder ones.

Both versions of the story have a similar ending when an hour or so later they realised that Abley had gone missing and they went in search of him. Abley was found stretched out on some old sacks in the stable groaning and clutching his stomach with both hands. It took two men to carry him home and put him in a warm bed. Unfortunately he died later that night.

At the inquest on Abley, all but one of the coroner's jury were satisfied that, since he was a pale thin man of indifferent health, to drink so much neat brandy on an empty stomach and then to lie in a cold stable for an hour or two had caused his death. They recorded a verdict of "Death from Natural Causes".

Edward Jenkinson the foreman of the Jury, however, strongly disagreed with the verdict of all the other jurors. At the inquest there were rumours about Palmer and Abley's rather buxom wife. Palmer was said to have fallen for her when she had been an outpatient at the Infirmary but that she would not have anything to do with Palmer saying that she would be faithful to her husband. A Times newspaper reporter however, in 1856, wrote in *The Illustrated Life, Career and Trial of William Palmer,* that, "*At the inquest there was a great deal of talk about Palmer and Abley's wife which was undoubtedly true.*"

In the local public houses Jenkinson freely told, anyone who was prepared to listen, his opinion of Palmer, stating that if only people had listened to him all the sordid events would not have occurred. Others at the time however reckoned that Jenkinson was a bitter man who disliked men like Palmer who were popular with the ladies, having himself received several refusals to his offers of marriage.

Abley was buried in Colwich churchyard. His Death Certificate issued on 30th November 1846 for the Stafford Sub-district of Colwich gives us some additional details: Abley was 27 when he died on the 24th October 1846; his occupation was given as "plumber and glazier" (rather than the occupation shoemaker given in some other reports). The exact cause of death given by the Stafford Coroner, William Ward, is recorded as "*Exhaustion the result of diseased blood vessels of the lung*". Note that the date on the death certificate is after Palmer had qualified as a doctor and some time after he had left Stafford Infirmary although all the stories printed in 1856 said that Abley died whilst Palmer was a "walking student" at the Infirmary.

Was it a case of natural causes? - Misadventure? - A prank gone wrong? - or Murder? We will never know for certain!

Chapter 10: Suspicious Deaths – Mother-in-law

Did alcohol or poison finish her off?

This is another of the deaths referred to in the newspapers of 1856 as one of the "Rugeley Tragedies". Mary Thornton (in her early life called Ann Thornton) was a dreadful, illiterate woman with good looks but a vile temper. Mary became the housekeeper to, and mistress of, Lieutenant Colonel William Brookes with whom she had a daughter called Annie who later became Palmer's wife. Colonel Brookes was a wealthy East Indian Army Officer who, having retired in 1820 with a healthy pension, returned to England where he bought several houses in Stafford.

Mary was regularly drunk and arguing with the Colonel, cursing him for never having married her and blaming him for driving her to drink. It was claimed that, when she was in one of her rages, Mary would attack the Colonel with whatever she could lay her hands on. He would often resort to hiding in one of the local hostelries, including the Noah's Arms which he owned, to escape from her but she would merely track him down to continue cursing him. Eventually in 1834 Colonel Brookes put a pistol to his head and shot himself. *(Three of the Colonel's four brothers also committed suicide).*

After the death of Colonel Brookes, Mary's drinking became worse and shortly, because of her drinking, Annie her daughter was made a Ward in Chancery and sent to live with one of her guardians Charles Dawson at his house at Abbots Bromley some 12 miles from Stafford. It was whilst living and attending school there that Annie met William Palmer.

Mary remained in a house behind St. Mary's Church in Stafford and, although she was then fairly wealthy, she employed no servants. She was in a poor state of health by then and her diet was said to consist of large draughts of gin with very little food to go with it. Her swarm of cats were left to fend for themselves. She did not

The Noah's Ark, now named the Surgery one of the properties formerly owned by Colonel Brookes. Photograph D. Lewis April 2001

like Palmer and, in spite of him arranging for her house to be repaired, she would regularly swear at him in a vile way accusing him of poisoning one or more of her many cats.

On the 6th January 1849, Mary was found in the street stretched out straight, she was in a state of delirium due, yet again, to an excess of alcohol. Palmer had her taken to his house where she died twelve days later on January 18th 1849 aged fifty. Mary was buried at Rugeley on January 22nd 1849.

When drawing up his will, there are two versions of the story – One that the colonel had not taken the necessary care that was needed when leaving money to a lady to whom he was not legally wed and to an illegitimate daughter. The second version was that the will was carefully worded so as to protect Annie by preventing his mistress, Mary Thornton, selling or forcing Annie to sell the property. Whatever the correct version was, the estate was "put into Chancery" to be administered for the benefit of the two ladies. Thus the nine houses that Colonel Brookes owned, which stood behind St. Mary's Church in Stafford and which Brookes left to Mary Thornton, were never inherited by Annie Palmer or William Palmer. Instead the Chancery Court ordered that the property be given to Mr. Shallcross Colonel Brookes' next heir with Annie receiving an annual allowance from the rents.

A report on January 19th 1856 in *The Illustrated Times* said only that his mother-in-law died soon after Palmer married. But a damning article on another day in the same newspaper on February 2nd 1856 (three months before Palmer's trial) carried the following damning report:-

The reader will not be surprised to learn that Mrs. Thornton, the mother of Mrs. Palmer, was a person of eccentric habits. She still lived at Stafford, not keeping any servants, though possessed of property. Some little time after Palmer's marriage, he called upon her, and requested her to lend him some money. He also invited her to go and live with her daughter. She refused to give him money, and he left her much incensed.

The poor woman afterwards, fearing that Palmer would ill-treat her daughter on his return home if she did not comply with his request, went to the bank, and having procured £20, forwarded it to him. She is reported to have said, that if she went to reside under the same roof with him, she would not live a fortnight. These forebodings proved to be true, for she subsequently went to live with her daughter, and four days afterwards she was a corpse. In accordance with Colonel Brookes' will, her property descended to her daughter, whose husband thus became possessed of a respectable income.

The last sentence in the article was not true as the property went to Mr. Shallcross. Annie continued to receive an annual income from the estate in Chancery but there was not the bonus of inheriting the nine properties. Gossips however said that Palmer didn't realise that this would happen and had assumed the properties would become the property of his wife and provide him with more income. This, gossips claimed, was a motive for him to murder his mother-in-law. In the newspaper report you might have noticed that there was no mention of the heavy drinking of Palmer's mother-in-law.

There were also reports that, as the landlord, Mary needed to repair many of the buildings. Mary was in such a poor state due to her drinking that Palmer, because it was claimed, he assumed he would inherit her house, had arranged for repairs to be carried out on the properties. It was further reported that Mr. Shallcross, after he had inherited the properties, refused to reimburse Palmer for the money he had spent on the repairs.

Mary had had a serious drink problem for most of her adult life but what we will never know is –
Did drink cause her death or did Palmer's poison "help" her on her way?

As the owner of the nine Stafford properties, which included the Noah's Ark, between 1834 and 1849 Mary Thornton would legally have been the licensee of the Noah's Ark. In the same way Annie, Palmer's wife would have been the licensee for a brief time until the Chancery Court awarded the properties to Mr. Shallcross. There is no suggestion that either Palmer's wife or his mother-in-law ever managed or worked in the Noah's Ark merely that, in law, they were the licensees. **Thus the gossips claimed that Palmer poisoned two licensees of the Noah's Arks.** When it was re-opened by Kevin Smith in 1999, to mark its links with Palmer the public house has been renamed The Surgery Café Bar and Lounge. In October 2003 he has mounted a permanent Palmer Display so that patrons can learn more about the infamous Palmer. *See the end of Chapter 47 for a few deatils of a Palmer display in the former Noah's Ark building.*

Chapter 11: Suspicious Deaths – Leonard Bladen

Died in Palmer's House in May 1850

This was another one of a number of mysterious deaths referred to as one of the "Rugeley Tragedies." **Was it a case of natural causes or poison?**

Palmer soon tired of being a country doctor and began spending more and more time running his own stables and gambling at various racecourses. One day in 1850 he went to Chester Races. He was very friendly with a 49-year-old man named Leonard Bladen who worked as a collector for Charrington Brewery. On that day Bladen won a considerable amount of money at the races and Palmer was known to have owed him money. After the Races, Bladen wrote to his wife telling her that he was going to Rugeley to collect what Palmer owed him and that, with his winnings and what Palmer owed him, he should come home with around £1,000. He also added that he would be in Rugeley for a couple of days. Palmer, "being a good loser" had promised Bladen "some sport with the gun". When Bladen first went to Rugeley he continued his journey on to Ashby in Leicestershire to see his brother Henry before returning to Rugeley.

Whilst he was back in Rugeley he was suddenly taken ill. Some time before, whilst he was working, Bladen had had an accident where he was hit in the chest by a cart. He suffered internal injuries and had been ordered to rest but, instead, he had gone to the races. Whether he died as a result of these injuries or as a result of poisoning is not known.

A Picture of Bladen's gravestone, taken by D. Lewis in March 2003

When he was first taken ill his wife was not sent for, as she had not wanted him to go to the races in the first place. A friend of Bladen's, however, sent for his wife. When she arrived in Rugeley she found that he was in great pain and so ill that he did not even recognise her. Later he died in agony in Palmer's house. His wife was surprised to find only £15 in his possessions and found that his betting books were missing. He was buried in St. Augustine's churchyard, Rugeley.

The Death Certificate dated 10th May 1850 registered the death, in Market Street, Rugeley of Leonard Bladen, male aged 49 years a "common brewer". The cause of death was given as, "*injury of the hip joint 5 or 6 months; abscess in the pelvis 12 days certified*". Wm. Palmer registered the death and was, "*present at the death*".

40

A damning newspaper report in *The Illustrated Times* on February 2nd 1856, published a full three months before Palmer's trial, stated that:

> *The year following Mrs. Thornton's*[1] *death - some few years ago - a Mr. Bladen, a collector for Charrington's brewery, who dabbled sufficiently in turf transactions to make him a defaulter to his employers, came to Rugeley on a visit to William Palmer. It would seem, if public rumour be worthy of credit, that Palmer had borrowed £400 from the sporting bagman, and it is possible that the hope of recovering this sum induced the unfortunate man to become the guest of his debtor. However this may be, he had no chance of taking it out of board and lodging. In less than a week he fell desperately sick and after William Palmer and his assistant and subsequent partner, Mr. Benjamin Thirlby, had exhausted their skill, old Dr. Bamford was called in to "prescribe a mixture". Nevertheless, the patient died. His wife arrived when he was already insensible, but in a few minutes she was hurried out of the room, and never again allowed to behold him - because decomposition had set in so rapidly! She was also dissuaded from carrying the corpse to London, the expense of which William Palmer greatly exaggerated. Rumour goes on to say that the latter handed the widow a cheque for £60, and some loose cash which he had found in the pockets of the deceased. On Mrs. Bladen expressing her surprise at the smallness of the amount, her husband having left London, as she believed, with £200 in his pocket. Palmer replied that, since Bladen had been in Rugeley, he had been betting heavily, and had been unfortunate. Poor Mrs. Palmer was greatly agitated when she heard of Bladen's death, and exclaimed, "My poor mother died when on a visit here last year - and now this man. What will people say?"*
>
> *What will people say, indeed! Beyond these deaths, there were also other grounds for suspicion. Of five children, the offspring of their marriage, four died in infancy - last in January, 1854. Er, too, a few short months had gone by, it was destined to be the poor mother's turn.*
>
> [1] *Mrs. Thornton was Palmer's Mother-in-law*

There is no doubt that Bladen died in Palmer's house but it is also a fact that he had gone to the races against medical advice having recently been injured at work. At the time Mrs. Bladen had not been suspicious being grateful for the supposed kindness shown towards her husband by Mr. Palmer and more especially by the kindness Annie Palmer had shown towards her. Later she was to be very suspicious.

Would Palmer's debts really have made him so desperate that he would risk murdering someone in his own home?

Chapter 12: Suspicious Deaths – Bly from Beccles

A suspicious death: Fact or fiction?

This story was not reported at the time of Palmer's trial but appeared later that same year when a story appeared in the Norfolk Chronicle; the story was then repeated in *The Illustrated Life and Career of William Palmer of Rugeley*, published in the same year as Palmer's execution by Ward Lock in 1856. A Mr. Bly lived at a place called Beccles in Norfolk and was supposed to be a friend of William Palmer. The pair would often attend the races together where Bly was a regular winner just as the unfortunate Palmer was a regular loser. It was claimed that Palmer owed Bly £800 when Bly suddenly became dangerously ill and was "*professionally treated*" by Palmer. The claims were rather vague suggesting that Palmer treated Bly either, "*at Rugeley, or at some town adjacent to a race course, by many said to be Leicester*".

The story continued that when Bly's wife heard that her husband was ill, she hurried to be with him and found Palmer treating him. Palmer tried to stop his wife seeing him but she insisted and, whilst she was sitting by his deathbed, she claimed Bly suddenly said that he believed that he was dying and regretted his misspent life. Mrs. Bly further claimed that her husband stated Palmer owed him £800.

When, after Mr. Bly had died, Mrs. Bly mentioned the money owed to her husband, Palmer replied that it showed just how bad a state her husband had been in. Palmer insisted that the truth of the matter was that Bly actually owed him £800 but that he would not have mentioned the matter had she had not brought up the subject.

Initially I was a more than a little sceptical about this story as it bore a great resemblance to the story of Leonard Bladen. Robert Graves commented in his 1957 book *They Hanged My Saintly Billy* that, "*Since Palmer's arrest, a great many new stories had come into circulation which represent him having killed scores of people in these years; but they prove without exception to be clumsy fabrications designed to assist the sale of the newspapers that publish them*". He quoted the example of *The Norfolk Chronicle* that printed a story but gave "*no exact date, nor even a certain location for the poisoning. It seems to have been concocted on the model of Bladen's murder, which Rugeley Police, after making due inquiries, decided to be no murder at all.*"

However, whilst this book was at the printers, Glen Chandler rang me with some fresh information. He had been reading an old book, which he had bought at a charity sale, entitled *The Diary of a Norwich Medical Student 1858 to 1860*, printed by Jarrold and Sons Limited, Norwich. On June 1st 1860 the author, Shephard T. Taylor M.B., had recorded:

Three operations this morning – amputation of the leg above the ankle for caries of bone and castration by Mr. Firth, and tenotomy for flexed fingers from malpraxis in fracture by Mr. Cadge.

Mr. Gooderson died this morning.

Dr. Robinson gave his final lecture on Medical Juris-prudence, in which strychnia was more particularly discussed, the cases of Palmer and Dove being alluded to, on which he commented at some length with considerable shrewdness. **Palmer undoubtedly poisoned a cousin of my mother's named Blyth ten years ago, but the evidence was not considered strong enough to justify taking legal proceedings against him.**

The "victim" was named as Blyth rather than "Bly" (the name quoted in the 1856 book) but there is the "Norwich link".

Does this cross-reference prove there really was a murder? Now we shall never know!

Cook's horse "Polestar" winning at the Shrewsbury Races from *Illustrated Life and Career of William Palmer of Rugeley* published 1856.

Chapter 13: Suspicious Deaths - The Cross Keys Mystery

Was there a murder? Was there a body?

This again was not one of the "stories" that the newspapers published in 1856 but a story I first heard in 1979. Unfortunately I cannot remember the source and would be delighted if anyone reading this book could track down the original source.

The story was centred on the Cross Keys Public House at Hednesford. Built in 1746 it was a regular stop for coaches on the road between London and Chester. The pub had been well known for its sporting connections having, in the past, been a venue for bare fist fights, cockfights and whippet racing. Philip Talbot told me a story of the times when illegal cock fights were held at the Cross Keys. Whilst cockfights were in progress a young boy would be put up in the rafters above the building to keep a watch out for "the Law". Philip was told that one such boy is supposed to have died whilst "on duty" and that his ghost still haunts the Cross Keys. Jockeys often stayed there, and "*Jealousy*" the winner of the 1861 Grand National was at one time stabled there. More recently, up until 1996, Hednesford Town Football Club had a ground immediately at the rear of the building. It was also thought to be a meeting place for Dr. William Palmer who had several horses in training with William Saunders at Hednesford.

Bob Brettle, a famous Birmingham bare-knuckle fighter, was training at Hednesford in readiness for his championship fight with "Gypsy" Jem Mace. Two of the main backers of Bob Brettle were the gamblers Dr. William Palmer and John Parsons Cook for whose murder Palmer was later hanged at Stafford.

The Cross Keys Public House as it looked February 2001
Photograph by D. Lewis

Cook and Palmer used to meet up each day with Brettle in the Cross Keys Public House, after his day's training, to check up on their fighter's progress.

One night in the Cross Keys their quiet drink was disturbed by a big brute of a navvy (an Irish labourer) who was taking great delight in playing tricks on customers or insolently drinking other people's drinks. Bob Brettle gradually became more and more fed up with the antics of the by now, drunken and loud navvy and was threatening "to sort him out". Palmer was naturally worried about his prize-fighter getting hurt before such an important fight and told Brettle to leave the bully to him.

Palmer got Brettle to order a drink for the navvy and then took a packet of white powder out of his pocket and put it in to the navvy's drink. They had no more trouble from the man until, at closing time, the landlord found him completely unconscious slumped at a table. The landlord made up a bed of straw for the navvy in the stables.

The navvy slept "like a corpse" in the stables. Brettle was worried about him and went in next morning and again several times during the day to check up on him. It appeared that the dope had not worn off and the man looked "as dead as a door nail". Brettle was so concerned that he got up early the following morning to go again and check up on the man but to his surprise the body had disappeared.

Had the navvy regained consciousness and slipped away or had Palmer disposed of the body? We shall never know!!

A lovely story but is it based upon fact? I have not found evidence of the story in the press from the Nineteenth Century. It is certainly true that Brettle and Mace fought on several occasions. My research on the Internet found three occasions when Brettle and Mace fought in championship fights but all the dates were after Palmer was dead. Mace was a pugilist, who became known as the "Father of Modern Boxing", born in Beeston, Norfolk, England on 8th April 1831 and died November 30th 1910. In September 1858 Brettles won the Welterweight Championship of England by beating Mace by a knockout in Round 2. They fought again in September 1860 with a "no decision" result after 6 rounds. They fought again the next day with Mace winning in 5 rounds.

From *Pugilistica* (The History of British Boxing written by Henry Downes Miles published in 1906), I read about a time of bare-knuckle fighters, a time when fights were not limited to a maximum number of three minute rounds. It was a time when steam trains with carriages loaded with 'fight fans' would be taken to a fight location in the countryside. Often the local constabulary would stop the fight and spectators would re-board the train to be taken to a reserve venue in another county.

Pugilistica stated that Bob Brettle was born in Portobello, near Edinburgh, in

January 1832. He was a glassblower by trade and *"was engaged in one of the larger establishments in the hardware districts"* (I take this to be in Birmingham because later he is referred to as the "Birmingham Pet"). The first record that the author could find of Brettle fighting was a fight on 14th February 1854 when he fought Malpas of Birmingham in a fight which lasted eighty rounds. Brettle was originally awarded the fight but after *"A wrangle took place; the referee gave two decisions, and ultimately the stakes were drawn."* His next fight was against Jack Jones of Portsmouth on 21st November 1854. Forty-nine rounds were fought in one hundred and five minutes, with Jones having the best of the fight, before darkness came and the referee ordered them to fight again on the following week. However, the following Saturday, Brettle did not show up and *"it being discovered subsequently that he had been apprehended, either through the kind offices of his friends or by his own negligence, the stakes were awarded to Jones"*. His only other fight, before Palmer was arrested, was on 20th November 1855 when he defeated Roger Coyne of Birmingham in 49 rounds and 48 minutes.

Unfortunately I have found no evidence, so far, that the fighters, Brettle and Mace, fought prior to Palmer's death. My research could not prove or disprove the suggestion that Brettle trained at Hednesford but would suggest that if he was being backed by Palmer and Cook it was unlikely to have been for a fight with Jem Mace. So is this merely another good tale that has grown around the Palmer story?

Chapter 14: Suspicious Deaths –
Four of His Five Children

Poison from Palmer's fingers? The wagging tongue of Matilda Bradshaw

The Palmer Family grave in the churchyard at Rugeley. From the Illustrated
Times *2ⁿᵈ February 1856.*
*Four of William Palmer's five children were buried here along with many of
the Palmer Family, with the notable exception of William himself who was
buried in the grounds of Stafford Gaol.*

Of the five children born to William and Annie Palmer four died in infancy
and these deaths contributed towards the so-called "Rugeley Tragedies". Death
certificates show that Elizabeth, their second child, died on 6ᵗʰ January 1851
aged 10 weeks, with the reason for death given as, "*Convulsions 2 days Certified*".
Exactly one year later on 6ᵗʰ January 1852 Henry Palmer died aged one month,
again with the reason for death given as, "*Convulsions 2 days Certified*". On
19ᵗʰ December 1852 Frank Palmer died aged 7 hours "*Convulsions 7 hours
Certified*" and finally on 27ᵗʰ January 1854 John Palmer died aged 4 days
"*Convulsions 2 days Certified*".

When a fourth child, John, died Matilda Bradshaw, Palmer's cleaning lady,
ran next door in to the Bell public house swearing that she would never go into
Palmer's house again and that he'd "done away" with another child. When she
was asked how he'd done it, she replied that she had been upstairs with baby
John when Palmer had come in and said that he would look after his son. She
declared that she had gone downstairs when she suddenly heard Baby John
screaming. After rushing upstairs she found the baby dead.

She maintained that Palmer poisoned his children because she heard him say that a growing family was too expensive for his slender purse and that he couldn't altogether blame providence for the deaths of his children. When asked, Mrs. Bradshaw claimed that Palmer murdered them by dipping his finger in poison and then in honey (or in some reports sugar) and would make them suck his finger. Matilda was asked if she had ever seen him do it and she replied, **"No, but I know it in my heart to be true".**

There could be an alternative explanation for the infant deaths. Kathleen Smith in her 1994 dissertation, "Sinner, Saint or Political Pawn", suggested an alternative explanation for the four children dying in infancy and the subsequent death of their mother. She wrote:

> *William had appeared a devoted husband and father and a devout churchgoer, were these deaths suspicious as rumoured? It was not uncommon for children to die in infancy at this time without speculation, it is also possible that William could have had RH Positive blood and Anne have RH Negative blood in which case the first born child would live while further pregnancies would be affected by blood poisoning in the womb*[1] and after a fifth pregnancy the mother could die. Elizabeth Hamilton*[2] in her book about the Mordaunt Family of Warwickshire mentions that the butler Tomlinson had five children who died at under a year old (c.1844). No one seems to have suspected foul play in this case so why in the case of William Palmer?*

> **[1]By May 1968 all RH Negative women were injected with Anti D after giving birth to prevent this.*
> **[2] Life on a Country Estate in the mid-nineteenth century, pub The Dugdale Society 1991.*

Could Palmer really have been such a monster that he callously murdered four of his five children? Or does Kathleen Smith's hypothesis provide a medical explanation that is a more probable reason for these deaths?

Palmer's only surviving son, **William Brookes Palmer,** was affectionately called "Little Willie" by his father. Shortly after his mother died Palmer placed "Little Willie", then aged between six and seven years of age, in the care of Mrs. Salt. She recalls that when Palmer brought the child to her he appeared greatly affected, and, with tears in his eyes said, *"I have brought dear little Willie to you. It was Annie's desire, and I wish to carry out my dear wife's last injunction, which was to place him under your care."*

When Palmer was in Stafford Gaol he would not let either his mother or his son visit him for fear that a visit would be too distressing for them. When his sister visited Palmer in gaol they discussed his anxiety about his son. *The*

48

Illustrated Life & Career of Dr. William Palmer (published by Ward Lock 1856) stated that:

> *The poor little thing was ignorant of the doom awaiting his father, or, indeed, of his confinement in gaol, he being led to believe that he was ill at Birkenhead. He says he is sure there must be something dreadful the matter with him, or that he would be certain to come home.*
>
> *Poor little Willie Palmer is a nice boy, about seven years of age; he lifts his hat in an old fashioned way when he is spoken to. He seems to be a general favourite with all who know him.*
>
> *His father's miserable position was, of course, studiously concealed from him; and he did not become acquainted with it, until within a few days of Palmer's execution. It seems that a little boy (attending on his father, who was thatching a barn for old Mrs. Palmer) was playing with him. Willie made some reference to "Papa".*
>
> *"Papa," said his little playmate; "your Papa is in Stafford jail."*

William Brookes Palmer lived to the age of 76 having moved down to London where he spent most of his working life as a solicitor. He was living at 121 Croydon Road, Anerley, Surrey. His death certificate stated that his body was, *"Found dead 29th April 1926"* at *"21 Old Buildings, Lincoln Inn"*. Robert Graves in his book, *They Hanged My Saintly Billy*, and John Godwin in his booklet *The Pocket Palmer* stated that he committed suicide, however, the inquest held 1st May 1926 gave the cause of death as "Syncope and Asphyxia Coal Gas poisoning – Misadventure". The gas tap had been left on!

Chapter 15: Suspicious Deaths -
Uncle Joseph and Aunt's Chickens

Uncle Joseph (Bentley) - Died after drinking with Palmer

The death of Palmer's Uncle Joseph was referred to by the newspapers as another of the "Rugeley Tragedies" but if Palmer did murder this uncle there are those who would say that he at least did the world a favour!

Uncle Joseph was a disreputable character who was suspected of several crimes including arson and robbery. When his first wife died he had inherited a great deal of money and when his second wife died from a broken neck the local gossips suspected him of pushing her down the stairs. After his second wife died he took a mistress who lived with him and by her he had a daughter.

Joseph was Palmer's mother's brother who had lived at Longdon Green near Lichfield before moving to the village of Dodsleigh near Uttoxeter where he married his third wife. His neighbours used to call him "Beau Bentley" because he was always so well dressed.

It was claimed in the *Illustrated Life and Career of William Palmer of Rugeley*, published by Ward Lock 1856, that he also had a child by his illegitimate daughter. There was even talk that, after he had taken a third wife, several times he was seen being "*over friendly*" with another servant girl.

One night only a few months after Palmer's mother-in-law had died, Bentley and Palmer were drinking brandy and water together, when Joseph, who had been drinking heavily, fell from his chair supposedly in a drunken stupor. Reports vary but either the next day or three days later Bentley died. *The Illustrated Life and Career of William Palmer of Rugeley* maliciously stated that, "*It is general opinion that Palmer wanted his uncle out of the way*".

Bentley's death certificate stated that on 27th October 1852 Joseph Bentley; Male; Aged 62 years; Occupation - gentleman; Cause of Death - Malignant Disease of the stomach.

Certainly Uncle Joseph would not appear to be a great loss to the world but was Palmer really guilty of murdering him?

An Aunt Survives – But her Chickens did not!

Was there an attempted murder? We shall never know for sure.

The *Illustrated Life and Career of William Palmer of Rugeley* added another story, which stated that Palmer had another Uncle Bentley who was rich but elderly. He was a cripple but had a devoted and very caring wife, who was so affectionate towards her husband that her father-in-law changed his will so that she would inherit the house in the event that her husband should die before her. Thus it was that, as long as she was alive, William Palmer had no chance, in the immediate future, of inheriting the house.

One day, when old Mrs. Bentley was visiting Palmer's house in Rugeley, she complained of feeling unwell. Palmer "kindly" mixed a couple of pills for her, giving clear instructions that she must take the pills that night at bedtime. She however felt better and, as she disliked taking tablets, deliberately did not take them. Early next morning a messenger came from Palmer to enquire as to the lady's health. The messenger appeared "*very much disconcerted*", when he heard that she had not taken the medicine and suggested that, "*Mr. William felt very anxious about her health*", and added that she must be sure to take the pills that very night. Fortunately for her she decided she did not need the pills and threw them out of the window.

The story continued that, unfortunately, the aunt chose to throw the pills out of the window that overlooked the yard where they kept their chickens. Overnight the chickens had eaten the pills and were found dead the next morning.

Was it merely gossip, plain fact or just a good story?
We will never know for sure!

From a print in the book -
Illustrated Life and Career of William Palmer of Rugeley, *published in 1856 by Ward and Lock, 158, Fleet Street, London.*

It was labelled
"THE ONLY AUTHENTIC LIKENESS OF WILLIAM PALMER".

It is perhaps a little more flattering than the print shown on Page 1 of this book.

Chapter 16: Suspicious Deaths - Other Children

Deaths of Other Children - Palmer Suspected

In 1856 gossips claimed that Palmer had several illegitimate children by various "lady-friends" and that he poisoned four or five of them. One lady-friend was actually named as Jane Mumford who is thought to have had a child by Palmer but the infant died after a visit from Palmer. In the book *Illustrated Life, Career and Trial of William Palmer of Rugeley* published in 1856, there is a claim that:-

> *We heard an old man at Haywood count upon his fingers as many as fourteen girls whom Palmer had got in the family-way. He had, by a foolish freak, been concerned in the death of Abley. An illegitimate child, which a woman in Haywood had by him, died suddenly; and he is suspected of foul play.*

Should this damning report, made by just one old man, have been published or even be believed?

In George Fletcher's *The Life & Career of Dr. William Palmer of Rugeley* published in 1925 can also found the following: –

> *His avarice and lustful passions, with love of gambling and the Turf, soon overwhelmed him financially and socially. An illegitimate child of one of his maid-servants, born eighteen months after he had brought his bride home died suspiciously after a visit to his surgery for him to see how it was progressing.*

"Eighteen months after he had brought his bride home", would have been in the spring of 1849. I cannot find any other reference to there being a pregnant maidservant at that time in any of the books published in 1856. I wonder if this story is a mistake having been mixed up with the story of Eliza Tharme, his maidservant (see Chapter 20), who gave birth to his son in June 1855?

In 2001 many web sites that I saw gave greatly exaggerated reports of Palmer's "activities" whilst with Dr. Tylecote in Great Haywood.

One site www.microwaredata.co.uk/murder-uk/bookhtml_p/palmer_w00.html it stated –

> *Palmer took to crime at an early age. By the time he was seventeen he had been dismissed from one apprenticeship for embezzlement and fled from another after having been discovered running his own abortion service.*

At www.terryhayden.free-online.co.uk/murder/serialkillers/williampalmer.htm, it is claimed that after his job in Liverpool –

> *He was later to be sacked again, after it was discovered that he was operating*

an illegal abortion clinic. However I was unable to find any mention of any "abortion clinic or abortion service" in any of my reading of the reports published in 1856.

Is it likely that Dr. Tylecote, a respected local doctor for whom Palmer had worked, would have kept quiet and let Palmer be taken on, as a "walking pupil" at Stafford Infirmary if he had been involved in abortions?

Chapter 17: Suspicious Deaths - His Wife Annie

English cholera (natural causes), suicide or poison?

The newspapers included the death of Palmer's wife Annie as another of the suspicious deaths making up the "Rugeley Tragedies".

Anne Thornton, known as Annie, was an amiable young lady well liked by all who met her. As stated in Chapter 10 she was the daughter of a retired Army Officer Lieutenant Colonel William Brookes and his housekeeper Mary Thornton. Her mother was much younger than the Colonel and was a dreadful woman, with her behaviour deteriorating, she was regularly drunk and rowing with Colonel Brookes, cursing him for never having married her.

Colonel Brookes, like three of his brothers, committed suicide (he was found with a pistol by his side, *"having blown his brains out"*). After his death it was found that he had bequeathed property to his daughter Annie that brought in an income of about £250 annually. The Chancery Council took Annie away from her mother and made her a ward of chancery. Annie went to Abbots Bromley, some seven miles from Stafford, where she lived with one of her guardians, Mr. Charles Dawson and his family. There she nursed his first and later his second wife.

Annie was sent to Miss Bond's school in Haywood at a time when Palmer was an assistant to Dr. Tylecote and often went to the school to treat pupils and, in fact, treated Annie who had strained a ligament in her ankle. That is where Annie fell in love with William.

During Palmer's trial Serjeant Shee, who headed the Defence team, read to the jury a love letter from Palmer to his wife-to-be Annie. It is thought that it was sent to Annie whilst Palmer was in London studying to become a doctor:

MY DEAREST ANNIE,

I snatch a moment from my studies to write to your dear, dear, little self. I need scarcely say that the principal inducement I have to work is my desire of getting my studies finished so as to be able to press your dear little form in my arms.

With best, best love, believe me, dearest Annie, your own,

"WILLIAM."

After a long courtship, and in spite of Mr. Dawson's dislike of Palmer, they got married on 7th October 1847 at the Parish Church of St, Nicholas, Abbots Bromley in the County of Staffordshire. The marriage certificate gave their ages as William 23 and Annie 20.

The Rugeley Number of the *Illustrated Times* February 2nd 1856 said of Annie Palmer: –

.... *She was a clever, amiable, accomplished, and lovable girl, having, moreover a clear income of £200 a-year; her mother gave her besides a present of £700. Many speak of her almost with affection, and the poor of Rugeley still deplore the loss of a most sympathising benefactress. With such a wife, one would have thought that William Palmer would have lived in contented obscurity in his snug two-storeyed cottage, standing a little off the street, with its three square windows above, and one on either side of the door.*

However earlier in the same article the paper was far less respectful of her parents and then gave an insight into the "Victorian" view of illegitimate children:

More than twenty years since a retired Indian officer pitched his tent at Stafford, with a low vulgar woman, who was at once his housekeeper and mistress. He was a Lieutenant-Colonel, and his name was Brooks. The name of the housekeeper was Mary Thornton, and she it seems was subject to wild fits of ungovernable passion. The old Colonel, evidently a man of feeble mind though strong appetites, would flee from her anger to a neighbouring tavern, and there seek refuge till the storm had blown over. Not infrequently, however, she would track him to his retreat, and drag him home in ignominious triumph, Indeed, as it was naively remarked in the neighbourhood, "he might as well have been married." One night the old colonel was found lying dead upon the floor - a recently discharged pistol by his side. This was in 1834. By a will dated July 27, 1833, he bequeathed to Anne Thornton, the illegitimate offspring of his liaison with his housekeeper, nine houses at Stafford besides land, and the interest of 20,000 sicca rupees, for herself and her children; and appointed Dr. Edward Knight, a highly-respectable physician of Stafford, and Mr. Dawson, her guardians and trustees. To Mary Thornton, the mother of Anne, the Colonel bequeathed certain property, which was to pass to the daughter at the decease of the mother.

Anne Thornton is reported to have been painfully sensible of her own false position as an illegitimate child, and it is said that she was habituated to look upon herself as an outcast - being of an inferior order - one who should be deeply grateful to any man who would bestow his name upon a creature unrecognised by the laws, and tainted from her birth. Her first love was unpropitious. But fountains of that great deep, a woman's heart, had been broken up. The ark of her existence now drifted to and fro, reckless at the helm, and hope in the hold, until the waters of disappointment decreased, and the keel grated on the strand. Her mountain of Ararat was William Palmer.

Although Palmer seemed genuinely fond of Annie she saw less and less of him as his love for horses took over, not to mention his many lady friends. Poor Annie must also have been greatly saddened by the loss of four of five of her children.

In April 1854 William insured Annie's life for £13,000 and had only paid one premium of £760 before she died. The Insurance was taken out with the Prince of Wales Insurance Company who subsequently offset some of the amount, £3000 with Scottish Equitable and the same amount with The Sun.

On Monday 18th September 1854 Annie had gone with her sister-in-law Miss Sarah Palmer to a concert at Liverpool's St. George's Hall. She wore only a light summer dress and it was thought that she "caught a chill". They slept that night in Liverpool and spent the following morning there before catching a train back to Rugeley. When she arrived home she appeared unwell and went straight to bed. The next morning Palmer took her breakfast of tea with sugar (no milk), and some dry toast. Soon after this the vomiting started. On Sunday the elderly Dr. Bamford was sent for and he thought it to be a case of English cholera and prescribed pills containing calomel and colocynth and an "opening drought".

Twice on the Monday another medical man, one of Anne's guardians, described in one article as "the near deaf Dr. Knight" and "one of the antiquities of Stafford", also visited her but she was too ill for them to hold a conversation. (In fact Dr. Knight was a well respected doctor and only 73 years old). Dr. Bamford returned on Tuesday evening to find that only one pill had been taken. That was the last time he was to see Annie alive. One other medical man, Palmer's assistant, Benjamin Thirlby also saw Annie. Witnesses stated that the only medicine that Palmer ordered for Annie was a small dose of diluted prussic acid to reduce the retching.

In the *Illustrated Life and Career of William Palmer of Rugeley* published in 1856 by Ward Lock, it states that, on Friday September 29th 1854, Palmer wrote in his diary *"My poor dear Anne expired at 10 past 1"*. However in Fletcher's 1925 book, *The Life & Career of Dr. William Palmer of Rugeley* he states Palmer wrote in his diary, *"My darling Annie was called to-day by her God to the home of bliss so well deserved."* And on the day of the funeral he entered, *"Saw the last of my dear wife for ever. How desolate life is!"*

At Annie's funeral it is said that Palmer appeared greatly distressed as Annie's body was placed in the family vault, which stood beside St. Augustine's Church in Rugeley. Fletcher stated Palmer was apparently overcome by grief at his wife's funeral and was heard to cry aloud *"Take me. O God take me with my darling treasure."* However within a day or two of the funeral he was consoling himself in the arms of his pretty young housemaid Eliza Tharm.

The 1856 book states that:–

> *Eliza Tharm, the maid-servant, openly stated several months since, that she was certain Palmer would have taken improper liberties with her*

before his wife's death, if she had only given him encouragement. Whatever may have been the relations existing between the parties during the lifetime of Mrs. William Palmer, Palmer's diary leaves us in no doubt as to the nature of their relations subsequent to this event. Whether or not he spent the night following his wife's decease in the guilty embraces of his servant-maid, is known, of course, only to themselves; but it is certainly pregnant with suspicion, that nine months afterwards Eliza Tharm gave birth to an illegitimate child in Palmer's own house.

There were suggestions that Palmer's wife, being in very low spirits, perhaps even suffering suicidal melancholia, after the death of four of her children and being extremely worried about her husband's debts, might have committed suicide in the hope that the insurance money would save the husband that she loved dearly. It has even been claimed that taking out life insurance was Annie's own idea. The death certificate gave the cause of death as English cholera and her age as 27. The death certificate was signed by a Dr. Bamford (almost 80 years old) and one of Annie's guardians Dr. Edward Knight, a well respected Stafford doctor both of whom accepted Palmer's word about the symptoms and cause of death.

Inquest on Annie

After Palmer's arrest, on December 15th 1855, on suspicion of poisoning John Parsons Cook, there was a great deal of public interest. The Home Secretary Sir George Gray ordered that the bodies of his wife Annie and his brother Walter be exhumed and checked for poison. Annie Palmer had been dead for fifteen months.

On December 22nd 1855 the bodies of Annie and Walter Palmer were exhumed and brought to the Talbot Inn on the corner of Anson Street and Wolseley Road (not to be mixed up with the Talbot Arms where Cook died). The "viewing" of the bodies took place in the commercial room, which was the only room large enough to hold the Coroner plus Dr. Monkton, Dr. Bamford, and the jurymen in addition to the two coffins. The coroner's jury was made up of 23 men, none of whom had been on the jury for Cook's Inquest. They were named in the Staffordshire newspaper as, Mr. Wm. Fowke of Hagley, foreman, and Messrs. B. Woodward, James Mills, H. F. Hawkins, Thomas Byrne, James Moxon, Mellard Ingram, Thomas Clarke, Robert Tunnicliffe, George Todd, Thomas Devall, Abraham Pass, Thomas Sherratt, James Loverock, John Wills, John Rowley, Henry Brown, Joseph Degg, Richard Cheshire, George Verough Gilbert, George Tunnicliff, William Fortescue and George Tunnecliff.

Annie's coffin, which was made of oak, was opened first and although the body had been buried for fifteen months, the body was still in fairly good condition and Dr. Monkton easily removed the stomach and intestines for analysis. After

Annie's body had been "viewed" great distress was caused when Walter's sealed lead coffin was opened (see Chapter 18).

On Wednesday January 9th 1856 they had been due to complete the formal inquest on Annie Palmer but Dr. Taylor's findings were not ready and it was proposed that the inquest be adjourned. The Foreman of the Jury, Mr. W. Fowke, intimated that it would be more convenient if the inquiry was adjourned until Friday, the 11th, as Lord Lichfield's rent day fell on Wednesday, and market day was on Thursday.

In the end the inquest on her exhumed body was finally completed in Rugeley Town Hall, on Saturday 12th January 1856, when, after small traces of a poison called antimony had been found in her body, the jury recorded a verdict of murder. (It should be noted that antimony, whilst being a poison, can also, in small doses, be used as an effective purgative medicine.) William Palmer was not brought to trial for her murder having already been charged with the wilful murder of Cook.

Was Annie poisoned by Palmer or, out of love for her husband, did she give herself poison knowing that her husband, who was so deeply in debt, might be saved by the money from the insurance? Or did she die from natural causes (as explained in Chapter 14, her death could have been from natural causes if her blood group was RH Negative and William's blood group RH Positive)?

✦ ✦ ✦ ✦ ✦

The Interior of the Town Hall, Rugeley, During the Inquest on Walter Palmer. From *Illustrated Times 2nd* February 1856.

Chapter 18: Suspicious Deaths - Brother Walter

Did alcohol or poison finish him off

The death of Palmer's brother, Walter, formed another part of the "Rugeley Tragedies". As a youth, Walter worked for Messrs. Procter and Company who were corn merchants in Brunswick Street, Liverpool. At the age of twenty-one he inherited the £7,000 left to him in his father's will. With this money he set up his own corn factors in Stafford. Soon after that he married the ladylike Miss Agnes Milcrest who had an inheritance of £450 a year.

He was a popular fellow and friends called him "Watty". Unfortunately Walter began to drink heavily, his business started to suffer and he had less money to gamble. He was finally declared bankrupt in 1849, and although they still had his wife's money, he could not afford to pursue his interest in horse racing but his drinking increased. For a few years he went to live on the Isle of Man (see Chapter 21) but there his drinking led to his first attack of *"delirium tremens"* and again he was declared bankrupt. He returned to Liverpool to live nearer his eldest brother Joseph, and to be nearer to his widowed mother. *"Much to her sorrow"*, his wife finally felt compelled to leave him after his second attack of *"delirium tremens"*. This prompted Walter to go and stay with his mother for a few months. He next set up home in a small terraced house at Castle Terrace in Stafford becoming even more of a drunkard and remaining heavily in debt.

Gossips later claimed that William Palmer thought that he had found a new way of gambling. With a doctor's "insider knowledge", he could insure the life of someone who, in all probability, had not got long to live or even the gossips claimed, he would use poison to absolutely ensure that he collected the insurance money.

Was insuring a person known to be in poor health just a natural gamble for a gambling man, or was it a sinister plot where, if the insured person didn't die quickly enough, he could always finish them off with poison?

Whatever the truth might be it appears that Palmer approached his brother with a proposition. He suggested that, with the amount Walter was drinking, he couldn't possibly live more than ten years, so, as a gambling man, he was prepared to offer Walter £400 straight away if he would let him insure his life. So in December 1854, less than three months after Palmer had collect £13,000 insurance money following his wife's death, William tried to insure Walter's life with six different insurance companies. The Insurance companies that William approached and the amount he tried to insure Walter's life for, were as follows - The Solicitors' and General £13,000; The Prince of Wales £13,000: The Universal £13,000; The Indisputable £14,000; The Athenaeum £14,000; The Gresham £15,000; a grand total of £82,000, a veritable fortune in the 1850s. It is unsure if William was trying to insure Walter with all of the companies or was just finding the best deal, but his approaching so many companies certainly gave additional ammunition to the gossips.

William did not tell his brother how much he hoped to insure his life for. One company offered to insure Walter for £13,000 but only if Walter lived for at least five years but William did not take up that option. In the end William Palmer employed a man called Tom Walkenden to keep Walter sober long enough to sign the forms and convince the doctors appointed by the insurance company that he was fit and healthy.

On April 5th 1855 Mr. Waddell, surgeon of Stafford pronounced Walter to be, "healthy, robust and temperate", so William was finally able to insure Walter's life for £14,000 with the Prince of Wales Insurance Company. William Palmer paid only the first premium of £710, 13 shillings and 4 pence yet the unfortunate Walter did not get the £400 he had originally been promised by William but was given £60 and promised unlimited credit to buy drink from a local innkeeper.

Walter Palmer died on August 16th August 1855. William Palmer in his diary recorded that on the 16th August, "*Went to see Walter, who was very ill*"; and later added, "*Walter Palmer died at half-past two, p.m.*". The death certificate stated that Walter Palmer, male, formerly a corn dealer, died at Castle Terrace, Castlechurch (Stafford), the cause of death was given as "General visceral disease and Apoplexy"; present at the death was Tom Walkenden of Earl Street, Stafford.

Was it just coincidence that, like Palmer's wife before him, Walter died after William Palmer had paid just one life insurance premium? Mr. Lloyd, the landlord at the Grand Junction Inn Stafford reported that within an hour of hearing of his brother's death William Palmer's thoughts turned to his love of "the turf" when he asked Lloyd to send a telegram to the Clerk of the Course at Shrewsbury asking, "*Please tell me who has won the Ludlow Stakes?*" (Palmer's horse did not win!)

Gossips maintained that Walkenden, employed by William Palmer to look after Walter was actually instructed to encouraged Walter to drink heavily. Reporters from the *Illustrated Times* published on February 2nd 1856 wrote the following:

The man of the name of Walkenden, who has obtained so much notoriety, not only from the suspicion that he was engaged by William Palmer at a weekly stipend to ply the unhappy Walter Palmer with drink, but also for his general conduct when examined before the Coroner, resides in Earl Street, Stafford, in a house that adjoins St. Mary's burial-ground. We had determined on visiting this fellow, simply because we could not imagine or believe that a man could, without vengeance or cause for hatred, coolly hasten on the death of a person who considered and treated him as a friend. We paid this visit, mostly for our own consolation, so as to try and rid ourselves of the idea that such iniquity could exist.

Having been let in to the house by Walkenden's son, the reporters met the man and wrote:

Walkenden is a broad-faced man. His countenance is singularly flat,, but coarse and hard-featured. At first he stubbornly refused to hold any conversation with us. "The paper men have written me down as a rogue – let it be so," said he. "I've been blackguarded up hill and down dale, and it's best to let matters be. People may think as they like. I've nothing to say."

This appeared to us to be singular evidence of Walkenden's character. As we afterwards found out, he is obstinate to a remarkable degree. On the smallest attempt to force him to speak out at the inquest he in return abused Coroner, jury, and lawyers. The instant any coercion is attempted, the man resists.

However after some twenty minutes conversation Walkenden made a statement which the newspaper printed, part of which was as follows:

I knew Walter Palmer well. I had as great a respect for him as my own brother. Up to the 8th of April last, he lodged and boarded in my house, eating at my table with me and my family. When he was drinking heavy, he never had any appetite for eating. We have many times tried to prevent him from drinking, by taking away the bottle and hiding it. He used to say, "If I can't have it here, I'll go out and get it." Of course, when he insisted upon it, we were forced to give way, and let him have it; we had no other chance – I had no power over him. If I had been selling it to him, it might have been different, and even then he could have gone out and got it. It was his own, and he insisted what he liked with it.

Later in his statement he said:

When he had the delirium, I would not give him any gin, because Dr. Waddell said he was only to have two or three small glasses a day. But I used to see that he was sinking, and perhaps I would give him a glass or two more than Dr. Waddell directed, when I saw there was any necessity. But what was I to do? The poor fellow used to beg and cry for it as if it was his life

He used to do all he could, and be cunning to get gin. One morning, after I had had been sitting up with him all night, I thought he was so ill that he could not possibly leave his bed, and went down stairs to the kitchen which was under his bed-room. Whilst I was eating a little breakfast, I heard a noise overhead. "Why," I said, "that sounds as if he is out of bed; but it's hardly possible." I ran up stairs and I found him crawling on his hands and knees, and searching for something under the dressing-table, in the same place where formerly he used to hide his gin, to prevent us taking it away from him. He went on to add, *He used to hide his gin bottle in all sorts of places – under his bed-head or under his mattress, or in his boots, or anywhere.*

The day after Walter had died William Palmer went to Liverpool to Walter's estranged wife. She naturally wondered why she had not been told that Walter had been so ill. She wanted to go to see his body but was told that the coffin had already been sealed. In fact Mr. Vittie the Stafford undertaker stated at Walter's inquest that, *"Dr. Palmer ordered on August 16th, within an hour of the death, for his brother Walter a strong oak coffin, and a lead coffin, to be sent at once, and the funeral took place on the following Monday"* (August 20th) He added that the undertaker's boy had told him that the corpse had no need of embalming for, **"there be enough gin saturated in the flesh to preserve him for a year"**. (The last comment was stricken from the record of the inquest as hearsay)

Walter was buried in the Palmer Family vault which is in St. Augustine's Churchyard on the north-eastern side of the church. Once Walter was buried and Dr. Day had supplied a death certificate William Palmer wanted to claim the insurance money. However the insurance company withheld payment. Palmer wrote to Walter's widow, Agnes (who was then lodging at Edith Lodge, Graham Road, Great Malvern, Worcestershire) asking her to pay £85 he loaned Walter who had said his wife would repay, plus a mysterious £40 and further bills totalling £200. Agnes replied that Walter had told her that William had insured his life for £1,000 and promised him £500 but that her husband had only been paid a few pounds. In those circumstances she, having received no money from her husband in all their married life, felt that she should not be responsible for his debts. It is obvious that neither Walter nor his wife realised how much insurance was taken out on Walter's life. Palmer sent his friend and family solicitor Jerry Smith to get Walter's widow to sign a paper surrendering any interest in the life policy. She however wished her solicitor to see the papers and although Smith agreed to this he nevertheless took the papers away with him.

The Prince of Wales Insurance Company who had already paid out £13,000 for the death of his wife was suspicious when Palmer claimed a further £13,000 for the death of Walter. Two Inspectors, Field and Simpson, were sent to investigate the proposed insurance of a George Bates, but they also decided to also investigate Walter's death. With the insurance company refusing to pay the insurance money William Palmer's financial worries were greatly increased

The post-mortem on Walter on 22nd December 1855 was started at the Talbot Inn. After Annie's coffin had been opened and the body "viewed" it was the turn of Walter's coffin. Unfortunately although he had only been dead for four months he had been buried in a sealed lead coffin. The outer wood coffin was removed and a hole cut into the lid of the lead coffin that encased the body. Immediately noxious gases escaped from the coffin, which were so strong that it made most of those present vomit and several of the jury were still feeling sickly up to four days later. When the lead coffin lid was lifted the corpse presented a hideous sight. The face and cheeks were terribly swollen and limbs much distended and described as "*a mass of corruption, dropsy and gangrene*". Dr. Monkton had an almost impossible task of making a post mortem on Walter. The inquests of Annie and Walter were then promptly adjourned much to the relief of the coroner and jury.

The smell from the opening of Walter's coffin persisted for months and some say even years. They removed the wallpaper and sanded the floorboards in an attempt to rid them of the lingering smell. The publican of the Talbot Inn complained bitterly that it had ruined his trade and eventually the inn closed down.

On Monday 14th January 1856 a formal inquest on Walter was opened and immediately adjourned to the 15th to await Dr. Taylor's findings then finally to 23rd January when a verdict of willful murder was returned in spite of the fact that no poison was detected in the body.

The cases for the willful murder of John Parsons Cook, Annie Palmer and Walter Palmer were then brought before a grand jury at Stafford Assizes in March 1856. The jury considered that Palmer had a case to answer for the deaths of John Parsons Cook and Annie Palmer but found the case not proven in the death of Walter. Dr. Taylor originally thought the cause of Walter's death to be poisoning by prussic acid but later changed to agree with the other six doctors (including Dr. Day who had treated Walter Palmer) who all decided that Walter died of 'apoplexy'.

Did Walter drink himself to death or did William Palmer use poison to finish him off more quickly so that he could get his hands on the insurance money?

The *Illustrated Times* dated February 2nd 1856 published the following report:

THE LANDLORD OF THE TALBOT INN AT RUGELEY

Mr. John Williss, the landlord of the Talbot Inn, where the bodies of Mrs. William Palmer and Walter were opened, is a stout, jolly-looking man, who is trying to appear unhappy and who talks of ruin, because commercial travellers have of late taken a dislike to his house. We found him sitting in his bar, with a fat child between his knees, and sighing and drinking ale by turns, whilst his wife - a pretty little woman, with a baby in her arms, was endeavouring to reason him out of his despondency.

There was a gun over the fireplace, and he kept his eyes fixed on it like a crow. He occasionally thrust his hand into his brown velvet waistcoat, and glanced round at the rows of ale mugs and barrels of spirits, as though he was calculating what they would sell for, if the worst came to the worst. When a customer entered and called for ale, he rose to draw it with an air of resignation, and it was difficult to tell whether he or the beer-engine was groaning. The fat child was munching an apple, and nearly choked itself; and as Mr. Williss extracted the fruit from its mouth, he muttered something about it's being perhaps better to die young before it had come to want.

Three commercial travellers with plenty of luggage would restore Mr. Williss to happiness. There is one good thing; Mrs. Williss doesn't seem at all anxious on her husband's account, but appears to know that their sorrows will soon pass away. Mr. Williss made the subjoined communication to us:-

Yes sir, I'm the landlord of the Talbot Inn - not the Talbot Arms - that's old Masters as is the landlord of that, but I'm Williss.

Some time after the murder of Cook, and while Palmer was under arrest with sheriff's officers, it was determined to exhume the bodies of Mr. Walter Palmer and Mrs. Palmer. I knew they were going to do so, because two police officers stayed here all night. About seven in the morning, when we were in bed, on a bright frosty morning (it was very bright, added Mr. Williss), one of the policemen, by the name of Chesham who lodged here, came to our room, and says he, "Here you must get up, they are going to bring these bodies into the house; Mr. Bergen says they are to come here." I told him there was an outhouse and coachhouse where he could take 'em. Then Bergen told me they was to come here, and that he had a letter from the Secretary of State, saying they were to go into the Talbot Inn. We have had the coachhouse all cleared out on purpose; but Bergen says it's too cold there, the doctors can't manage their work; they must come here because the Secretary of State says so. I told him we could warm up the coachhouse but he wouldn't. They brought the corpses here. We were obliged to put 'em into the commercial-room, because that was the only place where the passage would let the coffins enter. Mrs. Palmer was not so bad, but Walter Palmer was shocking. It's a blessing he was taken away the same night. Only fancy, twenty-three jurymen, and I among the number, for I was a juryman, the coroner, four police-officers, and lookers-on in that little room, as is only about five yards by three. When the lid was lifted up the stench was awful. Captain Whitgreave took his stick and bobbed it through the window to let in the air (it's a beautiful ventilated room, too); some of the jurymen was sick. I don't know as ever

I smelt anything like it, it was uncommon bad.

In the commercial-room it seemed to soak into everything. It was against the walls, and in the paint, and in the looking glass even. We were obliged to have the passage took down (and it near killed the man as worked), and the wood-work painted, and the ceiling whitewashed. I never see such a thing; it was as if the things had been soaked in a liquor, and took it up in 'em. Of course, the boards where the stuff dropped from the coffin was all done for, and had to be taken up and burned. Ah! It was a nasty business.

The affair has been as good as £200 or £300 out of my pocket. Ah! I can't say the loss, I don't know it yet. Commercial gentlemen that used to come here before, and have done, some of them, for 20 years, won't come to the house now. One of them, only the other day, said to me (he takes a glass of brandy and water just for friendship sake), "I won't go into the house, and I won't look at the room; perhaps in a twelvemonth I may." I used generally to have four or five, and often more commercial gentlemen in a week. Now they don't come. Worse than that, they have taken away the "rent meeting." We live under Lord Lichfield, and the tenants used to meet in my house to pay their rents. Now this year, they let me provide the dinner, but they would not come after all, but took what we had provided from here to the Talbot Arms to be cooked. I was brought to this house in arms. My father and mother had it. We're the Talbot Inn. What's called the Talbot Arms, used to be the Crown formerly. They didn't alter it out of opposition, but this is a fact. They held under Lord Talbot, and I under Lord Lichfield, so they thought they ought to change.

There is some talk about getting up a dinner at my house as a recompense for what I've put up with. I can't say if it'll come off or not; perhaps as I'm in bad luck it won't; but I hope to Heaven it will, for I'm particular worried about this exhuming business, and wants to see somebody or other in the house.

Chapter 19: Suspicious Deaths - Narrow Escapes?
(Bates and 'Boots')

Did Palmer's groom and the "boots" from the Grand Junction Hotel have lucky escapes?

Palmer had not gained any money from the insurance company following the death of his brother Walter; several accounts claim that he was looking to find someone else to insure, then murder, in order to collect insurance money. George Bates was described in some accounts as Palmer's groom but in an interview published in the *Illustrated Times* February 2nd 1856 he was described as "a decayed farmer" employed by Palmer as "a kind of farm-bailiff". Later in the same newspaper it states that Bates formerly "held" a farm of 250 acres at Ranton, from Lord Lichfield. It appears that he ran into difficulties and had to give up the farm. When this happened, Palmer, who had known him for a few years, offered him a job as his "overseer".

The newspaper printed a statement from Bates that started,

I was a friend, not as is reported, the groom of Palmer. I was occasionally employed to look after and take care of his breeding-stud, and see to the little bit of farming he did, and take care that the men did their work, and so on …

A plot was hatched and then sealed over dinner at William Palmer's house. Bates had been invited to dine with Palmer, John Parsons Cook, Samuel Cheshire (the later to be disgraced Rugeley postmaster), Jere. Smith (friend and solicitor of the Palmer Family) and William Saunders (a horse trainer from Hednesford). It was decided to pass Bates off as "a gentleman and an esquire", a well-to-do farmer and, unbeknown to Bates, insure his life, with several insurance companies, to the value of £25,000. Cheshire and Cook were to act as witnesses to Bates signing the proposal. Smith was

George Bates from the *Illustrated Times* 2nd February 1856

Inspector Field from the *Illustrated Times* 2nd February 1856

to act as solicitor and would make 5% commission on the deal. Smith wrote to the first insurance company, the Midland Insurance Company, and was appointed as their agent with a proposal to insure Bates for £10,000.

The insurance company appointed two detectives Inspectors Field and Simpson who came to Rugeley to investigate the insurance proposal. They first interviewed postmaster Cheshire who assured them that Bates had an income of three or four hundred pounds a year and was free of debts, leading a life as an independent gentleman. Furthermore he had a fine cellar of wine.

There are two versions of the next part of the story. One version is that the inspectors next met Bates hoeing turnips in a field, the other version that they met him in the Market Place in Rugeley. Whatever the case they found a man dressed less well than "a well-to-do gentleman". When questioned it was revealed that Bates did not understand what life insurance was all about. He was under the impression that the policy was worth £6,000 and that he would receive £2,000 with the inference that he hadn't even realised that the money only came after his death. In his book, *They Hanged My Saintly Billy*, Robert Graves suggested that Jere Smith, with Cook a willing participant, was playing a joke on Bates. It was their way of warning Palmer not to pursue his claim against The Prince of Wales Insurance Company to recover the insurance money due upon the death of Walter Palmer. When Palmer was tried for the murder of Cook the prosecution tried to question Bates about the insuring of his life. The Defence objected to the story as being irrelevant to the case and the judge agreed. The Prosecution did not pursue the matter. Bates was however questioned about his part in Palmer sending gifts to the Coroner.

**Was this a case of Bates having a narrow escape
or just humour that went too far?**

"Boots" at the Junction Inn poisoned?

Another witness that Inspectors Field and Simpson interviewed was Tom Myatt the "boots" (a man who polished the boots of residents) at the Grand Junction Hotel in Stafford. Palmer, finding that the inspectors had spoken to Myatt and wanting to know what had been said, bought him a glass of his favourite drink, a brandy and mixed it with water. Myatt later claimed that, at the time, the drink didn't taste funny but that later he was "took bad" and that he was ill for three or four days after drinking the brandy.

"Boots" was later to give evidence at Walter Palmer's inquest. He stated that, two days before Walter died, William Palmer brought two medicine bottles to the stable-yard at the Junction Hotel which he left with him. Palmer had returned the next day and asked "Boots" for the bottles and he had seen him add the contents to a half-full medicine bottle. Mr. Lloyd the landlord also saw this.

Fletcher in his 1925 book commented that this was "a curious place to select for compounding medicine". There had been evidence given by George Whyman, a shop assistant, that William Palmer had bought a quantity of jalap (a purgative drug) and prussic acid (a poison) from Mander & Co, wholesale chemists of Cock Street, Wolverhampton. The inference is that Dr. Palmer might have been mixing poison to give to his brother Walter.

Was "Boots" just a simple man inventing a story to enjoy the attention gained by claiming to be a "victim" of the infamous Dr. Palmer, or did Palmer really attempt to poison him?

"Boots" at the Grand
Junction Hotel, Stafford.
From the *Illustrated Times*
2nd February 1856

Chapter 20: Suspicious Deaths -
Eliza Tharme's Baby

Palmer's maid-servant and mistress – death of their illegitimate son 1855

Eliza Tharme was a pretty looking eighteen-year-old live-in maidservant at Dr. Palmer's house. She was the youngest of ten children born to James and Mary Tharme from Colton, a village near Rugeley. It is not known if they had a relationship before Palmer's wife died but there is little doubt that she soon became Palmer's mistress after Annie died.

In Palmer's own diary (later used in evidence at his trial) he recorded Eliza giving birth to a son at his home with the brief words, *"Eliza confined of a little boy at 9 o'clock at night"*. The diary entry was on June 26th 1855, just nine months after his wife had died on September 29th 1854. (Note that the birth certificate differed from Palmer's diary giving the date of birth as June 27th 1855). The diary also shows that when the boy was being born Palmer was away at Newcastle.

Eliza's child, Alfred, was sent to Armitage, some two or three miles from Rugeley, to be cared for by a "nurse". It was claimed that one day Palmer sent for the young child saying that he wished to see that the child was well. *The Illustrated Life and Career of William Palmer of Rugeley* published in 1856 added:

> *The reader will guess the result, the child was seized with convulsions while going home and died shortly after, or as some say on its journey back.*

The boy died on November 17th 1855 in the same year as he was born and just four days before John Parsons Cook died. In his diary Palmer did not record the death of Alfred. The registers of birth and death record that Eliza Tharme gave birth to Alfred Tharme, born on 27th June 1855 in Market Street, Rugeley (Benjn Thirlby present at the birth) no father's name was recorded, and that Alfred died at Armitage on 17th November 1855 aged 5 months, the cause of death being given as "Erysipelas 5 days Certified" (Benj'n Thirlby in attendance). (Erysipelas is also known as "St. Anthony's Fire" because it is a fever that produces deep red coloured skin).

In the Rugeley Edition of the *Illustrated Times* February 2nd 1856 (who spelt Tharme without an 'e') they wrote:

> *We next hear of William Palmer in Stafford gaol. Before, however, he is conveyed there, he took a farewell leave of Eliza Tharm, his maid-servant, throwing his arms round her neck, and requiting her illicit love with a £50 Bank of England note.*

Gossips and newspaper articles hinted that Palmer "might" have poisoned his illegitimate son. Was this the case, or, was it a case of the newspapers and gossips "giving a dog a bad name"? As Glen Chandler who researched Palmer before writing the T.V. drama The Life and Crimes of William Palmer pointed out to me, the cause of death in this case, St. Anthony's Fire, was so different from all the others deaths that made up the "Rugeley Tragedies", that it is doubtful if this actually was a case of murder.

Chapter 21: Suspicious Deaths - A Manx Murder and Ghost

In 2002, the year after I had written the Palmer web site for the Staffordshire Learning Net, I received an e-mail from Julie Laslett from the Manx Multimedia Centre. She asked me about Palmer's links with the Isle of Man and later she came up with a rumour that Palmer had committed a murder on the Isle of Man.

I was able to establish the link between Palmer and the Isle of Man, in that his brother moved to live on the Isle of Man for a few years after he first went bankrupt. With additional help from Howard (Pip) Phillips, from the Isle of Man Newspapers, another fascinating Palmer story was tracked down.

It is thought that William Palmer visited Walter on the Isle of Man and that William stayed at the old Marine Hotel in Crown Street, Peel. Whilst he was there he became acquainted with a man called Spurrier, a wealthy stagecoach driver from Onchan. The pair were frequently seen together on the front of the stagecoach running between Peel and Douglas.

It is alleged that one night in the hotel, after a heavy drinking session, Palmer bet Spurrier that he couldn't down 20 raw eggs. Unfortunately Spurrier accepted Palmer's challenge, became ill and needed to retire to his room. Dr. Palmer followed him up and remained with him all night. **Next morning Spurrier was dead**.

It was reported that Spurrier had arrived at the Marine Hotel with around a thousand pounds on him (apparently he did not believe in banks), however, not a single penny was found on the corpse. Although Palmer was suspected of foul play he was never brought to justice in the Manx courts and, with no charges brought against him, he was free to return to Stafford.

There are ghostly stories that Spurrier's fine coach and horses have been heard since on many occasions passing the site of the old hotel in the early hours of the morning being driven by the ghost of Spurrier. The old Marine Hotel burnt down in 1885. The new Marine Hotel was not built on the same site but was relocated to Peel Promenade where it still stands today. The old Marine site was rebuilt as private houses (Wavertree and Seaforth) and a ships provisions store with accommodation known as the "Dales".

Howard Phillips met a woman who had the building at the old Marine site exorcised. He asked why and she explained that items kept vanishing and turning up at different locations, but worse was an apparition that several people kept seeing of a male figure with a tall black hat. She claimed that she had never seen a picture of Palmer before but when Howard showed her a picture of Palmer (the one at the beginning of this book, Palmer the Gambler) she said it was "very scary".

**Did Palmer commit another murder on the Isle of Man,
or is this just another good story?**

Chapter 22: Palmer's Crimes Other than Murder

Theft, fraud, forgery, bribery etc, etc

Theft:

There were stories from Palmer's childhood of minor thefts from his sister and his mother, as well as tricking his father's workmen to obtain money. He was dismissed from his first job in Liverpool for stealing money sent by letter to his employers. Whilst at Dr. Tylecote's there was a story that he cheated a farmer out of £5. A widow and mother of nine children, by the name of Mrs. Hawkins, living at Grey Friars in Stafford, was "tossed by a bull" breaking her leg and two ribs. The farmer who owned the bull, Mr. Parker, sent for Dr. Tylecote her "club doctor" but he was ill and couldn't come. Another surgeon, Mr. Masfen, was sent for and Tylecote sent Palmer so that he could make up any medicines that might be required. After Masfen had left, Parker asked about Masfen's fee with Palmer stating it was two guineas. Seeing that the farmer had quite a bit of money Palmer asked if he could change a five-pound note for him. When the farmer gave him five sovereigns Palmer said that he had left the five pound note in the pocket of his other trousers but promised to send it over with the boy who was to deliver the medicine. Needless to say the five-pound note did not arrive and five weeks later the farmer met Dr. Tylecote and complained that he had not received his money. Palmer's mother eventually had to pay the farmer.

In the "suspicious deaths" of Bladen and Bly there were accusations made that Palmer had stolen money. Also as Cook lay dying Palmer collected Cook's winnings using them to pay off debts however Palmer would have claimed that it was money Cook owed him.

Fraud and Forgery

His debts grew and he obtained loans, supposedly with his mother's agreement to stand as guarantor that the money would be repaid. Eventually on January 20th 1856, almost five months before his murder trial, Palmer was taken from Stafford Gaol to London and appeared in the Lord Chancellor's Court at Westminster as a witness. A Mr. Padwick had brought an action against Palmer's mother, Sarah Palmer, to recover a bill for £2,000 dated July 3rd 1854. Palmer had been arrested on December 12th 1855 in connection with this matter on the same day that he was later put under house arrest for murder.

All witnesses testified that the signature on the original document was not that of Sarah Palmer. When testifying Palmer calmly stated that it was not his mother's signature but that he had persuaded his wife (now dead) to forge his mother's name and he had seen her do it. The case against Mrs. Sarah Palmer was dropped and Palmer was returned to Stafford Gaol. Robert Graves in his book *They Hanged My Saintly Billy* makes the suggestion that one of the spectators at the trial in Westminster was none other than Jane Widnall (Smirke) Palmer's former girlfriend returned, a widow, from Australia.

Debt

On one occasion when Palmer ran away from Dr. Tylecote's to Walsall with a girlfriend, Jane Widnall, they got into debt and his brothers had to pay his bills. Later in his life the heavy costs involved in maintaining a string of racehorses led him in to the clutches of moneylenders charging up to 60% interest, such as Mr. Padwick who sued Palmer's mother to recover some of the money owed to him and Thomas Pratt. In the early nineteenth century debt was considered a serious crime and those in debt were often given a sentence of transportation or at least, long jail sentences. At one time Palmer bought two top class horses at £2,000 guineas each even though he could not afford to buy them. His mother was rich and in desperation he forged her signature to guarantee the loans to buy the horses.

After his wife, Annie, died in September 1854 the insurance money, £13,000, was paid to him within just six weeks, but this only went part way towards settling his huge debts. By the autumn of 1855 he owed £15,000 and bills for a further £11,500 were due in the November. If these bills were not settled the fact that he forged his mother's signature was likely to be discovered. Palmer also owed money to many of the Rugeley tradesmen. Later he forged John Parsons Cook's signature to secure more loans.

Fletcher's book written in 1925 told us more of Thomas Pratt the solicitor and moneylender. On January 23rd 1856 Pratt was called to give evidence to the coroner's jury, at the inquest into Walter Palmer's death, about the insurance proposals that William Palmer had taken out on his brother Walter. However after just two questions he broke down and screamed excitedly, "*How can you ask such questions of a man with three young children and a wife who will probably be ruined by this affair?*" There was doubt as to whether he would be able to give evidence in Palmer's trial at the Old Bailey but he recovered to give evidence on 20th May. Fletcher states –

> *. . the cold, merciless manner in which he gave his evidence made a great impression at the trial, and in a few weeks he became raving mad and - I believe - died shortly afterwards in an asylum.*

Thomas Pratt was also the solicitor who obtained the life insurance on both Annie Palmer and later on Walter Palmer

Insurance fraud

Palmer tried to insure his brother with numerous insurance companies to the total value of £82,000 although in the end he settled for a more modest insurance of £14,000. By employing Tom Walkenden to keep Walter sober long enough to get the medical clearance needed for the insurance he was committing fraud. If he had indeed poisoned his wife and his brother, as was suggested, his motive must have been to defraud the insurance companies.

Fixing horse racing /doping horses.

Palmer, with his knowledge of medicines and drugs, is reputed to have been a "nobbler" using this knowledge to attempt to fix the result of several races by doping horses. Although never proved there were numerous rumours surrounding him, which was made worse in racing circles, when he got a reputation for not paying all his bets. On occasions he even had to borrow money to pay off debts before his horses were permitted to start a race.

Bribery

Before Palmer's trial the newspapers carried the story that Palmer had offered a bribe of £10 to the postboy if he would "upset the vehicle", which he was going to drive to the railway station, carrying the jar carrying the organs removed at John Parson Cook's post mortem. The postboy refused. Another of Palmer's friends was Samuel Cheshire, the Rugeley Postmaster. Palmer had been in the habit of letting Cheshire borrow his carriage on Sundays to take his wife for a drive. Cheshire agreed to open letters addressed to the Coroner (Cheshire was later sent to prison for opening the mail). Cheshire went to Palmer's house where Palmer was in bed ill; he brought the news that Dr. Taylor had written to the Coroner to say that no poison had been found in the samples sent to him from Cook's post mortem. It is reported that Palmer, on hearing the news, said to Cheshire "I am as innocent as a baby". *The Illustrated Times* February 2ⁿᵈ 1856 added:-

> *No doubt this little bit of information helps to raise Palmer's spirits. All he has to do now is to make it right with the coroner W. Webb Ward Esq., so on the 8th December, he writes first of all a note to Mr. Frantz, the poulterer of Stafford, ordering some "nice pheasants and a good hare," and then a note to the Coroner to accompany the said game. In this latter note he lets out that he has seen "in black and white," Dr. Taylor's statement to the effect, that no poison had been found, and he coolly enough suggests to the Coroner, that he should like a verdict, "died of natural causes, and thus end it." These notes Palmer commits into the hands of Mr. George Bate, who starts off to Stafford. He goes to Mr. Frantz, the dealer in game, who says he is a pheasant short of the order, but will send the other things to Bate, at the Junction Hotel. Bate redirects the parcel, and gives the lad 3d. to carry it to Mr. Ward's office. He next goes in search of Mr. Ward, whom he unearths in the smoking-room of the Dolphin Inn which owns the only billiard-room in Stafford. George having "tipped him a knowing wink," the Coroner came out to the foot of the billiard-stairs,*

and there received the said letter.

On Thursday, the 13th, George Bate is again wanted on a similar errand. The adjourned inquest meets on the morrow, and Taylor's evidence will then come out. Palmer is still ill in bed, and when Bate arrives, he is sent to Thirlby (Ben that used to be at Salt's), to borrow a £5 note. This he came back with, but Palmer, in the meanwhile, seems to have thought the amount too little for his purpose. He therefore sets Bate to hunt for bank notes in a looking-glass drawer. George can only see one for £50, which Palmer we suppose thinks too much, and yet it is a question of life and death with him. At this juncture, a sheriff's officer is announced.

A Sheriff's officer was to arrest Palmer for being in debt. Bate was ordered out whilst Palmer talked to the officer but then Bate was summoned again. The article continued:-

When he comes back again, Palmer hands him a letter to take to W. W. Ward, Esq., which he is to be sure no one sees him deliver. George did not like so much secrecy, and he asked Mr. Palmer if he could not send some one else. Palmer replied, "Why, George, as for this poor fellow Cook, they will find nothing in him; for he was the best "pal" I ever had in my life, and why should I have poisoned him? and he added, "I am as innocent as you George." George thereupon goes off to Stafford. This time he catches William Webb Ward, on the road between the Station and the Junction Hotel, and there slyly slips the note into his hand. Not a word passed; both of them no doubt understood each other.

Palmer was guilty of many crimes and desperate to get out of debt, but was he desperate enough to poison his friend and racing companion John Parsons Cook?

Chapter 23: Palmer Owner of Racehorses
Palmer neglects doctoring to pursue his love of the 'Turf'

Palmer had soon tired of being a country doctor and turned his attentions to horse racing thus spending less and less time on his patients and in effect, retired from being a doctor. The "Turf" was not an uncommon hobby for the men in Rugeley. Rugeley was famous for its annual horse fair and had its own racecourse at Etching Hill on the edge of Cannock Chase (the racecourse has long since disappeared) and there were several other racecourses within easy reach of Rugeley, such as Hendesford, Penkridge and Wolverhampton.

As was suggested in the case of Abley and Walter, Palmer loved to bet. However, Palmer was not content with just the occasional wager, he wanted to own and run his own horses, a pursuit normally exclusive to the rich gentry. He acquired his own stables and started to buy horses, paying high prices for them. A broadside printed in Stafford tells us that - *The first race-horse he possessed was purchased from Mr. John Meeson, late of the Swan Inn, Stafford and bore the ominous name of "Doubt." With this horse he won the Leamington Stakes, in 1848, realising the sum of £1,000, which it is said he paid for the mare.* However an article in Gibbons Stamps Monthly in January 2001 states - *His first horse "Goldfinger" was unplaced in its first appearance but made up for this by two second and two third places in its first season and in 1853 despite carrying top weight, won the "Tradesman's Plate" at Chester to win a purse of £2770. Palmer also backed his horse to win at thirty to one.* Whichever horse he first purchased, it would appear that his love of the turf was the start of his downfall for he certainly did not have the funds needed to maintain a whole string of horses when, on his own admission, keeping each race-horse cost £700 a year. At one time he had seventeen horses many of whom he sent to train at Hednesford. His own stables were on the outskirts of Rugeley consisting of a paddock with stables and several adjacent fields. Though at first he was fairly successful with his horses and his betting, soon his debts mounted. He was no longer gambling as a sport but desperately attempting to win enough money to clear his debts as he fell into the hands of the moneylenders charging up to sixty percent interest.

After just one year in racing Palmer was known as a "defaulter" for not paying his debts and at one time was stopped from running one of his horses "Goldfinder" and had to be lent money to pay his bets. His 'money problems' led him to being banned from being a member of Tattersall's the leading European bloodstock auctioneers where most top class horses were bought and sold. Palmer also gained a reputation as a "nobbler" who tried to fix the results of races by doping a horse that was thought to have a chance of beating his own horse. The "Racing Authorities" were a powerful body and by upsetting them Palmer made many enemies who were keen to see him convicted when his trial came to court. It was claimed that the Attorney General, who prosecuted Palmer, had a personal friend who told him Palmer had "nobbled" his horse.

In the *Illustrated Life, Career and Trial of William Palmer of Rugeley* published in 1856 they printed the words of an anonymous gentleman who claimed to know Palmer:-

> *I knew him, sir - I have done business with him - I had great difficulty in getting my money - he was bad pay, sir - he was not admitted at Tattersall's, nor was he received by the first-class betting men. I've seen him over and over again take his place in a sort of corner immediately under the grand stand just with two or three, - and, amongst them, a little dwarf of a man, name of Dyke, who used to stick pretty close to him - but none of the nobs went anear him.*

Palmer was known as "a very good loser" accepting with good grace when he lost. Unfortunately he lost far too often. George Bates who was employed by Palmer claims that his downfall and his troubles stemmed from one particular race. Palmer's horse "Nettle" had been entered in the Oaks and in fact was, at one stage, handily placed in second place. Unfortunately just after the mile-post the horse swerved to the left and stumbled over the chains beside the track. Nettle's jockey Marlow, wearing Palmer's colours of all yellow, was thrown to the ground landing in furze bushes fracturing his thigh. It was claimed that Palmer calmly accepted the incident and merely said when friends commiserated with him, *"It is a bore though isn't it?"*

To pay off his debts, after his arrest, seventeen of Palmer's horses were auctioned at Tattersall's. The publicity arising from the murder case helped to

One of Palmer's horses "The Chicken", renamed "Vengeance" by new owner.
From the Illustrated Life and Career of William Palmer *published in 1856*

swell the crowd attending the auction and the keen competition to own one of his horses led to the sale raising a total of £3,906. The most expensive purchase was the four year old "The Chicken" which was bought by Mr. Horlock for 800 guineas. The Prince Consort, "Albert the Good", bought another of the horses, 8 year old "Trickstress", for 230 guineas.

With Palmer branded as a callous murderer, books and newspapers of the time painted a picture of riotous behaviour from Palmer and his racing friends. One picture (below) was said to depict part of their return journey after The Derby.

Palmer and Party in a Fix Returning from the Derby
from *Illustrated Life, Career, and Trial of William Palmer of Rugeley*
published 1856

The account from the *Illustrated Life and Career of William Palmer of Rugeley* published in 1856 stated:

> *The fun commenced at the very edge of the race-course, where a solemn-looking old gentleman driving quietly home in his four-wheeler was hit on the head by a pincushion thrown by a moustached swell on a drag, and, becoming indignant, was immediately assailed with a very frail storm*

of musical pears, snuff boxes, pincushions, dolls, and all variety of "knock-'em-down," prizes. There was a van filled with cheap crockery, a bad investment to bring to the Derby, and that is, of course, immediately stormed. Every carriage, cab, or omnibus that passed was assailed with chaff, mild in the first instance, but growing stormy and abusive under provocation; long peashooters were produced, and a volley of missiles blown against the windows of the houses in Cheam and Sutton; post-horns, which during the day had, by the simple insertion of a cork in the mouth-piece, been turned into drinking goblets, now once more became post-horns, and blow defiant, sentimental, and drunken notes. Palmer's party were more uproarious than any on the road; and when they pulled up at the Cock, at Sutton, so much additional liquor was imbibed, that even the driver lost his head; and just before they reached Kennington-gate, ran into a gig, in which a stout old gentleman was quietly driving home with his wife, and, to use Mr. Watkin's elegant expression, "upset the whole biling of 'em." Such an accident as this, however, was but little thought of on the Derby-day, and, after a few minutes, Palmer and his friends were again on their way to town, to wind up a day of excitement with a night of debauchery.

Chapter 24: The Trial –
How the Trial differed from Today

Palmer not permitted to give evidence

After the Criminal Evidence Act 1898 prisoners could, if they so wished, give evidence and be cross-examined, from the witness box. In fact from 1898 if the accused did not wish to give evidence they ran the risk of the jury making the assumption that they had something to hide. However in the 1850s prisoners, such as Palmer, were not allowed to give evidence on their own behalf.

About three weeks after the Coroner's inquest there was a suggestion that there should be a magistrates hearing into Cook's murder. However when John Smith, Palmer's solicitor, heard this he immediately wrote to the Home Secretary to remind him that Lord Campbell had strongly expressed a wish that there be no further discussion in newspapers or elsewhere for fear that the prisoner's case might be prejudiced. Had there been a magisterial investigation, Palmer would have had the right to give evidence and speak in his own defence. **So it was that Palmer was tried without ever having had the opportunity, at any stage, to give his own account of events.**

In addition Palmer's Defence were not permitted to make a closing speech summing up the case on behalf of the prisoner. This changed with the introduction of the Denham Act 1865, just nine years after Palmer's trial, which gave a Defence lawyer the right to make a second speech, after the prosecution, summing up their case.

In 1856 there was no Court of Criminal Appeal and after the verdict the only way Palmer could appeal against his sentence was by appealing directly to the Home Secretary.

A couple of petitions were made to the Home Secretary, on Palmer's behalf, on the grounds that strychnine was not found in the body of the deceased John Parsons Cook. Another issue raised was that the timing of the execution, 14th June 1856, was the day on which, together with France, Britain was celebrating the ending of the Crimean War and also the day on which the Prince Imperial was to be baptised. They suggested that the execution of a man, about whose guilt there was some doubt, would surely spoil such a festive day. Sir George Gray, the Home Secretary, replied that he could, "*see nothing in the points pressed upon his attention to justify his interfering with the due course of the law.*" and, therefore, he refused to reduce or postpone the sentence.

Nowadays there is a Court of Criminal Appeal. The setting up of a Court of Appeal was considered at the end of the Nineteenth Century. The "final nudge" came as a result of another Staffordshire case. On May 17th 1907 the Home Secretary advised His Majesty to grant George Edalji a free pardon, without compensation. Edalji was the son of the Vicar of Great Wyrley in Staffordshire and had been sentenced to seven years penal servitude in 1903 following a series of incidents in which horses were badly maimed. Sir Arthur Conan Doyle, the author famous for his Sherlock Holmes books, was one of the men who campaigned on Edalji's behalf. Following Edalji's release in 1907 a Commission of Enquiry was set up to look at criminal appeals. Edalji returned to his job as a solicitor but never had the satisfaction of receiving an official apology for his wrongful conviction.

The Power of the Press to comment *"sub judice"*, (before a trial has reached a verdict), has now been limited by the Contempt of Court Act 1981. Under the Contempt of Court Act of 1981 so-called "background" material, which has not been heard by a jury, cannot be published until a trial is finished.

For months before Palmer's trial, almost on a daily basis, the newspapers published material that, without doubt, would be certain to prejudice any jury. Reporters had interviewed all of the main witnesses and published damning statements as well as publishing accounts of the so-called "Rugeley Tragedies", suspicious deaths that they implied might have been murders committed by Palmer. Each new story cast further doubt upon the possibility of Palmer being innocent. The swift passing of a new Act of Parliament that then permitted the case to be switched to London only served to produce even more adverse publicity.

The *Times Report of the Trial of William Palmer* published in 1856 shows that even the Attorney-General who personally conducted the prosecution against Palmer commented, in his opening speech, upon the fact that the details of the case had been widely reported and discussed.

> *Gentlemen of the jury, the duty you are called upon to discharge is the most solemn which a man can by possibility have to perform - it is to sit in judgment and to decide an issue on which depends the life of a fellow human being who stands charged with the highest crime for which a man can be arraigned before a worldly tribunal. I am sure that I need not ask your most anxious and earnest attention to such a case; but there is one thing I feel it incumbent on me to urge upon you. The peculiar circumstances of this case have given it a profound and painful interest throughout the whole country.*
>
> *There is scarcely a man, perhaps, who has not come to some conclusion on the issue which you are now to decide. All the details have been seized on with eager avidity, and there is, perhaps, no one who is not more or less acquainted with those details. Standing here as a minister of justice, with no interest and no desire save that justice shall be done impartially, I feel it incumbent on me to warn you not to allow any preconceived opinion to operate on your judgment this day. Your duty - your bounden duty - is*

to try this case according to the evidence which shall be brought before you, and according to that alone. You must discard from your minds anything that you may have read or heard, or any opinion that you may have formed.

In asking the jury to, *"discard from your minds anything that you may have read or heard, or any opinion that you may have formed"*, the Attorney-General was surely asking the impossible of them. All of the jury must have been aware of much of the sensational publicity surrounding the case for Palmer had been tried and found guilty by the newspapers and the case was the talk of the nation.

Chapter 25: The Trial – Setting the Scene

The twelve days that sealed Palmer's fate

Palmer's trial started on May 14th 1856. Robert Graves in his Foreword to his book *They Hanged My Saintly Billy* (first published in 1957 now published in paperback by Xanadu Books ISBN 1-85480-004-3), started his book with the following words:

> *Today is the centenary of Dr Wm Palmer's public execution for the alleged poisoning of his friend John Parsons Cook; and all opponents of capital punishment should be wearing black. "I am a murdered man," Dr Palmer told the Prison Governor after his twelve-day trial, one of the best attended, and most scandalous ever staged at the Old Bailey; which was the truth. The medical evidence against him had broken down completely, and the circumstantial evidence conflicted, but the Lord Chief Justice and the Attorney General were both out to secure a verdict of guilty from the handpicked jury.*

Dudley Barker in his book *Palmer, The Rugeley Poisoner*, one of the Rogues Gallery Series published in 1935 wrote:-

> *The trial of Palmer was one of the greatest trials in the whole of English law, if not the greatest. Certainly there have been few trials that have aroused such tremendous interest, not in this country only, but all over the civilised world. And yet two-thirds of the evidence of expert witnesses was highly technical, and consisted of the evidence of expert medical witnesses as to the symptoms of the administration of strychnine.*

> *It is interesting to analyse the cause of the excitement that the trial produced. First of all, it was due to the social position of the characters involved, all middle-class people, well-educated and apparently in respectable positions in life. There is no class of murder that arouses as much public interest as this. A murder in the slums, no matter how sensational, has always an atmosphere of sordidness; a murder in high society is scandal enough, but it seems a little remote, a little too much on the plane of history. But a murder among the middle class is both "respectable" and familiar. It is happening to people whom one might meet and mix with in the ordinary. It is drama set on a stage that everybody knows.*

> *Palmer's case had that element of popular appeal very strongly, for was not Palmer himself a doctor in practice, and his victim a young fellow with a slightly discreditable and wild reputation for gaming and racing and other interesting vices? But the case had much more than that*

as well. It became almost a State trial, it involved a special Act of Parliament, it drew to itself some of the most eminent scientists of Europe as witnesses, and even Royalty as audience, and it evoked some of the finest examples of legal oratory in the whole of the English literature of the Bar.

The build up to the trial was sensationally covered in great detail by the newspapers. The suspicious death of Cook, then the stepfather ordering an inquest and getting the famous Dr. Taylor to provide evidence was swiftly followed by the coroner's verdict of willful murder. After Palmer's arrest and the Home Secretary's involvement in ordering that two more bodies be exhumed, keen reporters unearthed stories of other suspicious deaths and of Palmer's debts. Immediately prior to the trial there was another court hearing at Westminster involving admissions of forgery. Then the passing of a new Act of Parliament so that the trial could be held at the Old Bailey in London, supposedly because it was felt that he would not receive a fair trial at the Stafford Assizes. All these factors added to the public's interest in the case with Palmer widely portrayed as a cold blooded, and mercenary killer.

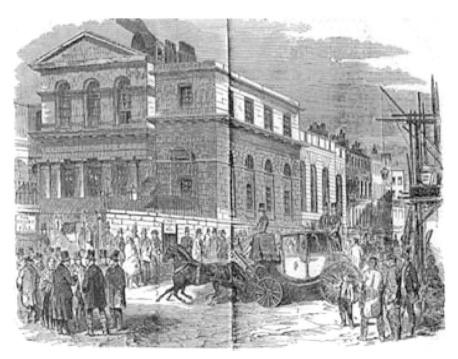

Outside of Central Criminal Court during Palmer Case
from the *Times Report of the Trial of William Palmer* published 1856

84

As one of the most famous in trials English criminal history it attracted many famous spectators who huddled into the court to see the drama unfold. Politicians (including Mr. Gladstone), the Lord Mayor of London (who once lived in Rugeley), famous doctors, judges and even the Nobility including Prince of Saxe-Weimar, the Dukes of Cambridge and of Wellington, the Marquis of Anglesey, the Earl of Derby (our Prime Minister three times), the Earls of Albemarle and of Dufferin and the Chief lord of the Admiralty Sir John Parkington all were present at some time during Palmer's trial.

Palmer was charged with –

"The willful murder of John Parsons Cook, who died at Rugeley upon the 21st of November last."

Palmer replied in a clear, low, but perfectly audible and distinct tone, **"Not Guilty."**

Chapter 26: The Trial - The Judges
The three judges selected for the Palmer Trial

As was the custom in the 1850s three judges presided over the trial. They were Lord Chief Justice Campbell, Baron Alderson and Justice Cresswell. Lord Chief Justice Campbell, the senior judge for the trial, was seventy-six or seventy-seven years of age. Dudley Barker, in *Palmer the Rugeley Poisoner* published in 1935 described Campbell as "*an old man then, past his real greatness, but eager still to preside at such a trial, and painstaking, if not brilliant in his long summing-up*". That he had been very keen to preside over the trial was never doubted but, it was said, he was also very keen to see Palmer convicted. He even took the unusual step, at the conclusion of the trial, of personally passing sentence on the prisoner, a role normally given to one of the junior judges.

Baron Alderson, Lord Chief Justice Campbell, Justice Cresswell
From the Times Report of the Trial of William Palmer, published 1856

In George Fletcher's Book on Palmer published in 1925 and from newspapers at the time we learn that Campbell had thought of retiring before the "Palmer Act" led to the trial being switched to London. Fletcher even suggested that he was too old for such a trial. Lord Chief Justice Campbell used the whole of the eleventh day of the trial (May 26th 1856) to sum up the case for the jury, commenting on the whole of the evidence. He continued his summing-up on the twelfth day finishing at eighteen minutes past two o'clock. The jury then retired to consider their verdict. Fletcher's book also tells us that, after Campbell had summed up the case, and before the jury retired to consider their verdict, he finished with the words, "*May God direct you to a right finding*". At this point the book tells us there was a most unusual interruption by Serjeant Shee who

86

was leading Palmer's Defence:

..... Serjeant Shee caused a somewhat unseemly interruption by stating the question left by the Lord Chief Justice was whether, "the evidence proved that Cook's symptoms were consistent with death by strychnine." This ought to be followed by the questions "Is it inconsistent with death from natural causes?" and "does the medical evidence establish the death of Cook by strychnine?" In the middle of the arguments Shee invoked the Almighty with the words, "It is my duty not to be deterred by any expression of displeasure - I am accountable to a much higher tribunal than even your Lordship's - to submit what occurs to me to be the proper question." At the end of the argument the Judge said to the jury, just before they retired: "The question whether the symptoms were consistent with death from strychnine was not THE question, but it was most material in finding your judgment as to whether he died from natural disease, or from poison administered by the prisoner. If the symptoms were consistent with death by strychnine, then you must consider the other evidence in the case as to whether the death was due to natural causes or whether he did not die by poison - by strychnine. And if it were, was it administered by the prisoner. If you so believe, then it is your duty to God and man to find a verdict of guilty." The jury retired to their room to consider their verdict.

After the trial there were pamphlets published which were highly critical of the judges. In the William Salt Library, Stafford there is an 1856 pamphlet comprising of a letter, supposedly written by the Reverend Thomas Palmer, to the Lord Chief Justice Campbell which contains derogatory remarks on the conduct of the Prosecution and of the three judges. There is also another 1856

pamphlet entitled *The Rugeley Tragedy Revealed; being a review of all the startling disclosures of Rev Thomas Palmer proving the innocence of his brother William Palmer*, published by T. Duggan. However it is thought that Palmer's brother Thomas was not the actual author of either of these pamphlets.

Lord Chief Justice Campbell. From *The Trial of William Palmer* (from the *Notable Trials Series*) 2nd Edition published in 1923 revised by Eric R. Watson

Chapter 27: The Trial - Counsel for the Prosecution

A strong team against Palmer

The Attorney-General, in England, is the principal law officer for the Crown and is the Head of the English Bar, a post which carried great political importance. In 1856 the Attorney- General was General Sir Alexander Cockburn who was widely regarded as the finest orator of his generation and, like the government of the time, he badly wanted to convict Palmer. Cockburn was determined that he would personally lead the prosecution against William Palmer as he was shortly due to "leave the Bar" to become a judge and was determined to make a high profile departure. With the Palmer case making headline news in the press both here and abroad, outraging the nation as more and more revelations were fed to the public at large, he was given an opportunity to make a memorable farewell.

Counsel for the Prosecution
Mr. Huddlestone Q.C. Mr. Bodkin,
Mr. Welsby , The Attorney-General,
Mr. Edwin James Q.C.
From the *Times Report of the Trial of William Palmer,* published 1856

Not all of the prosecution team were themselves honest and law-abiding citizens. One member of the Counsel for the Prosecution who helped convict Palmer was Mr. Edwin James, Q.C. He had also been the prosecuting counsel who lost the case brought against Mrs. Sarah Palmer, at Westminster, when William Palmer testified that he had seen his wife, Annie, forge his mother's signature. Five years after the trial, James had become a Member of Parliament but, like Palmer, he got himself into financial difficulties and was disbarred for fraud concerning amounts of over £60,000. However, when he got into trouble, he was able to flee to America leaving behind debts of £100,000. Once in New York he was not only able to continue his legal work but also became a successful actor, even performing at the Winter Garden Theatre. Later he was able to return to England where, in 1882, he died poor aged 70.

Apart from the Attorney General and Edwin James there were three other members of the Counsel for the Crown, they were Serjeant Huddlestone, Sir William Bodkin, and Mr. Welsby.

Serjeant Huddlestone had been asked to defend Palmer and had, in fact, appeared for Palmer in the successful bid to have the trial switched to London. In January 1856 he had successfully appeared for Mrs. Sarah Palmer at the case at Westminster and had represented Palmer's friend, Samuel Cheshire, when he was tried for opening mail addressed to the coroner. Unfortunately for Palmer, very late on, he changed sides to work for the Crown in prosecuting Palmer. Surely this must have harmed Palmer's case?

Some time after the trial Sir William Bodkin (1791-1874) became an assistant judge at Middlesex Sessions and a Counsel to the Treasury. I could find no further information about Mr. Welsby the fifth member of the Prosecution Team.

The Attorney-General, Sir Alexander Cockburn, unrivalled at the time as an orator began the prosecution in hushed silence and went on to deliver a masterly speech setting out the background to the charge of murder. He held the attention of the courtroom for nearly four hours not missing one point in setting out, with admirable clarity, the case against Palmer. It was said that he eclipsed even his most notable performances. If this was not enough, on the tenth day of the trial, his closing speech lasted six hours and he spoke for all that time without referring to any notes. Fletcher, in his 1925 book, described Cockburn's closing speech as, "*tightening the rope round Palmer's neck with every detail, and tearing to pieces the weak defence which had relied mainly on the medical aspects of the case, and showing completely how the crushing circumstantial details had ALL remained unanswered*".

Robert Graves in his 1957 book claimed that the Attorney-General had a personal grudge against Palmer. He claimed that on the evening after the second day of the trial the Attorney-General, who enjoyed betting on the horses, dined with some racing friends and was told by one of his guests, Frank Swindell, that he thought that Palmer had tried to "doctor him to death" at Wolverhampton Races.

Sir Alexander Cockburn: From *The Trial of William Palmer* (from the *Notable Trials Series*) Second Edition published in 1923 revised by Eric R. Watson.

Chapter 28: The Trial – Counsel for the Defence

Fighting for Palmer's life

John Smith known as "Honest John Smith of Brum" (Birmingham), was the solicitor for the Defence and was responsible for hiring the men who were to defend Palmer in court. He chose Mr. Serjeant Wilkins who had studied medicine before he took up law and would have been ideal to conduct the Defence. Wilkins agreed and represented William Palmer in January 1956 when at Westminster Court, Padwick had unsuccessfully sued Mrs. Palmer.

Unfortunately, just three weeks before the trial, Wilkins withdrew from the Palmer case. He claimed ill health but the real truth is that he had got into debt and had to escape quickly to avoid arrest himself. He succeeded in getting away to Dieppe in France by travelling on a "fishing-smack".

Back row - Mr. Gray, Mr. Kenealy. Front row - Mr. Serjeant Shee, Mr. Grove Q.C. From the *Times Report of the Trial of William Palmer*, published 1856

This left Smith with the daunting task of finding a good, last minute replacement to lead Palmer's Defence. He unsuccessfully approached Sir Frederick Thesiger before choosing **Mr. Serjeant Shee, Q.C.** who was the Member of Parliament for Kilkenny. He was an able barrister but was a devout Roman Catholic. Robert Graves, in his book *They Hanged My Saintly Billy*, suggested that there was a strong "anti-catholic sentiment" which was particularly rife among London trades people of the "Roundhead tradition". It should be noted that most of the jurors were London tradesmen.

Mr. Serjeant Shee's surname led to a comedian in the court cracking the following poor joke – "Why cannot Palmer be hanged for poisoning his wife?" Answer, "Because 'Shee' was in court!"

One unusual occurrence, almost unique, was that Shee, the leader of the Defence Team, told the jury that he personally believed in Palmer's innocence. The Attorney- General replied to this quietly and pointedly, *"You have had from my learned friend the unusual, I think I may add the unprecedented, assurance of his personal belief in his client's innocence. It would have been better if he had abstained from so strange a declaration."*

He continued *"If he was sincere in that - and I know he was - there is no man in whom the spirit of truth and honour is more keenly alive - he said what he believed. But what would he think of me if, imitating his example, I at this moment stated to you, upon my personal word and honour as he did, what is my personal conviction from a conscientious consideration of the whole case?"*

A few days before the execution, Serjeant Shee sent a sympathetic letter and a bible to Palmer whilst he languished in Stafford Gaol. Shee went on to become a judge in 1863 and died in 1868 aged sixty-three.

The second member of the team was **Mr. Grove Q.C.,** who came from a scientific background. He was no doubt chosen as someone who might be able to fully understand the complicated arguments of the medical witnesses who could not agree upon the symptoms attributed to poisoning by strychnine or agree upon the cause of death. Grove was appointed as a barrister and a judge to the Court of Common Pleas in 1871. He also served in the High Court of Justice. Grove had become famous, or perhaps infamous, as the defender of Dr. William Palmer, the "Rugeley Poisoner" but Grove was also scientifically oriented, and would sometimes get sidetracked in patent cases where he often ended up suggesting improvements in the product's design, rather than worrying about mere legalisms. Grove was knighted in 1872. Ill health interrupted his law career, and he turned to science. After retirement from the bench in 1887, he resumed his scientific studies. He is also credited with inventing the "fuel cell", the forerunner of today's batteries.

The third member of the team was **Mr. Kenealy** who was a scholar and gifted in many ways but he also is said to have had "a touch of madness". Sometime after the Palmer trial he was "struck off" for his conduct and abuse of the judges in the "Tichborne" trial. After being struck off he then became a Member of Parliament for a few years. He died in 1880 aged 61. I could find no additional information about the fourth member of the Defence Team, **Mr. Gray.**

Mr. Serjeant Shee, from *The Trial of William Palmer* (from the *Notable Trials Series*) Second Edition published in 1923 revised by Eric R. Watson.

Chapter 29: The Trial –
The Prosecution's Circumstantial Evidence
The Prosecution starts their attack

The Attorney-General started the prosecution with a masterly four-hour speech in which he clearly and precisely outlined each part of their case against Palmer. Dudley Barker in his book *Palmer* published in 1935 as part of the *Rogues Gallery Series* said of the opening speech:

> *It is impossible to quote effectively from the speech, for its supreme brilliance is its completeness, its compact presentation of a most difficult case, and its triumphant prose, sentence knit to sentence throughout, harmonized like a symphony. People who heard the Attorney-General deliver that opening speech must have been conscious from the first that they were listening to some of the finest oratory that was ever to be heard in a court of law. It is comparatively easy, with flashy metaphor and trumpet gesture, to give a semblance of dramatic intensity to a speech, but this speech was none of that kind. Its first characteristic was its clarity, an exposition of the case that has never been equalled. It held the fascination of a perfect piece of craftsmanship, no matter what the medium. Its second characteristic was its restraint. Cockburn spoke his accusations with dignity. Never once did he descend to a fiery partisanship, or vehement plea for vengeance on the man whom the jury was trying. He referred to him humanely, almost pitifully, avoiding, as only a great lawyer can, the impression that a criminal, even before he is convicted, is a thing apart, something inhuman, and devoid of all natural feelings.*
>
> *Just because that speech was so dignified and restrained, it was therefore highly dramatic. Before the case had opened the public knew that it was an important case. When the Attorney-General had finished his opening speech it was realised that this was a case that would go down into history; and the promise of that opening speech has been fulfilled.*

The Attorney-General then called the prosecution witnesses one by one, organising them just as carefully as he had logically arranged his opening speech, starting with witnesses to the fact that Cook began feeling unwell in Shrewsbury.

Wine merchant **Ishmael Fisher** stated he was present in Shrewsbury when Cook complained that his drink burned his throat and that Palmer had dosed him. He also said that Cook had given him between £700 and £800 to look after whilst Cook was ill. **Thomas Jones**, law stationer, was present at Shrewsbury and saw Cook when he was ill and complaining about his throat burning. **George**

Read, a "sporting housekeeper", was at Shrewsbury when Cook complained about a drink burning his throat. Under cross-examination he agreed Cook was never a strong man but one who had "delicate health".

William Scaife Gibson, a surgeon of Shrewsbury, stated Cook complained of pain in his stomach and heat in his throat. He added that Cook said he thought he had been poisoned. Gibson had recommended an emetic to make Cook be sick but when he inspected the vomit it proved to be "perfectly clean" and Cook's tongue was also "clean".

Ann Brookes, "a lady from Manchester who attends races", stated she had visited Palmer to ask him about a jockey. When she first saw Palmer, he was pouring some fluid from a small bottle in to a tumbler and then he shook it up and down before putting it up to the gaslight. She added that Palmer did not seem distressed that she had seen him doing this and that Palmer had just said that he would be with her in a minute.

Although the Prosecution tried to prove that Palmer had poisoned Cook's brandy, they never successfully proved that Palmer could have switched the glasses so as to poison Cook. **That Cook was ill in Shrewsbury was established, but not that Palmer was necessarily the cause of his illness. The prosecution then brought witnesses linked to the time that Cook spent in Rugeley, in the days before his death**.

Firstly **Elizabeth Mills**, chambermaid at the Talbot Arms, gave her evidence claiming that Cook had been ill after drinking coffee that Palmer had ordered for him. She also stated that she had been ill after tasting only two tablespoonfuls of some of Cook's broth sent from Palmer's house. When asked why she had not mentioned this earlier at the post-mortem or at the inquest she replied that she had not been asked, adding that she had only been asked a few questions by the coroner. At Dolly's Hotel, in the presence of Cook's stepfather, she had given an additional statement to a gentleman. In this later statement she talked of the symptoms Cook displayed. She agreed that she had not, before then, mentioned Cook beating the bedclothes or crying out "Murder!" twice, or mentioned the toast and water being given to Cook

Elizabeth Mills from the Times Report of the Trial of William Palmer published in 1856

on Palmer's orders or that he had snapped at the spoon, and bit it so hard that it was difficult to get it out of his mouth.

Shortly after Cook's death she had left Rugeley to work at Dolly's Hotel, Paternoster Row in London where, she admitted, Cook's Stepfather Mr. Stevens visited her six or seven times. She also received visits from Mr. Gardner, the solicitor for Mr. Stevens, and Captain Hatton Chief Constable for Stafford. She claimed that she did not know if they discussed the trial and they did not ask her what she could prove. The Defence also tried to discredit her by asking her questions about her relationship with a man called Dutton. She admitted that she had lived at his house but insisted that she slept with his mother who also lived at the house. Again she repeated, "*I swear that I slept with his mother.*"

The evidence of Elizabeth Mills was very strong and she stood up well to almost three hours cross examination by Serjeant Shee, some suggested too well and questioned if she had been "coached" believing that her evidence had been rehearsed.

Her evidence, as reported in the Times Report of the trial, gave a most graphic description of the agony suffered by Cook on the Monday/Tuesday night before his death in the early hours of Wednesday. She stated that:

About eight or ten minutes before 12 o'clock the waitress, Lavinia Barnes, called me up. While I was dressing I twice heard screams from Cook's room. My room is above, but not immediately over Cook's. I went down to Cook's room. As soon as I entered the room I saw him sitting up in bed. He desired me to fetch Palmer directly. I told him Palmer was sent for, and walked to his bedside. I found the pillow upon the floor. There was one mould candle burning in the room. I picked up the pillow, and asked Cook if he would lay his head down. He was sitting up, beating the bedclothes with both his hands and arms, which were stretched out. When I asked him to lay his head down, he said, "I can't lie down; I shall be suffocated if I lie down. Oh, fetch Mr. Palmer!" The last words were very loud. I did not observe his legs, but there was a sort of jumping or jerking about his head and his neck, and his body. Sometimes he would throw back his head upon the pillow, and then raise it up again. He had much difficulty in breathing. The balls of his eyes were projected very much. He screamed again three or four times while I was in the room. He was moving and knocking about all the time. Twice he called out aloud, "Murder!" He asked me to rub one hand. I found it stiff. It was his left hand.

(Questioned about the hand by one of the judges) It was stretched out. It did not move. The hand was about half shut. All the upper part seemed to be stiff.

Examination resumed - I did not rub it long. As soon as he thought I had rubbed it sufficiently he thanked me, and I let off. Palmer was there while I was rubbing the hand. While I was rubbing it the arm and also the body seemed to twitch. Cook was perfectly conscious. When Palmer came in he recognized him. He was throwing himself about the bed, and

94

said to Palmer, "Oh doctor, I shall die." Palmer replied, "Oh, my lad, you won't!" Palmer just looked at Cook, and then left the room, asking me to stay by the bedside. In about two or three minutes he returned. He brought with him some pills. He gave Cook a drought in a wine glass, but I cannot say whether he brought that with him. He first gave the pills, and then the drought. Cook said the pills stuck in his throat, and he could not swallow them. Palmer desired me to give him a teaspoonful of toast and water, and I did so. His body was jerking and jumping. When I put the spoon to his mouth he snapped at it and got it fast between his teeth, and seemed to bite it very hard. In snapping at the spoon he threw forward his head and neck. He swallowed the toast and water with the pills. Palmer then handed him a draught in a wineglass, which was about three parts full. It was a dark, thick heavy-looking liquid. Cook drank this. He snapped at the glass as he had done the spoon. He seemed as though he could not exactly control himself. He swallowed the draught, but vomited it immediately into the chamber utensil. I supported his forehead. The vomit smelt like opium. Palmer said he hoped either that the pills had stayed on his stomach or had not returned. He searched for the pills in the vomit with a quill. He said "I can't find the pills," and then he desired me to take the utensils away, and pour the contents out carefully to see if I could find the pills.

Mills said that she had spoken to Cook later that day when he asked her if she had ever seen anyone suffer such agony as he did last night? That night she said that at about ten to midnight the bell in Cook's room was rung violently. Cook asked for Palmer to be sent for. She had gone to Palmer's house and rung the surgery bell and looking up had seen Palmer at his bedroom window. Palmer came to Cook's bedside immediately and she said he commented that he had never before dressed so quickly. The Defence objected because she implied that Palmer was already dressed as if expecting to be called.

Mr. Gardner was a Rugeley solicitor acting for Cook's stepfather. In his evidence he stated that he was unhappy with the way in which the Coroner had conducted the inquest on Cook. **Lavinia Barnes**, waitress at the Talbot Arms, gave details of the time leading up to Cook's death. She also stated that she had seen Palmer looking in Cook's coat pockets after he had passed away. She also stated that, in death, Cook's eyes were, "wild looking and standing a great way out of his head." The Defence questioned the differences between the statements of Elizabeth Mills and Lavinia Barnes.

Mr. William Henry Jones, Cook's friend and personal doctor, stated Cook's health had been generally good but not robust. Palmer had summoned him to Rugeley in a letter dated November 18th 1855. He arrived in Rugeley at 3.30 p.m. on the Tuesday 20th November and found Cook was slightly recovered. He had examined Cook in Palmer's presence. The same day he visited Cook several times as did Dr. Bamford. Palmer suggested that Bamford make up some morphine pills. At 11 p.m. Palmer brought the pills in a box, which he opened remarking that Bamford had excellent handwriting for an old man. Cook eventually was persuaded to take the pills but shortly vomited but did not appear to bring up the pills. Jones stated that the pills couldn't have caused the vomiting.

Later Cook had called out, *"Doctor get up, I am going to be ill! Ring the bell and send for Palmer"*. Palmer arrived within some three minutes saying, *"I never dressed so quickly in my life"*. Cook then started having convulsions (violent irregular motions of the limbs due to involuntary contraction of muscles) that lasted five or ten minutes and his body went rigid and he asked to be sat up. They could not raise the body because he was so rigid, his whole body was bent upwards like a bow and they had to lay him on his left side. Cook gradually weakened, his heart gradually ceased and about 1 o'clock in the early hours of Wednesday morning he died.

Jones said Cook died of tetanus, which caused the action of the heart to stop. Palmer remained half an hour after the death. Jones left the room to send for someone to "lay out" the body. When he returned, Palmer had Cook's coat in his hand and handed in to Jones with the suggestion that, as Cook's nearest friend, he should look after his possessions, which included a watch and a purse containing five sovereigns and five shillings. Jones saw no betting book. Soon afterwards Palmer told him that Cook's death was bad for him (Palmer) as they had debts of £3,000 or more and he hoped Cook's friends would assist him or all his horses would be seized. Jones did disclose that Cook had been worried about secondary symptoms resulting from syphilis.

Also called were **Ann Rowley,** Palmer's charwoman, who had brought broth from the Albion Inn on the Saturday and taken it to Lavinia Barnes at the Talbot Inn to give to Cook. **Charles Horley** Palmer's gardener who, on the Sunday before Cook's death, had also taken some broth across from Palmer's house for Cook to eat. **Sarah Bond** housekeeper at the Talbot Arms gave evidence of Cook being at the Talbot Inn. She said that Cook had asked for coffee *(whereas Elizabeth Mills, when Palmer ordered coffee for Cook, had said she had never known Cook to order coffee)*. As part of her statement she said that passengers coming from London by express train usually arrived about 10 o'clock. Finally **Dr. Henry Savage,** physician and one time doctor to Cook, who stated that Cook had been well before going to Shrewsbury Races.

The Prosecution then brought witnesses who claimed Palmer had purchased strychnine. As **Charles Newton** entered the courtroom a murmur ran round the spectators as only in the previous twenty-four hours had the public known that he had come forward, on the eve of the trial, saying that Palmer had purchased strychnine.

96

Charles Newton, an assistant to Mr. Salt the chemist claimed that Palmer had bought 3 grains of strychnine from him at 9 p.m. on Monday 19th November (Cook died in the early hours of 21st November). He claimed he had not said anything to his employer Mr. Salt because Salt and Palmer were not friends. Mr. Salt had born a grudge against Palmer since Thirlby left his employment to become Palmer's assistant. The first time he said anything about the purchase was to Mr. Boycott clerk to Mr. Gardner, the solicitor of Cook's stepfather, on Rugeley Station as they and a number of other witnesses were waiting to catch the train down to London in readiness for the trial. He had not entered the sale of strychnine in the book at Mr. Salt's surgery. He stated that he had also seen Palmer purchase strychnine from Hawkins' shop the next day on the 20th November.

He went on to claim that he had gone to Palmer's house on 25th November (the Sunday after Cook had died) and, over a drink of brandy and water, Palmer had asked him how much strychnine it would take to kill a dog and had answered a grain. He added that Palmer had asked what the appearance of the stomach would be like after death and had replied that there would be no inflammation. He also stated that Palmer, on the morning of the post-mortem, had said that the post-mortem would be a "dirty job" and given him two wineglasses of neat brandy. He said that he had not told the Coroner at Cook's inquest that he had sold strychnine to Palmer on the 19th November.

Charles Joseph Roberts apprentice to Mr. Hawkins, druggist of Rugeley gave evidence that on Tuesday 20th November he had sold two drachms of prussic acid to Palmer and six grains of strychnine along with some solution of opium. Palmer had not bought drugs in his shop for about two years. He admitted that he had not made entries of any of these sales in the books and was not in the habit of making entries in the books.

Were either of these two, Newton or Roberts, reliable witnesses? Why did Newton not mention Palmer buying the strychnine until the eve of the trial? Palmer wrote to his solicitor categorically denying that he was even in Rugeley at the time Newton claimed, as his train did not get in to Stafford until 8.45 p.m. a claim that his friend Jere Smith was to support. Palmer and Mr. Salt were not on friendly terms so why would Palmer have risked going to Newton in Salt's shop to buy poison?

The Attorney General for the Prosecution in his summing up of their case asked, "*Did the prisoner at the bar obtain possession of strychnia on the Monday night? Did he get it again upon the Tuesday morning? The fact of his having got it on the Monday night rests, it is true, upon the evidence of an individual whose statement, as I have said to you at the outset, and as I repeat now, requires at your hands the most careful and anxious attention before you adopt it easily. . . . It is for you to say whether you are satisfied with his explanation. It is unquestionably true that it detracts from the otherwise perfect credibility which would attach to his statement. But then gentlemen, on the other hand, there is a consideration which I cannot fail to press upon you. What possible conceivable motive can this young man have, except a sense of truth, for coming forward to make this statement?"*

In his summing up the senior Judge, Lord Chief Justice Campbell, commented that Newton did not alter his statement but the jury must consider the possibility that Newton had wickedly invented his evidence. He further commented that Newton had no ill-will towards Palmer and nothing to gain by lying and, *"if you believe him, certainly the evidence against the prisoner is much strengthened, and a fearful case is made out against him."*

The Attorney- General stated that **Dr. Bamford** was seriously ill and unable to attend so his deposition was read out. (See Chapter 30).

The Prosecution then called **Cook's stepfather Mr. Stevens** into the witness box. He stated that he had married Cook's father's widow some fifteen years ago. He said he was on affectionate terms with Cook and had tried to persuade him to give up "the turf". He had last seen Cook on the 5ᵗʰ November when he appeared well, although the previous winter he had had some illness. Mr. Jones had brought news of Cook's death on the Wednesday evening and the next day he had gone to Lutterworth to look for Cook's will. He went to Rugeley on the Friday and when he saw Cook's body he was struck by the tightness of the face muscles. He had talked to Palmer about Cook's financial affairs and was told that Cook owed £4,000. When he asked Palmer, had not Cook any property or horses, Palmer replied yes but that they were mortgaged. Stevens stated that he had told Palmer that Cook would need to be buried whether he was in debt or not.

He stated that Palmer immediately replied, *"Oh! I will bury him myself, if that is all."* And he had responded, *"I certainly cannot think of you doing that; I shall do it."* and told him he was going to be buried in London in his mother's grave. To which Palmer replied, *"Oh! That is of no consequence, but the body ought to be fastened up at once."*

He had asked Palmer to recommend an undertaker to which Palmer replied that he had already ordered a coffin. Stevens was surprised, as he had not given his authority to do so. He had questioned Palmer about the missing betting book. He also told Palmer that he was going to insist upon a post-mortem. - Also called was **Mary Keeley** who had "laid out" Cook's body and found the corpse to be the most rigid she had ever encountered.

The Prosecution witnesses called to give evidence of misconduct at the post-mortem were **John Thomas Harland** the surgeon who oversaw the post-mortem on Cook and whose evidence confirmed the general opinion that he had been too feeble to oversee such a crucial event; **Charles Devonshire** undergraduate of the University of London who made the post-mortem on Cook; **Dr. Monkton**

physician who conducted the post-mortem on Annie Palmer and the second examination of Cook's body. **John Boycott,** solicitor's clerk, then gave evidence that he had received the samples from the post-mortem and had passed them on to Professor Taylor. He also stated that the day before the trial on Birmingham railway station he was approached by Newton who had informed him that he had sold strychnine to Palmer.

James Myatt, the postboy at the Talbot Arms, accused Palmer of trying to bribe him. He alleged that Palmer asked him if he was driving Mr. Stevens (taking the samples from the post-mortem) to the railway station? Myatt claimed that Palmer said, "*Do you think you could upset them?*" and offered him £10 to do so. Serjeant Shee for the Defence suggested that Palmer had actually said, "*I wouldn't mind giving £10 to break Steven's neck*". Myatt then said that he could not recollect the words "*break his neck*" but when asked if Palmer had said, "*I wouldn't mind giving £10 to upset him*", Myatt replied "*Yes, I believe those were the words*".

James Myatt, postboy at the Talbot Arms. From the *Times Report of the Trial of William Palmer,* Pub. 1856

Next the Prosecution dealt with evidence that the Coroner's mail had been tampered with and of Palmer's attempts to bribe the Coroner. **Samuel Cheshire**, former postmaster of Rugeley was brought direct from Newgate Prison where he was serving a sentence of two years imprisonment for tampering with mail addressed to the Coroner. **Captain Hatton**, Chief Constable of Stafford produced a letter from Palmer to the Coroner that proved Palmer must have read the letter that Cheshire had intercepted. Then **Ellis Crisp,** Inspector of Police in Rugeley, stated he searched Palmer's house and found, amongst other things, a medical book about poisons in which Palmer had written a note on one page saying "*Strychnia kills by causing tetanic fixing of the respiratory muscles*". **Elizabeth Hawkes**, keeper of a boarding house, gave evidence that Palmer had a hamper made up to send to the Coroner.

Additional circumstantial evidence was provided by George Herring, a man of independent means, who was asked about financial dealings. He had met with Palmer during the Shrewsbury Races and stated Palmer needed to pay moneylenders Pratt and Padwick £450 and £350 respectively. Herring was an eminent, rich man, a respectable turf accountant who was said to have been furious that Palmer had involved him in collecting Cook's winnings from

Tattersalls. He stared in front of himself as he gave his evidence in a bitterly cold voice leaving a lasting impression on everyone who heard his evidence. **Frederick Slack**, a porter at Mrs. Hawkes' boarding house, said Palmer had given instruction to address the hamper to Ward the Coroner. The Attorney-General tried to ask **George Bates** an ex farmer who worked at Palmer's stable about his attempt to insure Bates' life, but the Defence objected and the Judges ruled in their favour. Bates was then questioned about a letter, which contained a £5 note for the Coroner and obtaining a basket of game as a gift for the Coroner. Bates became somewhat surly when asked about Palmer's horses and couldn't, "*tell their value*," or "*say whether the mares were in foal*". Also he "*never saw any dogs 'run' them*," and was "*not aware that Goldfinger's dam slipped her foal*," and although he had seen a gun at the paddock "*couldn't say if it belonged to Palmer*". **The implication was that the Defence wished to prove that Palmer purchased some strychnine and a gun to rid them of the dogs that were worrying his horses and had caused his broodmares to lose their foals.**

The Juror's Retiring Room
From the *Times Report of the Trial of William Palmer*, published 1856.

Up until this point all the evidence had been circumstantial and next the Prosecution moved on to call up its medical experts (see Chapter 30)

before they called further witnesses who could comment upon Palmer's financial difficulties.

Daniel Scully Bergen, Chief Superintendent of Police at Stafford, had searched Palmer's house for papers relating to the case. Next came **Henry Augustus Deane** an attorney and solicitor to the Prince of Wales Insurance Office who was responsible for employing Inspector Field to investigate the proposed insurance of George Bates. Then **John Espin**, solicitor, employed by moneylender Mr. Padwick gave evidence of a cheque bearing Palmer's handwriting and a forged signature supposed to be that of his mother.

Then came **Thomas Pratt** a solicitor and moneylender who had been lending money to Palmer, since 1853 at 60% interest and who surely must have known that the signatures of Palmer's mother guaranteeing the money were forged. In an extremely cold manner he gave further evidence of Palmer's dire financial affairs. Fletcher in his 1925 book quoted a Mrs. Tennyson Jesse who described Pratt as, *"One of the most repulsive characters in the trial."* Also called were **John Armshaw**, Rugeley attorney acting for Rugeley traders whose money was paid back later on the morning that Cook died. **John Wallbank**, Rugeley butcher; **John Spillbury**, a farmer near Stafford, who was owed forty-six pounds two shillings which was paid back in cash the day after Cook died. **Mr. Strawbridge**, Rugeley bank manager who said in evidence that Palmer's bank balance was less than £9 and **Herbert Wright** a Birmingham solicitor acting for his brother who was owed £10,400. **Charles Weatherby** who received a letter from Palmer on the 21st November containing a cheque from Cook asking him to send a cheque to Palmer for the same amount but they were unable to honour the cheque. **Mr. F. Butler,** a jockey, was owed seven hundred pounds and got forty pounds but one of Palmer's cheques for two hundred and fifty pounds upon the Rugeley Bank was not paid.

With this evidence the Prosecution's case against Palmer was concluded.

Chapter 30: The Trial –
Prosecution's Medical Evidence
Trying to establish the cause of death

WARNING: If you have got this far without losing interest, then readers should note that they might find their interest flagging when reading the next two chapters. These chapters give a flavour of the complex and often contradictory medical evidence. These chapters have been included for the completeness of the story and to include fully the characters appearing in the court room drama. Less avid readers might prefer to go directly to Chapter 32 on page 121.

Palmer's was the first ever trial in Britain where someone was accused of murder using strychnine. For anyone who is not from a medical background it can be difficult to follow all the medical evidence. For this reason I have written two chapters devoted to this element of the case, separated from the chapters on circumstantial evidence. Surely it must have been equally difficult for the jury to fully comprehend the disagreements between the numerous so-called medical experts called by each side.

It was not until the fourth day of the trial that the Prosecution called upon their first medical expert. Previously all the evidence, apart from some descriptions about Cook's symptoms and general health, had been purely of a circumstantial nature.

Both the Prosecution and the Defence agreed that Cook died from tetanic convulsions (tetanus), with Cook suffering an horrific form that racked his body and, at times, left his body so agonizingly bowed that he rested on the back of his head and the heels of his feet. However the Prosecution and the Defence could not agree upon what caused the tetanus. Basically tetanus is a disorder of the nervous system, which manifests itself by painful and lengthened spasm of the voluntary muscles throughout the body. The direct causes of tetanus were not known until a Japanese man called Kitasato discovered the bacillus *Chostridium tetani* in 1889 more than thirty years after Palmer's trial.

At the time of the trial there were considered to be three main types of tetanus, the first type being *idiopathic tetanus*. The term "idiopathic" is applied to indicate that the cause of a disease is not known. Idiopathic tetanus could be caused by a chill or by a stomach disorder but fortunately this is a very rare form of tetanus. The second tetanus type is *traumatic tetanus*, which is also referred to in England as "*lockjaw*". A wound such as a deep cut or a gunshot wound usually causes this type of tetanus. The tetanus can start as quickly as three days after the wound or as long as four weeks afterwards when the original wound has healed.

Thirdly there is the type described in the trial as *tetanus due to strychnine*. This is now known not to be a form of tetanus. The symptoms of strychnine poisoning bear a strong resemblance to tetanus but are more acute and less prolonged than in a case of tetanus.

The Prosecution set out to prove, through the testimony of their expert medical witnesses, that Cook had <u>not</u> died from idiopathic or traumatic tetanus or in fact from any known disease that the Defence might suggest.

Firstly **Thomas Blizard Curling**, member of the College of Surgeons, gave a general description of idiopathic tetanus and traumatic tetanus and denied that Cook's symptoms were consistent traumatic tetanus. He reasoned that the sudden onset of Cook's disease contrasted with the normal mild symptoms of tetanus gradually proceeding to the complete development of tetanus.

Dr. Todd, for 20 years a physician at Kings College Hospital who had lectured on physiology, anatomy and on tetanus and diseases of the nervous system, gave his opinion that the term tetanus ought not to be applied to disease produced by poison. He stated traumatic tetanus begins with stiffness about the jaw, gradually developing to extend to muscles of the trunk and although there are periods of remission, these are not complete but merely a lessening of the severity of the symptoms. He ruled out apoplexy and epilepsy as possible causes of death in Cook's case.

At this stage the Attorney General revealed that **Dr. Bamford** was so unwell that the octogenarian, Rugeley doctor was unlikely to be able to give evidence and asked that Bamford's deposition be read to the court. After hearing from two doctors, who stated that Dr. Bamford was in fact suffering from English cholera, Dr. Bamford's evidence was read out by the Clerk of the Court.

In the deposition, Dr. Bamford mentioned making his first visit to Cook, at Palmer's request, at 3 o'clock on the Saturday when Cook was suffering from violent vomiting. He detailed his visits and the medicine he prescribed but stated that he had not given Cook antimony. He stated that, "*I consider death to have been the result of congestion of the brain when the post mortem examination was made, and I do*

Print from the Illustrated Times 2ⁿᵈ February 1856 of Dr. Bamford the Rugeley doctor who was over eighty years old. He signed the death certificates for eight of Palmer's "supposed victims".

not see any reason to alter that opinion." (The death certificate signed by Dr. Bamford gave the reason as apoplexy, which is a malady arresting powers of sense and motion caused by effusion of blood in the brain) He also stated *"I attended Mrs. Palmer some days before her decease; also two children, and a gentleman from London, who was on a visit at Palmer's house, and who did not live many hours after I was called in. The whole of these patients died."* His statement also said, *"Mr. Palmer said he was of the same opinion as myself with respect to the death of the deceased. I never knew apoplexy produce rigidity of the limbs. Drowsiness is a prelude to apoplexy. I attributed the sickness on the first two days to a disordered stomach."*

The questioning returned to **Dr. Todd** who declared that, *"Having heard the deposition of Dr. Bamford read, I do not believe that the deceased died from apoplexy or from epilepsy. I never knew tetanus arise either from syphilitic sores or from sore throat. There are poisons which will produce tetanic convulsions. The principal of these poisons are nux vomica and those which contain as their active ingredients strychnine and bruccia. I have never seen life destroyed by strychnine, but I have seen animals destroyed by it frequently."* He talked of differences between Cook's symptoms and those of tetanus finding it "remarkable" that the deceased was able to swallow, and that there was no fixing of the jaw, which would have been the case with tetanus proper, resulting either from a wound or from disease. Before cross-examination he concluded, ***"From all the evidence I have heard, I think that the symptoms which presented themselves in the case of Mr. Cook arose from tetanus produced by strychnine."***

Under questioning from the Defence he replied, *"There is nothing in the post mortem examination which leads me to think that the deceased died from tetanus proper. I think that granules upon the spinal chord, such as I have heard described, would not be likely to cause tetanus."* He did know that morphia (Cook had been given this) sometimes produces convulsions but thought that they would be of an epileptic nature.

Sir Benjamin Brodie, a senior surgeon to St. George's Hospital, also President of the Royal College of Surgeons, gave his evidence with great clearness, slowly, audibly and distinctly. He stated that death from idiopathic tetanus was rare in this

Sir Benjamin Brodie.
From the *Times Report of the Trial of William Palmer* published in 1856

country and that ordinary tetanus in this country was traumatic tetanus. He agreed that the general contraction of muscles resembled traumatic tetanus but the course of Cook's illness was different entirely. He said, "*I do not believe that death in the case of Mr. Cook arose from what we ordinarily call tetanus – either idiopathic or traumatic. I never knew tetanus result from sore throat or from a chancre, or of any other form of syphilitic disease. The symptoms were not as a result either of apoplexy or of epilepsy.*"

The Times Report of the Trial from 1856 quoted Brodie as saying, "*Perhaps I had better say at once that I never saw a case in which the symptoms that I have heard described here arose from any disease.*" Following this quote they wrote "(Sensation)" presumably to mark the reaction, of the spectators within the courtroom, to the implication of these words. Brodie continued, "*When I say that, of course I refer not to particular symptoms, but to the general course which the symptoms took.*"

Dr. Daniel, by then out of practice but for many years a surgeon to the Bristol Hospital, agreed with Sir Benjamin Brodie with respect to the difference between ordinary tetanus and tetanus caused by strychnine. He said that Cook's symptoms were not those usually associated with ordinary tetanus where symptoms developed from firstly a stiffness of the lower jaw with the contraction of the muscles always a later symptom. He suggested that the clenching of the fist and the twisting of the foot were unusual symptoms not normally associated with tetanus. He did not know of a case of tetanus where death had come so quickly, ruled out apoplexy and epilepsy as possible causes of death and stated that he knew of no cases where syphilitic sores caused tetanus.

Mr. Samuel Solly, for twenty-eight years a lecturer and surgeon of St. Thomas's Hospital, stated that, in his experience of tetanus, there had always been, "*a marked expression of countenance*" as a first symptom and that once you saw this "*sort of grin*", peculiar to tetanus, you could never mistake it. In his judgment Cook's death could not be attributed to apoplexy, epilepsy or any disease he had ever witnessed.

Mr. Henry Lee was a surgeon to King's College and Lock Hospitals, which were devoted to treating up to three thousand cases a year of a syphilitic character but had never known an instance of that disease terminating in tetanus. He was not cross-examined.

After the evidence relating to what might or might not have been the cause of Cook's death the prosecution brought evidence from four cases of accidental strychnine poisoning. In three of the cases the patient died but in the other case the patient recovered.

Dr. Henry Corbett, a physician of Glasgow, recalled a patient, Agnes Sennett, who in 1845 had taken strychnine pills and died an hour and a quarter later. He described some of the symptoms, the red face; pupils of eyes dilated; head bent back; spine curved; muscles rigid and hard like a board; the arms stretched out; the hands clenched and severe paroxysms recurring every few seconds. **Dr. Watson**, surgeon at Glasgow Infirmary, **Dr. J. Patterson**, from their laboratory and **Mary Kelley** a former patient of the Infirmary all gave their recollections of the symptoms of Agnes Sennett. All mentioned the rigidity of the body with Mary describing it as, *"like a poker"*.

Witnesses **Caroline Hickson**, who, in 1848, had been a nurse and lady's maid in the family of Mr. Sarjantson Smyth and **Mr. Francis Taylor**, a surgeon from Romsey, described the symptoms leading up to the death of Mrs. Smythe. Her symptoms were very similar to those of Cook even to the fact that the victim asked to be "turned over". **Charles Blocksome** who had been an apprentice to Mr. Jones a Romsey chemist gave evidence that his employer had made a grave mistake having made up her prescription with strychnine instead of salacite (bark of willow). It was stated that after his mistake, Mr. Jones had committed suicide.

Jane Witham, a lady's attendant, stated that the previous March she had attended a lady, but was advised by the learned counsel not to name the lady. She described the symptoms before her death. The lady was attended by the next witness, Mr. Morley a surgeon from Leeds, who gave evidence that he had also helped at the post-mortem for the lady. In her stomach they had found, *"appearances characteristic of strychnine"*. They administered the strychnine taken from the stomach to a few mice and rabbits and a guinea pig. They had then observed, in each of the animals, *"more or less the effects produced by strychnine – namely, general uneasiness, difficult breathing, convulsions of a tetanic kind, muscular rigidity, arching backwards of the head and neck, and violent stretching out of the legs"*.

When questioned, by Mr. Grove Q.C. for the Defence, Morley conceded that in his experiments on frogs where he had given strychnine he had, in almost all cases, found the strychnine where it was known to have been administered. He had even detected strychnine in the stomach nearly two months after death, when decomposition had proceeded to a considerable extent.

Mr. Edward D Moore, a former surgeon, talked of a patient who suffered from paralysis and, for treatment, was actually given small doses of strychnine. His dosage was increased and this caused him have spasms with every limb stiffened and his head drawn back. However he survived the attack and his paralysis was better after the attack.

Mr. Moore was the last witness to give his evidence on the Saturday and the trial was adjourned until the Monday at 10 o'clock. Before the jury left the box the senior judge, Lord Campbell, exhorted them not to, *"form any opinion upon the case until they had heard both sides,"* and that they should even, *"abstain from conversing about it among themselves."* His lordship also expressed a hope that, if the jury were taken out upon the following day (Sunday), they

106

would not be allowed to go to *"any place of public resort,"* and mentioned an instance in which a jury, under similar circumstances, had been conducted to Epping Forest. The jury members were then conveyed back to the London Coffee House where they had their lodgings for the duration of the trial but I have been unable to find out where they spent their Sunday.

The Jurors Lodging House – From a book of the Palmer story, found in the William Salt Library, Stafford, written in Greek, published 1860.

On the Monday morning the first witness to be called was **Professor Alfred Swaine Taylor**, Fellow of the College of Physicians and a lecturer at Guy's hospital, who had made a study of strychnia but had never witnessed its action on a human subject. He gave evidence for nearly a whole day. He stated that strychnia is first absorbed into the blood, then circulates through the body, and especially acts on the spinal cord, from which proceed the nerves acting on the voluntary muscles. He answered several leading questions put to him by the Attorney-General as follows:

"You have heard the descriptions given by the witnesses of the symptoms and appearances which accompanied Cook's attacks?"

"I have."

"Were the symptoms and appearances the same as those you have observed in the animals to which you administered strychnine?"

"They were."

And later: *"How do you account for the absence of any indication of strychnia in cases where you know it was administered?"*

"It is absorbed into the blood, and is no longer in the stomach. It is in a great part changed in the blood."

He was asked if the *"parts"* sent to him for analysis were in a *"favourable condition"*? He replied, *"The most unfavourable that could possibly be,"* and added that, *"the stomach had been completely cut from end to end, all the contents were gone, and the fine mucous surface, on which any poison, if present, would have been found, was lying in contact with the outside of the intestines – all thrown together."*

He said that he had heard the four cases mentioned by earlier witnesses and agreed that the deaths in those cases were caused by strychnine and that Cook's symptoms appeared to be of a similar character. To the question, *"As a professor of medical science, do you know any cause in the range of human disease except strychnine, to which the symptoms in Cook's case can be referred?"* he answered, *"I do not."*

Professor Taylor had been chosen by Cook's stepfather to examine the samples taken at Cook's post-mortem prior to the inquest. Before Cook's inquest he had originally diagnosed that antimony (a poison which can be used in small quantities as a medicine) had caused the death of Cook.

When questioned by Serjeant Shee for the Defence, in spite of agreeing that the quantity of antimony found in the body was not sufficient to account for death, Taylor claimed that, before the inquest, he had been justified in suggesting that antimony (not strychnine as was later suggested) caused death, reasoning, *"We could infer nothing else."*

He continued, *"I was told that the deceased was in good health seven or eight days before his death, and that he had been taken very sick and ill, and had died in convulsions. No further particulars being given us we were left to suppose that he had not died a natural death. There was no natural cause to account for death, and finding antimony existing throughout the body we thought it might have been caused by antimony."* Referring to the statement that Cook had been in good health Shee asked if Taylor, *"allowed his judgment to be influenced by the statement of a person* (Cook's stepfather) *who knows nothing of his own knowledge?"*

Taylor stated that he had been present for part of the inquest and heard some of the witnesses and had had some evidence read to him. He had experimented upon five rabbits some twenty-three years previously and on some more rabbits since the inquest stating that this was, *"the only knowledge of my own that I had of the effect of strychnia upon animal life."* He claimed to have, *"a great objection to sacrifice of life."* When the Defence Council suggested that he might have been better choosing to experiment upon dogs rather than rabbits, his answer of *"Dogs are very dangerous to handle"*, caused some laughter in the court. The

Defence quipped, did he not mean to answer that, *"Dogs and cats bear a greater analogy to man because they vomit, while rabbits do not, but rabbits are much more manageable?"*

He was asked, *"Do you think it your duty to abstain from all public discussion of the question which might influence the public mind?"* and, *"Did you write a letter to the Lancet?"*

He answered "Yes" to both questions but claimed in justification that he had written to the Lancet so as to, *"contradict several misstatements of my evidence which had been made."* He also wished to correct the impression, *"circulated in every newspaper that a person could not be killed by tartar emetic."* (Tartar emetic is a purgative medicine containing antimony).

He was also questioned upon the following quote from his letter, *"During the quarter of a century which I have now specially devoted to toxicological inquiries I have never met with any cases like these suspected cases of poisoning at Rugeley. The mode in which they will affect the person accused is of minor importance compared with their probable influence on society. I have no hesitation in saying that the future security of life in this country will mainly depend on the judge, the jury, and the counsel who may have to dispose of the charges of murder which have arisen out of these investigations."*

When Serjeant Shee for the Defence asked *"Do you adhere to your opinion that 'the mode in which they will affect the person accused,' that is, lead him to the scaffold, 'is of minor importance compared with their probable influence on society'?"*

Taylor replied *"I have never suggested that they should lead him to the scaffold. I hope that, if innocent, he will be acquitted."* Asked what he meant by - *"The mode in which they will affect the person accused is of minor importance"*? Taylor replied *"The lives of 16,000,000 of people are, in my opinion, of greater importance than that of one man."* Taylor continued, *"As you appear to put that as an objection to my evidence, allow me to state that in two dead bodies I find antimony. In one case death occurred suddenly, and in the other the body was saturated with antimony, which I never found before in the examination of 300 bodies. I say these were circumstances which demanded explanation."*

Shee asked, *"You adhere to the opinion that, as a medical man and a member of an honourable profession, you were right in publishing this letter before the trial of the person accused?"*

To which Taylor responded, *"I think I had a right to state that opinion in answer to the comments which had been made upon my evidence."* He agreed that no comments had been made by the prisoner, Palmer, but claimed, *"Mr. Smith, solicitor for the Defence, circulated in every paper statements of 'Dr. Taylor's inaccuracy'. I had no wish or motive to charge the prisoner with this crime. My duty concerns the lives of all."*

Drs. Taylor(left) and Rees, the Analytical Chemists.
Published in the Illustrated Times

Shee switched his attack to ask Taylor if he had given permission to Mr. Augustus, Mayhew the editor of the Illustrated Times to publish the caricature (see picture left) of himself.

Professor Taylor claimed that he had been tricked by Mr. Mayhew and had not given his permission for the caricature. He claimed that he had given an interview on the subject of poisons without thinking about the links to the Rugeley cases. In fact he claimed he had not realised that Mayhew was the editor of the *Illustrated Times*. Taylor responded, *"On my oath. It was the greatest deception that was ever practiced on a scientific man. It was disgraceful. He called on me in company with another gentleman, with a letter from Professor Faraday. I received him as I should Professor Faraday, and entered into conversation with him about these cases. He represented, as I understood, that he was connected with an insurance company, and wished for information about a number of cases of poisoning which had occurred during many years. "* (It should be noted that, after the trial, Mr. Mayhew entirely denied Dr. Taylor's statements.)

Taylor denied claims made by a Mr. Johnson, in a letter to Sir George Gray (a member of the Defence team), that Taylor had once said about Cook, *"He will have strychnia enough before I have done with him."*

There was some further discussion about Cook's symptoms with Taylor stating that, *"Cook's symptoms were quite in accordance with an ordinary case of poisoning by strychnia."* Asked if he knew of a case where a patient, seized by tetanic symptoms, sat up in bed and talked, he pointed out that it was after he sat up that he was affected by the symptoms. He was also asked if he knew of any cases in which the symptoms of poisoning by strychnia commenced with the patient beating the bedclothes. He replied that this was a symptom which might be exhibited by a person suffering from a sense of suffocation whether caused by strychnia or other causes.

Questioned about why he had suggested questions for the coroner to ask at the inquest, he replied that the coroner, *"did not put questions which enabled me to form an opinion"* and commented that, *"There was an omission to take down the answers"*. He said that, at the time of the inquest he wrote to Mr. Gardner (the solicitor for Cook's stepfather) *"I had not learnt the symptoms which attended the attack and death of Cook. I had only the information that he was well seven days before he died, and had died in convulsions. I had no information which could lead me to suppose that strychnia had been the cause of death, except that Palmer had purchased strychnia. Failing to find opium, prussic acid, or strychnia, I referred to antimony as the only substance found in the body."*

In spite of their finding only small traces of the poison antimony and absolutely no traces of strychnine in the deceased's body, Professor Taylor stated that, *"Cook's symptoms were quite in accordance with an ordinary case of poisoning by strychnia."*

In his book, *They Hanged My Saintly Billy*, Robert Graves quotes a "wag" from the time of the trial:

> *In antimony, great though his faith,*
> *The quantity found being small,*
> *Taylor's faith in strychnine was yet greater,*
> *For of that he found nothing at all.*

Dr. G. O. Rees, a lecturer at Guy's Hospital, had assisted Taylor in making the post-mortem examination and had been present when antimony had been discovered. He stated that the tests that they had employed had all failed to discover the presence of strychnia but said that the stomach was, *"in a most unfavourable state for examination; it was cut open, and turned inside out; its mucous surface was lying upon the intestines and the contents of the stomach, if there had been any, must have been thrown among the intestines, and mixed with them. These circumstances were very unfavourable to the hope of discovering strychnia."* He was present at experiments on animals undertaken by Professor Taylor and the symptoms accompanying the deaths of the animals were very similar to those described in the case of Mr. Cook. He had heard the cases discussed in the trial and suggested that the symptoms in every one were similar to those in the case of Mr. Cook.

Professor Brande, professor of chemistry at the Royal Institution was present at the analysis of Cook's liver and spleen and was able to state positively that antimony was found.

Professor Christianson was professor of Materia Medica to the University of Edinburgh and stated that strychnine, the poison, had been first discovered in Paris in 1918 where two years later he had worked. He stated that, *"I have heard the evidence of what took place at the Talbot Arms on the Monday and Tuesday,* and *the result of my experience induces me to come to the conclusion that the symptoms exhibited by the deceased were only attributable to strychnia,* *or the four poisons containing it. There is no natural disease of any description that I am acquainted with to which I could refer these symptoms.*" He went on to say that, "*When death is the consequence of the administration of strychnia, if the quantity is small, I should not expect to find any trace in the body after death.*" and later "*The colour tests for the detection of strychnia are uncertain.*" and also, "*The stomach of the deceased was sent in a very unsatisfactory state for examination, and there must have been a considerable quantity of strychnia in the stomach to have enabled any one to detect its presence under such circumstances.*"

Professor Christianson's evidence brought a close to the fifth day of the trial and with it the main medical evidence for the Prosecution. The sixth day and the start of the seventh day was taken up with more of the Prosecution's circumstantial evidence (described in Chapter 28), before the Attorney-General completed the Prosecution case with a masterly eight hour address that summed up their case.

Chapter 31: The Trial –
Defence's Medical Evidence
Trying to establish that death was not caused by strychnine

On the resumption of the case on the eighth day, as the Defence started to bring their own expert medical witnesses, Palmer's demeanor was described as having been, *"as on the previous days of his trial, calm and attentive, but betrayed no additional anxiety"*.

The Defence's case rested upon them proving that Cook's symptoms, although similar in some respects to the effects brought about by strychnine, were not necessarily those produced as a result strychnine. Their medical witnesses did not agree about what had caused Cook's death but offered eight different possibilities. They also brought witnesses who felt that Dr. Taylor should have been able to trace evidence of strychnia in Cook's body had he in fact been poisoned using strychnine.

First to give evidence for the Defence was **Mr. Thomas Nunneley**, Professor of Surgery at Leeds School of Medicine, called as a man who had a large practice and had seen cases of both traumatic and idiopathic tetanus. He was, *"of the opinion that death was caused by some convulsive disease"*.

*Mr. Thomas Nunneley
From the Times Report of the
Trial of William Palmer
published in 1856.*

From the evidence he had heard he continued, *"I assume that Cook was a man of very delicate constitution – that for a long period he had felt himself to be ailing, for which indisposition he had been under medical treatment; that he had suffered from syphilis; that he had disease of the lungs; and that he had old standing disease of the throat; that he lived an irregular life; that he was subject to mental excitement and depression; and that after death appearances were found in his body which show this to have been the case. There was an unusual appearance in the stomach. The throat was in an unnatural condition. The back of the tongue showed similar indications. The air vessels of the lung were dilated. In the lining of the aorta there was an unnatural deposit, and there was a very unusual appearance in the membranes of the spinal marrow. One of the witnesses also said that there was a loss of substance from the penis. That scar on the penis could only have resulted from an ulcer. A chancre is an ulcer, but an ulcer is not necessarily a chancre. The symptoms at the root of the tongue and the throat I should ascribe to syphilitic inflammation of the throat. Supposing these symptoms to be correct, I should infer that Cook's health had for a long time not been good, and that his constitution was delicate. His father and mother died young. Supposing that to have been his state of health, it would make him liable to nervous irritation*

That might be excited by moral causes. Any excitement or depression might produce that effect. A person of such health and constitution would be more susceptible of injurious influence from wet and cold than would one of stronger constitution. Upon such a constitution as that which I have assumed Cook's to have been convulsive disease is more likely to supervene. I understand that Cook had three attacks on succeeding nights, occurring about the same hour. As a medical man, I should infer from this that the attacks were of a convulsive character. I infer that in the absence of other causes to account for them. According to my personal experience and knowledge from the study of my profession, convulsive attacks are as various as possible in their forms and degrees of violence. It is not possible to give a definite name to every convulsive symptom. There are some forms of convulsion in which the patient retains consciousness. Those are forms of hysteria, sometimes found in the male sex. It is also stated that there are forms of epilepsy in which the patient retains consciousness."

He had seen cases where convulsions recurred with the time of recovery from a violent attack of convulsions varying from a few minutes to many hours. He stated that with convulsions death comes from asphyxia, a spasm of the heart. He was familiar with idiopathic tetanus, as his own child had suffered from the disease. He had also, within the previous twelve months, made post mortem examinations on two people who had died from strychnia and in each case, using chemical analysis, he had been able to find strychnine.

Mr. Nunneley thought that Cook's symptoms on the Saturday night did not resemble those that, from experience, he would expect following the administration of strychnia. Cook had more power of voluntary movement. Cook had, "*sat up in bed, and moved his hands about freely, swallowed, talked, and asked to be rubbed and moved, none of which, if poisoned by strychnia, could he have done*". He also believed that the convulsions were not caused by strychnia because of the length of time that had elapsed between Cook taking the pills, which were alleged to have contained strychnine and the commencement of the screaming and vomiting. He felt that strychnine ought to have been detected if it had actually been given to Cook and he had found strychnia in a patient forty days after death. When he experimented on animals he had worked jointly with Dr. Morley who had been a medical witness for the Prosecution and disagreed with the doctor's evidence. He did not know of any cases of strychnine where rigidity after death was any greater than with the usual rigor mortis.

He concluded that, "*I judge that he died from convulsions, by the combination of symptoms.*" He supposed that Cook was, "*liable to excitement and depression of spirit,*" giving as justification the reason that, "*The fact that after winning the race he could not speak for three minutes.*" And, "*Mr. Jones stated that he was subject to mental depression. Excitement will produce a state of brain which will be followed, at some distance, by convulsions. I think that Dr. Bamford made a mistake when he said the brain was perfectly healthy.*" He went on to add, "*With the brain and the system in the condition in which Cook's were I believe it is quite possible for convulsions to come on and destroy a person. I do not believe that he died from apoplexy. He was under the influence of morphia. I don't ascribe his death to morphia, except that it might assist in producing a convulsive attack. I should think morphia was not very good treatment, considering the state of excitement he was in.*"

Mr. William Herapeth, professor of Chemistry and Toxicology at the Bristol Medical School had performed experiments on animals and in all cases had been able to detect poison. The Defence asked, "*Are you of the opinion that where strychnia has been taken in a sufficient dose to poison it can and ought to be discovered?*"

To which Herapeth answered, "*Yes; unless the body has been completely decomposed; that is unless decomposition has reduced it to a dry powder. I am of opinion, from the accounts given by Dr. Taylor and other witnesses, that if it had existed in the body of Cook it ought to have been discovered.*"

There is no doubt that he was a great scientist and chemist but the Attorney General tried to undermine the value of Herapeth's evidence of by asking, "*Have you not said that you had no doubt that strychnia had been taken, but that Dr. Taylor had not gone the right way to find it?*" Herapeth's comments had been made at a private function in Bristol. He replied that he might have made some initial comments based upon the impression given in various newspaper articles that strychnine had been given to Cook. There seems to be little doubt that there was professional rivalry between Professor Herapeth and Professor Taylor and that he wished to publicly prove Taylor to be wrong. Herapeth maintained that he could detect as small a quantity of strychnine as one fifty-thousandth part of a grain if unmixed with organic matter or one-tenth part of a grain if in water. However the suggestion of rivalry had been made and there is no doubt that this weakened the credibility afforded to Herapeth's evidence.

Mr. Rogers, Professor of Chemistry at St. George's School of Medicine, had made experiments upon a dog poisoned by strychnia and said of Cook's case, "*Strychnia must unquestionably have been discovered in this case if it had been present and the proper tests had been used.*" Adding, "*If the contents of the stomach were lost it would make a difference, but not if they were only shaken up.*" Finally adding that, "*If strychnia were in the stomach a portion would probably be smeared over the mucous membrane, and then I should expect to find it on the surface.*"

Dr. Henry Letheby, a Medical Officer of Health to the City of London, had been engaged for a considerable time in the study of poisons and concluded that the symptoms described in Cook's case "did not accord" with the symptoms he had witnessed. He stated that he, "*had no hesitation in saying that strychnine is of all poisons, either mineral or vegetable, the most easy of detection.*" He claimed that, "*When it is pure the 20,000th part of a grain can be detected. I can detect the tenth part of a grain most easily in a pint of any liquid, whether pure or putrid.*" Adding, "*I never failed to detect strychnine where it had been administered.*"

When asked his opinion of the cause of Cook's death he replied, "*We are learning new facts every day, and I do not at present conceive it to be impossible that some peculiarity of the spinal cord, unrecognizable at the examination after death, may have produced symptoms like those which have been described. I, of course, include strychnia in my answer; but it is irreconcilable with everything I have seen or heard of. It is as irreconcilable with strychnia as with everything else; it is irreconcilable with every disease that I am acquainted with, natural or artificial.*"

Mr. R. E. Guy, member of the Royal College of Surgeons, described the symptoms of a Mr. Foster whom he attended and who undoubtedly died of idiopathic tetanus with symptoms that were, in his opinion, the same as those of Cook.

Mr. J. B. Ross, a house-surgeon to the London Hospital spoke of a case he had seen where, after death, no poison was found but where old ulcers had left sores on the arm. He stated that these sores had led to death from tetanus. He had also seen old chronic syphilitic wounds in patients, which could account for tetanus.

Mr. Rymers Mantell also a house-surgeon to the London Hospital appeared briefly to agree with the evidence of Dr. Ross that, in the case he mentioned, the patient died from tetanus produced by the sores on the arms.

Dr. Wrightson had been a pupil of Leibig's at Giessen and was then a teacher of chemistry in a school in Birmingham. He had been involved in another case where poison was detected. He stated that, "*I have found no extraordinary difficulties in the detection of strychnia. It is certainly to be detected by the*

116

usual tests."

Professor Partridge a Professor of Anatomy in King's College lectured at the same college as the Prosecution witness Dr. Todd but disagreed with Todd's assertion that granules on the spine couldn't cause tetanus. He stated, *"I have heard the statements as to the granules that were found on his spine. They would be likely to cause inflammation, and no doubt that inflammation would have been discovered if the spinal cord or its membranes had been examined shortly after death. It would not be likely to be discovered if the spinal cord was not examined until nine weeks after death. I have not seen cases in which this inflammation has produced tetanic form of convulsions, but such cases are on record. It sometimes does, and sometimes does not produce convulsions and death."*

When asked if he could form any judgement as to the death in Cook's case he replied, *"I cannot. No conclusion or inference can be drawn from the degree or kind of contractions of the body after death. - Hypothetically, I should infer that he died of tetanus which convulses the muscles. Great varieties of rigidity arise after death from natural causes. The half-bent hands and fingers are not uncommon after natural death. The arching of the feet in this case seemed rather greater than usual."*

Asked, *"You heard Mr. Jones state that if he had turned the body upon the back it would have rested on the head and the heels. Have you any doubt that that is an indication of death from tetanus?"*

He replied, *"No; it is a form of tetanic spasm. I am only acquainted with tetanus resulting from strychnine by reading. Some symptoms in Cook's case are consistent, some are inconsistent with strychnine tetanus. The first inconsistent symptom is the intervals that occurred between the taking of the supposed poison and the attacks."* He also added other inconsistent symptoms namely, *"sickness, beating the bed-clothes, want of sensitiveness to external impressions, and sudden cessation of the convulsions and apparent complete recovery".*

Mr. John Gay, a Fellow of the Royal College of Surgeons and surgeon to the Royal Free Hospital, recalled a case he had been involved in 1843. A boy had suffered an accident when a large stone had fallen upon the middle toe resulting in him having to have his toe amputated. A week later he suffered from a stiff neck and could not open his mouth and this was followed by intermittent convulsions. The injury to the toe had given rise to affection of his spinal cord and this irritation of the spinal cord ended in tetanic convulsions.

Dr. W. Macdonald a licentiate of the Royal College of Surgeons, Edinburgh, stated that epileptic convulsions sometimes have the same appearance as tetanic convulsions. He disagreed with all his colleagues by stating lock-jaw is generally a late symptom. He doubted if a patient who had been given strychnine could pull a bell violently as Cook had done and stated, *"**I think that death was in this***

case caused by epileptic convulsions, with tetanic complications." Adding, "*I form that opinion from the post mortem appearances being so different from those that I have described as attending poisoning with strychnia, and from the supposition that a dose of strychnia sufficient to destroy life in one paroxysm could not, so far as I am aware, have required even an hour for its absorption before the commencement of the attack. If the attack were of an epileptic character the interval between the attacks of Monday and Tuesday would be natural, as epileptic seizures very often recur at about the same hours of successive days.*"

Asked by the Defence, "*Assuming that a man was in so excited a state of mind that he was silent for two or three minutes after his horse had won a race, that he exposed himself to cold and damp, excited his brain by drink, and was attacked by violent vomiting, and that after his death deposits of gritty granules were found in the neighbourhood of the spinal cord, would these causes be likely to produce a death as that of Cook's?*"

He replied, "*Any one of these causes would assist in the production of such a death.*"

A picture of some the jurors: *From a book of the Palmer story, found in the William Salt Library, Stafford, written in Greek, published in 1860*

Dr. Bainbridge, a medical officer to St. Martin's Workhouse who had much experience of convulsive disorders, suggested that, "*In both males and females hysteria is frequently attended by tetanic convulsions.*" And, "***Hysteric convulsions*** *very rarely end in death. I have known one case in which they have done so.*"

Mr. Edward Austin Steddy, a Member of the Royal College of Surgeons and of Chatham, told the court of a patient called Sarah Ann Taylor who had **convulsions brought on by depression,** brought about by a quarrel with her husband. Sarah had had convulsions that lasted for a week before recovering and she had had another attack lasting a week a year later.

118

Dr. George Robinson was a physician to the Newcastle-on-Tyne Dispensary, who having heard the medical evidence, had come to the conclusion that Cook died of tetanic convulsions by which he meant, not the convulsions of tetanus, but convulsions similar to those witnessed in that disease. **He believed that gritty granules in the region of the spinal cord would be very likely to produce convulsions similar to the ones Cook experienced.** He also stated that Cook's "mode of life" would have predisposed him to epilepsy but he had never seen a case of epilepsy where the body was so stiff as to rest upon head and heels. He agreed that the symptoms spoken of by Cook's friend Mr. Jones could indicate death from strychnine but if there were no other cause of death suggested he would have said that death in Cook's case arose from epilepsy.

Dr. Richardson, a physician practicing in London, knew of many cases of death by convulsion often tetanic in appearance without being strictly tetanus. There are cases of angina pectoris in which the patient has recovered and appeared perfectly well for a period of twenty-four hours, and then the attack returned. **Dr. Richardson was of the opinion that the fact that Cook had a second fit was more likely to be the symptom of angina pectoris than of strychnia poison.**

Dr. Wrightson was recalled and said, that although strychnia poison is absorbed into the system, he would have still expected to find it in the spleen and liver and blood. **Catherine Watson** from Garnkirk gave evidence that, in the previous October, she had been attacked by a fit but had not suffered from a wound or taken poison.

Oliver Pemberton a lecturer on anatomy at Queen's College, Birmingham and a surgeon at the city's General Hospital, stated that he had been present at the examination of Cook's body after its exhumation in the January. He could not form any opinion as to the state of the body immediately after death. After this witness Mr. Serjeant Shee intimated that this concluded the medical evidence on behalf of the prisoner.

The Defence Team's own experts had given their opinions upon what caused Cook's death; however, they could not agree suggesting many different possibilities other than strychnine. The jury had to decide upon an issue that divided the medical experts, though the decisive factor was undoubtedly the masterly way in which the Attorney-General summed up the evidence for the Prosecution.

The Central Criminal Court at the Old Bailey
From The Times Report of the Trial of William Palmer published 1856

Chapter 32: The Trial –
Circumstantial Evidence for the Defence

Jere fails Palmer in the witness box

Serjeant Shee followed the Prosecution's case by taking eight hours, on the seventh day of the trial, delivering his address for the Defence before later using the whole of the eighth and ninth days to present his medical evidence (outlined in the previous Chapter).

Shee stood up to begin Palmer's defence with the words:

"In rising to perform the task which it now becomes my duty to discharge, I feel, gentlemen of the jury, an almost overwhelming sense of responsibility. Once only has it fallen to my lot to defend a fellow-creature charged with a capital offence. You can understand that to take a leading part in a trial of this kind is sufficient to disturb the calmest temper and try the clearest judgment, even if the effort only lasts one day. But how much more trying is it to stand for six long days under the shade, as it were of the scaffold, conscious that the least error in judgment may consign my client to an ignominious death and public indignation! It is useless for me to conceal that which all your endeavors to keep your minds free from prejudice cannot wholly efface from your recollection. You perfectly well know that for six long months, under the sanction and upon the authority of science, an opinion has almost universally prevailed that the blood of John Parsons Cook has risen from the ground to bear witness against the prisoner; you know that a conviction of the guilt of the prisoner has impressed itself upon the whole population, and that by the whole population has been raised, in a delirium of horror and indignation, the cry of blood for blood. You cannot have entered upon the discharge of your duty – which, as I have well observed, you have most conscientiously endeavoured to perform – without, to a great extent, sharing in that conviction. Before you knew that you would have to sit in that box to pass judgment between the prisoner and the Crown you might with perfect propriety, after reading the evidence taken before the coroner's jury, have formed an opinion with regard to the guilt or innocence of the prisoner. The very circumstances under which we meet in this place are of a character to excite in me mingled feelings of encouragement and alarm. Those whose duty it is to watch over the safety of the Queen's subjects felt so much apprehension lest the course of justice should be disturbed by popular prejudice which had been excited against the prisoner – they were so much alarmed that an unjust verdict might, in the midst of that prejudice, be

passed against him, that an extraordinary measure of precaution was taken, not only by her Majesty's Government, but also by the Legislature. An act of Parliament, which originated in that branch of the Legislature to which the noble and learned Lord who presides here belongs, and was sanctioned by him, was passed to prevent the possibility of an injustice being done through an adherence to the ordinary forms of law in the case of William Palmer. The Crown, also, under the advice of its responsible Ministers, resolved that this prosecution should not be left in private hands, but that its own law officer, my learned friend the Attorney-General, should take upon himself the responsibility of conducting it. And my learned friend, when that duty was entrusted to him, did what I must say will for ever redound to his honour – he resolved that in a case in which so much prejudice had been excited, all the evidence which it was intended to press against the prisoner should, as soon as he received it, be communicated to the prisoner's counsel. I must therefore tell my unhappy client that everything which constituted authorities of the land – everything which the Legislature and the law officers of the Crown could do to secure a fair and impartial trial has been done, and that if unhappily an injustice should on either side be committed, the whole responsibility will rest upon my Lords and upon the jury. A most able man was selected by the prisoner as his counsel not many weeks ago, but, unfortunately, was prevented by illness from discharging that office. I have endeavoured to the best of my ability to supply his place; but I cannot deny that I labour under a deep feeling of responsibility, although the national effort, so to speak, which has been made to insure a fair trial is a great cause of encouragement to me. I am moved by the task that is before me, but I am not dismayed. I have this further cause for not being altogether overcome in discussing the mass of evidence which has been laid before you. When the papers in the case came into my hands, I had formed no opinion as to the guilt or innocence of the prisoner. My mind was perfectly free to form what I trust will prove to be a right judgment upon the case."

Serjeant Shee then took the most unprecedented step of declaring his own personal belief in the prisoner's innocence with the words, ***"I say it in all sincerity – having read these papers, I commenced his defence with an entire conviction of his innocence. I believe that there never was a truer word pronounced than the words which he (Palmer) said, 'Not guilty,' to the charge."***

It is interesting to note that Shee seemed genuinely convinced of Palmer's innocence and on the Tuesday prior to the execution, whilst Palmer was in prison awaiting execution, Shee sent Palmer a gift of a beautiful bound Bible accompanied by a "most affecting note". The bible was later given to the Palmer

Family.

Serjeant Shee had first dealt with medical evidence (as detailed in the previous chapter), then on the tenth day, after his first witness of the day, he moved on to more circumstantial matters concerning Cook's general state of health and to trying to provide an alibi for when Palmer was alleged to have purchased strychnine from Newton.

The day's first witness was **Henry Matthews,** the Inspector of Police at the Euston-Square Railway Station, who gave evidence that the fast train from Euston was due in Stafford at 8.42 p.m. but was three minutes late. **(Rugeley is nine miles from Stafford by rail longer by road. The implication was that Palmer could not possibly have been in Rugeley at 9.00 p.m. the time that Charles Newton claims he sold him strychnine.)**

Joseph Foster, a farmer, gave evidence that Cook had suffered bilious attacks for several years before his death. **George Myatt,** a saddler from Rugeley, stated that Cook had been "the worse for liquor" at the Raven in Shrewsbury but he had not seen anything put into Cook's drink. **John Sergeant**, "an attendor of race meetings", gave evidence that shortly before the Shrewsbury Races Cook's throat was full of ulcers and very much inflamed and his tongue swollen. He said that Cook had told him that his throat had been in that state for weeks and months and now he didn't even notice it.

The Defence returned to attempting to disprove the evidence of Newton that Palmer bought strychnine from him at 9 o'clock at night and called as their next witness Jeremiah (Jere.) Smith, a friend and solicitor to the Palmer family, (Jere. Smith should not be mixed up with John Smith Palmer's solicitor for the trial).

The *Times Report of the Trial of William Palmer* published by Ward and Lock in 1856, gives us Smith's words given in evidence:

> . . . *I know Mrs. Palmer the prisoner's mother. In consequence of what passed between me and her on the Monday evening, I went about 9 o'clock to the prisoner's house to see if he had arrived. I did not find him. About ten minutes past ten I saw him. He was coming in the direction from Stafford in a car. He said, "Have you seen Cook to-day?" I said, "No. I have been to Lichfield on business." He said, "We had better run up and see him before I go to my mother's, or it will be too late." We then went up to Cook's room together. Cook said, "You are late to-night, doctor, I did not expect you to look in. I have taken the medicine which you gave me." We did not stay more than two or three minutes. I think he asked me why I had not called in earlier, and I told him I had been to Lichfield on business.*

The Attorney-General did not cross-question him about this evidence but sought to discredit Smith as a reliable witness by questioning him

about his relationship with Palmer's mother. In his book, *The Life & Career of Dr. William Palmer of Rugeley*, George Fletcher gave the following account of Smith suffering under cross-examination:

> *When in the witness-box this Jere Smith made a most sorry exhibition of himself at the hands of the Attorney-General, who, merciless in his attitude and language, found an easy prey in this man. After five minutes he shook like a leaf, trembling all over, with the perspiration running off his head, and stammered out his replies. Once he commenced an answer with:*

"Mr. Attorney, I am — —"
"Don't 'Mr. Attorne' me sir. But answer honestly, if you can, my questions. Where, in the course of 1854 or 1855 were you living? In Rugeley?"—
"In 1854 I think I resided partly with William Palmer; sometimes I was at his mother's."
"Did you sleep at his mother's?"
"Sometimes."
"When you slept at his mother's, where did you sleep?" —
"In a room."
"Was it in hers?" —
No."
"I ask you upon your oath, whether you were not intimate with her — you know what I mean?" —
"I was not; no more intimate with her than the proper intimacy that ought to exist."
"How often were you in the habit of sleeping at her house, having your own place of residence in Rugeley?"—
"Frequently I slept there; I cannot say the number of times, but frequently."
"Two or three times a week?" —
"Yes, I should say I did."
"Having your own place of abode in Rugeley?" —
"Yes."
"Are you a single or a married man?" —
"Single."
"How long did this habit and practice of sleeping two or three times a week at Mrs. Palmer's continue?" —
"Several years."
"Had you your own lodgings at Rugeley at the time?" —
"Yes, my own chambers at Rugeley at the time; I had chambers in Rugeley; lodgings."
"Your own bedroom, I suppose?" —

"Yes, I had a bedroom."

"How far is your house from Mrs. Palmer's?" —

"I should say it is nearly a quarter of a mile."

"Will you be so good as to explain how it happened that, having your own place of abode and your own bedroom, for several years you slept two or three times a week at Mrs. Palmer's house?" —

"Sometimes some of the members of the family used to come and visit her; her sons."

"It was too far, I suppose, when you went to see the members of the family, to dine and drink tea, to return a quarter of a mile?" —

"I used to stop and have a glass or two of gin and water, and play cards."

Lord Campbell: *"You went to the mother's to see them?"* —

"Yes."

Attorney-General: *"But you did not sleep at the mother's to see them. How was it that you did not go home?"* —

"I had no particular reason why I did not."

"Why did you not?" —

"I used to have some gin and water and smoke, and if it was late they used to say 'You had better stop all night.' "

"Did this go on three times a week for several years?" —

"Yes; but I used to stop there frequently when there was no one there, neither the mother, nor the sons nor anyone."

In the Times Report of the Trial of William Palmer published by Ward and Lock in 1856, we can see how the Attorney-General mercilessly switched his questioning of Jere Smith to his involvement with Palmer's attempts to get money by insuring people. Jere's answers were faltering and evasive:

The Attorney-General: "Now, I will turn to another subject. Were you called upon to attest another proposal for £13,000 by Walter Palmer in the Universal Office?" —

"I cannot say; if you will let me see the proposal I shall know."

"I ask you sir, as an attorney and a man of business, whether you cannot tell me whether you were applied to by William Palmer to attest a proposal for an assurance for £13,000 on the life of Walter Palmer?" —

"If I could see any document on the subject I dare say I should remember it."

"Do you remember getting a £5 note for attesting an assignment by Walter Palmer to his brother of such a policy?" —

"Perhaps I might. I don't recollect positively."

The Attorney-General (handing a document to witness), "Is this your signature?"

"It is very like my signature."

"Have you any doubt about it?" —

(After considerable hesitation) "I have some doubt."

"Read the document, and tell me on your solemn oath, whether it is your signature?" —

"I have some doubt whether it is mine."

"Read the document, sir. Was it prepared in your office?" —

"It was not."

"I will have an answer from you on your oath one way or another. Isn't that your handwriting?" —

"I believe that it is not my handwriting. I think that it is a very clever imitation of it."

"Will you swear that it is not?" –

"I will. I think that it is a very good imitation of my handwriting."

Baron Alderson (one of the three judges): "Did you ever make such an attestation?" —

"I don't recollect my Lord."

The Attorney-General: "Look at the other signature there, 'Walter Palmer', is that his signature?" —

"I believe that is Walter Palmer's."

"Look at the attestation and the words 'signed, sealed and delivered,' are they in Mr. Pratt's handwriting?" —

"They are."

"Did you receive it from Mr. Pratt?" —

"Most likely I did; but I can't swear that I did. It might have been sent to William Palmer."

"Did you receive it from William Palmer?" —

"I don't know; very likely I did."

"Did William Palmer give you that document?" —

"I have no doubt he did."

"If that be the document he gave you, and those are the signatures of Walter Palmer and of Pratt, is not the other signature yours?" —

"I'll tell you, Mr. Attorney —"

"Don't 'Mr. Attorney' me, sir! Answer my question. Isn't that your handwriting?"

"I believe it not to be."

"Will you swear that it isn't?" —

"I believe that it is not."

By now Smith's reputation was left completely in tatters. The Attorney-General in his summing up said of Smith: -

"Had we known what Smith was going to prove, we should have been able to

meet him with contradictory evidence. I need not say that any would have been
better than the evidence of that miserable man whom we saw exhibited today."

Such a spectacle I never saw in my recollection in any Court of Justice.
He calls himself a member of the legal profession. I blush for it to number
such a man upon its Rolls.

There was not one man who heard him to-day that is not satisfied he
came here to tell a false tale. There cannot be a man who is not convinced
he had been mixed up in many a villainy with Palmer which, if not
perpetrated, has been attempted, and he comes here now to save, if he
can, the life of his companion and friend, the son of the woman with
whom he has had that intimacy which he sought to-day in vain to disguise."

Even the Judge, Lord Chief Justice Campbell, in his summing up of
the evidence against Palmer, said of Jere Smith - *"Can you believe a man*
who so disgraces himself in the witness-box? It is for you to say if you think
Smith spoke the truth." **The Defence had left Jere Smith as their last witness**
and was relying upon his evidence to disprove Newton's evidence that Palmer
had bought strychnine from him. Smith's poor performance did nothing
to aid Palmer. What little reputation Smith had left was totally ruined by
his performance in court.

Palmer wrote two letters to Jere Smith from his prison cell. The Prison
Governor showed these letters to George Fletcher who reproduced copies of
these letters in his 1925 book. They read:

DEAR JERE, —

No man in the world ever committed a grosser case of Perjury than
that vile wretch Newton - he positively swore last Friday 16th May, that
he let me have 3grs. of Strychnine the Monday night before Cook's death
and that I went to Mr. Salt's Surgery for it, and got it from him at 9
o'clock.

It is a base lie for I left London on that very night at 5 o'clock by
Express and arrived at Stafford at 10 minutes to 9, brought a Fly from the
Junction and arrived at Rugeley at Masters' door about 10 o'clock.

Now as there is a God in Heaven (I am sure you can't have forgotten
it) you know that you were waiting for my coming and when I got out of
the Fly you told me that my mother wanted to see me particularly, and
after bidding Cook good night we walked together down to the YARD
{Mrs. Palmer's house}, and got a good brushing from the old Lady about
a writ of Brown's that Arminshaw had sent for; that Arminshaw told to
George and George to my mother - and if you recollect she was very cross.

We then walked back to my house and you said, "Well let me have a
glass of spirit." I went to the cupboard and there was none — you said

"Never mind" and bid me good night. This must have been after 11 o'clock — now I should like to know how I could get to Mr. Salt's shop at 9 o'clock on that night. You can also prove this truth, that Cook dined with me (and you) at my house on the Friday before his death and that we had a quantity of wine. Cook then went with you and had a glass of Brandy and water — and that he was then the worse for liquor. You can further prove that Cook handed me some money on this day, for he told you so in my presence when he gave you the £10. He told you at the same time I had won over £1,000 on his mare at Shrewsbury, and lastly you can prove that he and I betted for each other, that we had "Pyrrhine" jointly, and that we had had bill transactions together. These are solemn truths and I am fully persuaded that they cannot have escaped your memory.

Therefore let it be your bounden duty to come forward and place yourself in the witness-box and on your oath speak these great truths. Then rest assured you will lie down on a downey pillow and go to sleep happy.

Bear in mind I only want the truth. I ask for no more.

Yours faithfully,

W^M. PALMER.

Newton no doubt calculated upon my coming by the luggage train, but this had been discontinued more than a month - thus my reason for going to Stafford.

And another letter:–

DEAR JERE, -

Do, for God's sake tell the Truth — if you will only consider I am sure you will recollect meeting me at Masters' steps the night Monday the 19th of Nov. I returned from London and you told me my mother wanted to see me. I replied, "Have you seen Cook? And how is he?" You said, "No." I then said, "We will go upstairs and see him." We did so. When upstairs Cook said "Dr., you are late, Mr. Bamford has sent me two pills which I have taken," and he said to you, "Damn you Jere, how is it you have never been to see me." You replied that you had been busy all the day settling Mr. Ingram's affairs and we then wished him good night and went to my mothers.

Yours ever faithfully,

W^M. PALMER.

Do these letters prove that Palmer was innocent or were the letters telling Jere Smith what to say in court to provide Palmer with an alibi?

(Smith didn't live long after the trial, Rugeley Parish Church Burial Records show that Smith, Jeremiah aged 47, solicitor, was buried on January 1st 1858.)

After the Defence had put their case the Attorney-General took the rest of the tenth day replying to the evidence of the Defence and in doing so he delivered his second great speech of this trial.

Chapter 33: The Verdict and Sentence
The Decision of the Jury May 27th 1856:

The judge, Lord Chief Justice Campbell, used two of the days to slowly, methodically and with extreme dullness, sum up the case. After this the jury retired to consider their verdict. Palmer passed a note concerning Campbell to Shee which read, *I wish there were 2½ grains of strychnine in old Campbell's acidulated draught solely because I think he acts unfairly.*

The jury, as was the custom at that time, comprised of twelve men. They were largely respectable City tradesmen. A criminal broadside printed in Bristol in 1856 gives us some detail about ten of the twelve jurors. William Fletcher was named as foreman of the jury. (Later it is stated that the foreman William Mavor (a veterinary surgeon) gave their verdict. The others named were Richard Dumbrell, William Newman, (bootmaker), George Miller, George Oakshott, William Eccleston (grocer), Samuel Mullin, John Over (grocer), and William Nash. In the Verbatim Report of the trial I found the names and addresses of the missing jurors namely Thomas Knight and Charles Bates (and a juror named Samuel Mullett rather than Samuel Mullins). A Mr. Mason was chosen but released when he stated that he felt prejudiced against Palmer and the reporter could not catch the name of his replacement. The broadside also states that the jury retired at 2.45 p.m. and the verdict was delivered at 3.35 p.m. just 50 minutes later. This is different to Fletcher's versions that states the jury retired to consider their verdict at 2.18 p.m.

The *Illustrated Life and Career of William Palmer of Rugeley* published in 1856 refers to a letter from one of the jurymen published in the *"Times"*. In the letter the juryman states that on reaching the jury room there was dead silence for twenty minutes, followed by a discussion of the facts presented to them lasting for about ten minutes. Then each juryman took pen and paper and wrote his decision and signed his name, it having been decided that no one should pronounce his opinion in case they might influence others. The papers were laid on the table and the foreman opened them and read them aloud. Guilty was the unanimous verdict. There then followed an earnest conversation having no relation to William Palmer. He further stated that it was quite untrue that they were absent a longer time for the mere sake of appearance.

After an extremely complex trial lasting twelve days involving much conflicting evidence, the majority of which was circumstantial, the jury took just one hour seventeen minutes (or even less according to the account given in the *Times*) to reach their verdict of guilty.

Does just one hour seventeen minutes seem long enough to make a decision when the verdict was certain to bring with it the death penalty?

The jury's early return was met by a buzz of excitement. The prisoner, Palmer, was returned to the dock at the same time. The formal question silenced the spectators as the "Clerk of the Arraigus", put the question, *"Gentlemen of the Jury, are you all unanimous in your verdict?"*

The Foreman replied, *"We are."*

The "Clerk of the Arraigus" continued, *"How say you, gentlemen, do you find the prisoner at the bar guilty, or not guilty?"*

The Forman rose to his feet and in a distinct and firm tone replied, *"We find the prisoner GUILTY."*

The *Times Report on the Trail of William Palmer for the poisoning of John Parsons Cook at Rugeley* published by Ward Lock in 1856 stated that:

The prisoner, who exhibited some slight pallor and the least possible shade of anxiety upon the return of the jury to the box, almost instantly recovered his self-possession and his demeanor of comparative indifference. He maintained his firmness and perfect calmness after the delivery of the verdict; and when the sentence was being passed, he looked an interested, although utterly unmoved spectator. We think we may truly say that during the whole of his protracted trial his nerve and calmness have never for a moment forsaken him.

The "Clerk of the Arraigus" spoke again, *"Prisoner at the bar, you stand convicted of murder; what have you to say why the court should not give you judgment to die according to law?"*

Palmer made no reply.

The Lord Chief Justice then took the unusual step of delivering the sentence himself whereas, in those days, the usual custom was for one of the assisting judges to pronounce sentence. Justice Campbell "assumed the black cap" the placing of a flat black cap upon his head signaling that the death sentence was to be given. He then solemnly delivered the following words of the sentence:

William Palmer, after a long and impartial trial you have been convicted by a jury of the crime of willful murder. In that verdict my two learned brothers, who have so anxiously watched this trial, and myself entirely concur, and consider that verdict altogether satisfactory.

The case is attended with such circumstances of aggravation that I do not dare touch upon them. Whether it is the first and only offence of this sort which you have committed is certainly known only to God and your own conscience. It is seldom that such a familiarity with the means of death should be shown without long experience; but for this offence of which you have been found guilty your life is forfeited. You must prepare to die; and I trust that, as you can expect no mercy in this world, you will, by repentance of your crimes, seek to obtain mercy from Almighty God.

The Act of Parliament under which you have been tried, and under which you have been brought to the bar of this court at your own request, gives leave to the Court to direct that the sentence under such circumstances shall be executed either within the jurisdiction of the central criminal Court or in the county where the offence was committed. We think that, for the sake of example, the sentence ought to be executed in the county of Stafford.

Now I hope that this terrible example will deter others from committing such atrocious crimes, and that it will be seen that whatever art, or caution, or experience may accomplish, such an offence will be detected and punished. However destructive poisons may be, it is so ordained by Providence that there are means for the safety of His creatures, for detecting and punishing those who administer them. I again implore you to repent and prepare for the awful change that awaits you.

I will not seek to harrow up your feelings by any enumeration of the circumstances of this foul murder. I will content myself now with passing the sentence of the law, which is, that you be taken hence to the jail of Newgate, and thence removed to the jail of the county of Stafford, being the county in which the offence for which you are justly convicted was committed; and that you be taken thence to a place of execution and be there hanged by the neck until you are dead; and that your body be afterwards buried within the precincts of the prison in which you shall be last confined after your conviction; and may the Lord have mercy upon your soul!

Amen.

Before leaving the court Palmer wrote a note to his solicitor, which said, "*It was the riding that did it*". Later the phrase Palmer had used caused a great deal of discussion as to the exact meaning of his words. Some believe he meant that it was not the strong circumstantial evidence that resulted in him being found guilty but the masterly way in which the Attorney General arranged and presented the evidence. Others think he meant that Judge Campbell's summing up was the decisive factor against him. There was also an opinion that Palmer was referring to both the Attorney-General's powerful speeches and Judge Campbell's hostility in his summing up. One last suggestion was that Cook had in fact died from tetanus caused by a wound that Cook got when he fell from a horse.

Palmer was immediately removed from the dock. When he left the court he first went to a cell where he complained to the Under-Sheriff that, **"I did not receive a fair trial"**. The Under-Sheriff pointed out that all the judges agreed with the verdict of the jury but Palmer replied, **"Well, Sir, but that don't satisfy me"**. In the courtroom, after Palmer had left, Mr. James applied to have the bills, supposedly signed by Mrs. Palmer but shown to be forgeries, impounded.

A request the court granted without hesitation.

The Lord Chief Justice Campbell then turned to the jury and said:

> *"I beg to return to you, Gentlemen, the warm thanks of my learned brothers and myself for the service which you have rendered to your country upon this occasion. Your conduct throughout this protracted trial, which you have attended, no doubt, at much serious inconvenience to yourselves, has been such as to merit our utmost commendation. I only hope, and I doubt not, that you will be rewarded for your patient attention and for the sacrifices which you have made by the approbation of your own consciences and the approving voice of your country."*

He turned to the Sheriffs and continued:

> *"We have also to thank the Sheriffs of London for the manner in which the court has been kept during the trial, for their excellent arrangements, and for the facilities which they appear to have afforded to every one who had any business here to transact."*

The learned judges remained at the bench long enough to sign the warrants for the removal of the prisoner to the gaol in Stafford, and the warrant for the execution to be carried out there by the Sheriffs of Stafford.

Meanwhile Palmer was returned to his cell at Newgate Prison where he changed back into prison clothes then he was handcuffed, his ankles chained and he was then chained to a warder. That evening, at twenty minutes to eight, two "Black Marias" (horse-drawn convict vans) were brought to the prison. One went in to the prison gates the other remained outside the door of the Governor, Mr. Weatherhead. Weatherhead and two officers got Palmer into the cab outside the Governor's door and drove rapidly across to Euston Railway Station in time to catch the eight o'clock train to Stafford. When the second Black Maria came out of the prison gate empty the crowd that had gathered realised they had been tricked and ran after the first van shouting, "Poisoner" and "Murderer".

At Euston station there was great excitement as he was recognised when he arrived on the platform still dressed in convict's uniform but covered by a cloak. He was bundled in to the middle compartment of a first-class carriage. The party was met at Stafford by Woollaston, the Superintendent of Stafford Police, who took one of Palmer's arms. Palmer is said to have commented that it was very wet and asked if they had had much rain. Later, when he stumbled he complained about it being difficult to walk properly in his chains. The party was driven, in a prison van, straight to Stafford Gaol where Palmer was to await his fate.

"The Prisoner in the Dock" taken from a print in *The Times Report on the Trail of William Palmer for the poisoning of John Parsons Cook at Rugeley*, published by Ward Lock in 1856

Chapter 34: The Trial – Reasons for Doubt

Is circumstantial proof, however strong, sufficient in the
absence of concrete proof?

In this chapter, I could be accused of failing to provide a balanced summary; especially if one merely judges the case upon the column inches that I have devoted to supporting the guilty verdict, as apposed to the greater column inches given to casting doubt upon Palmer's guilt. I make no apologies, however, as it is important that each reader form their own opinion as to the weight of importance they feel should be attached to each individual thread of the evidence.

The main reasons supporting a guilty verdict were:

- The overwhelming circumstantial evidence brought against Palmer.
- The fact that nine experts stated that, in their opinion, the symptoms of death were consistent with strychnine poisoning, with several claiming that Cook's symptoms could not be attributed to any other known disease.
- Palmer had an extremely strong motive to commit murder:
  - his heavy debts from running fifteen race-horses (at the very least he could have received a heavy gaol sentence or might even have been transported to one of the colonies for being a debtor);
  - the exorbitant rates charged by the moneylenders were increasing his debts daily;
  - if debts weren't paid it was likely that he would be found guilty of forging his mother's signature to secure the loans.
- At one time Cook had claimed to have been "dosed" by Palmer.
- Palmer had the medical knowledge of, and access to, poisons.
- The inquest on Cook was so poorly conducted that the Prosecution could argue it was impossible to find traces of strychnine in Cook's body.
- The coroner's jury felt Palmer was guilty of administering poison to Cook.
- Many strongly believed that Palmer was responsible for Cook's death, even if there was a doubt as to whether the poison used had been strychnine.
- At Stafford Assizes the jury also judged Palmer to have a case to answer for in the death Cook as well as for the death of his wife.
- The jury at the Old Bailey seemed in little doubt, and very quickly returned a unanimous verdict of "guilty".
- Palmer was clearly shown to be dishonest and capable of many other crimes.
- The sheer number of suspicious deaths around Palmer, all of which could be shown to have a financial motive.
- It could be argued that the Crown took every precaution to counteract the

bias against the prisoner, which was widely encouraged by the daily reports in the national newspapers, to the extent of rushing through an Act of Parliament to have the trial switched to London.

Palmer's supporters, however, would argue that, in the absence of concrete proof, the judgement was "unsafe".

Some reasons that Palmer's supporters put forward for doubting Palmer's guilt:

- Dr. Jones, a long time friend who was Cook's own doctor, was present at his death and under oath gave the cause of death as 'tetanus'.
- Medical experts could not agree that Cooks death was caused by strychnine. At least 18 so-called experts were called and were split in their opinions as to why Cook died
- Strychnine was never found in the body of John Parsons Cook.
- Palmer always insisted that Cook did not die of strychnine.
- The newspapers of the time had virtually tried Palmer and found him guilty. It would have been impossible to find a jury who could not have been influenced by what had been reported in the newspapers. The scandal was the talk of the country.
- Much was made of Newton's evidence that he had sold Palmer 3 grains of strychnine at 9.00 p.m. on 19th November 1855. However Palmer's train from London did not arrive at Stafford Station until 8.45 p.m. and it would have been impossible for a fly, the horse drawn equivalent to today's taxi, to reach Rugeley in just 15 minutes. It should be remembered that Newton was one of the two men who carried out the botched post-mortem on Cook.
- Why was the driver of the "fly" never called as a witness? Mr. Bergin, a constable from Stafford, had given the driver of the fly a temporary job in a remote part of Staffordshire where he could not easily be contacted. Neither was the station ticket collector called to give evidence. Had there been a conspiracy to keep a vital witness away?
- Another witness who made an impression upon the jury was Elizabeth Mills the chambermaid at the Talbot Arms where Cook died. She claimed to have been sick after sampling some broth sent to Cook from Palmer's house. She had not mentioned this at the time of the post-mortem or inquest. She also had not commented on the manner of Cook's death but, at the trial, stated that Cook was "twitching" in the time leading up to his death. When questioned at the trial she claimed that she had not mentioned these things at the inquest because she was not asked.

136

- After the inquest Mills got a job as a hotel maid down in London. Here Cook's stepfather Mr. Stevens, Captain Hatton of Staffordshire Police, solicitor Mr. Gardner and Lavinia Barnes, a maid from the Talbot Arms, all visited her. She claimed that on these visits, their only topic of conversation was the question of whether she enjoyed living and working in London. Under cross-examination she eventually agreed that Cook's stepfather had visited "six or seven times" in the five-month period leading up to the trial. So many visits and not discussed the case, is this likely? Had Mills been "coached" in the evidence she was to give?

Even back in 1856 not everyone was convinced by the reporting of the case in the newspapers or by the verdict of the jury. In the William Salt Library there is a 16-page pamphlet, priced one penny that was produced in the month between the verdict and the hanging. The pamphlet written by a coroner Mr. Thomas Wakley, published by C. Elliot of 2 and 3 Shoe Lane, Fleet Street, published it in 1856 and having the exceedingly long title of:

"THE CRIES OF THE CONDEMNED OR PROOFS OF THE UNFAIR TRIAL AND (IF EXECUTED) THE LEGAL MURDER OF WILLIAM PALMER, LATELY SENTENCED TO DIE ON A CHARGE OF POISONING AND Reasons why he should not be HANGED, From circumstances that have since Transpired, unknown to the Public, and which were not mentioned at his trial. with suggestions as to WHAT SHOULD BE HIS PROPER FATE INSTEAD OF SUFFERING DEATH. Including a Strong Parallel Case of the Uncertainty of Circumstantial Evidence, the Weakness of Human Judgment and the Danger of Sacrificing Innocent Life."

A selection of additional Points made in the pamphlet:
- Professor Taylor who analysed the contents of the stomach stated that he found neither strychnia nor any poison that could account for the death of Cook. As the senior judge said with a sneer, "*of course the whole defence rests upon this.*" In spite of the judges scepticism it struck the pamphlet's writer as a very feasible defence.
- In Palmer's case, the old axiom – "Give a dog a bad name, you had better hang him at once," has been too truly realised.
- Newspaper articles and correspondent's letters, and even pamphlets entitled, "An account of the Life of the Notorious Murderer," have inundated the country, until the tables and sideboards of almost every household have been covered with exparte and unreasonable appeals to the passions.
- A man is tried and condemned by mob-reasoning and brutal prejudice, before the time of his legal trial. In that case, who can deny the glaring fact that an individual charged with a serious offence like the one attributed

to Palmer, is often found guilty and bespoke for the gallows before an impartial jury has had the opportunity to calmly and dispassionately investigate every circumstance bearing upon the case, according to true evidence, on the oath of trustworthy witnesses?

The pamphlet further claimed:

- The condemned man has not yet had a fair trial.
- Circumstantial evidence, however apparently strong it may appear, is not to be always relied on for a proof of guilt.

The pamphlet which had started with the words, **"Let not passion but reason be your guide"** had a final paragraph which said:

"When the circumstances in Palmer's case, by the re-investigation he justly asks for, have been clearly proved against him then *we object to his being executed* to satisfy the brutal thirstings of "blood for blood;" but rather, we would suggest, for raising the moral standard of society, and the *greater punishment of criminals*, inflict upon them the more lasting and terrifying scourge of hard labour and solitary confinement for life."

Chapter 35: The Public Execution
The fateful day, the crowd, the scene, the "drop"

In the days leading up to his execution Palmer ate regularly, slept well and in no way gave the impression that he was depressed. Twice on the Sunday before the execution he attended the prison chapel and was given a seat screened off from the other prisoners.

The public execution was set for 8.00 a.m. on Saturday June 14th 1856. His brother Thomas (a clergyman) unsuccessfully made a last minute appeal for a reprieve. He stressed in the appeal the dangers of convicting a man on circumstantial evidence alone. On the Friday it was announced in Stafford that the Home Secretary Sir George Grey, in reply to the petition for Palmer's reprieve, had decisively and solemnly, stated that the law must take its course.

The Staffordshire Advertiser 21st June 1956 told us that on the Friday night before the execution –

> *Mr. John Smith, the prisoner's attorney arrived at half-past ten o'clock to take a farewell of his unhappy client, whom he had not seen since his conviction. The Governor of the gaol, with the discretion which has characterised his conduct throughout the whole proceedings, accompanied Mr. Smith to the prisoner's cell. After a few words of greeting the Governor informed Palmer that, if he had anything to say to Mr. Smith upon family matters, of a confidential nature, he might rely upon his keeping, whatever he might say upon that subject, secret. Palmer replied, "No," and that he "hoped all he might say the Governor would lose no time in publishing to the world." He then remarked that all he had to say was, that he thanked the chaplain for his great attention to him, and that he was also grateful to the officers of the prison for their kindness, finishing his remarks by saying that Cook did not die from strychnine. The Governor made an observation in reply, to the effect that he "trusted, in the awful condition in which he was placed, he was not quibbling." "The question," added the Governor, is 'aye', or 'no', did you or did you not murder Cook?" Palmer answered directly, "Lord Campbell summed up for poisoning by strychnine." The Governor replied, "Are you guilty of the murder – it is of very little importance how the deed was done!" Palmer replied that he had, "nothing more to add," and that, "he was quite easy in his conscience and happy in his mind."*

Later the newspaper gave John Smith's version which was that Palmer stated –

> *"I am innocent of poisoning Cook by strychnine. All that I have to ask is that you will have Cook's body exhumed, and that you will see to*

my mother and boy." Mr. Smith promised to fulfil his last behest, and in *grief parted with the prisoner, who presented Mr. Smith with a book, in which he wrote in a firm hand, 'The gift of William Palmer, June 13th, 1856.' The book was headed 'The Sinner's Friend,' and the following couplet formed its prelude, to which the prisoner referred:-*

'Oh! Where for refuge should I flee,
  If Jesus had not died for me.'

Late on the night before his execution, Palmer was visited by both his surviving brothers and his sister. It was said that he had accepted his fate and that, apart from a slight nervous twitch in the corner of his mouth, he was calm. After his visitors had left he was given brandy and water and at 1.00 a.m. he slept. He was awoken at 2.30 a.m. to prepare himself for a visit from the Prison Chaplin the Reverend R. H. Goodacre.

On the morning of the hanging the Reverend Goodacre stayed with Palmer from 2.30 a.m. until 5.00 a.m. and tried unsuccessfully to get Palmer to confess that he was guilty. Goodacre returned at 6.30 a.m. and remained until 7.30 a.m. All through Palmer categorically maintained that John Parsons Cook was not murdered by strychnine. He was also visited by another clergyman the Reverend Henry Sneyd.

7.30 a.m. Palmer was given a cup of tea and more brandy and water.

7.40 a.m. Palmer was joined in the condemned cell by the High Sheriff Lt. Col. Dyott, the Under Sheriff R.W. Hand and the Prison Governor. They told him that the time had come to carry out the sentence and he was quietly led to the pressroom. Here they were joined by George Smith the hangman who was introduced to Palmer who showed no emotion. Smith tied Palmers hands and Palmer asked that Smith did not draw the cord (rope) too tight before the drop. It is said that Palmer was extremely calm at this point. He was then taken to the Chapel where he received the "Sacrament". The Chaplain made another visit. He asked Palmer if he was satisfied with the justice of his sentence. Palmer replied emphatically "No!" The chaplain left and Palmer told the officers that he had never changed his version of the events and asked them to pray for his child. The chaplain came again and tried unsuccessfully to get Palmer to confess his guilt, he then told Palmer, "Then your blood be on your own head".

7.53 a.m. At seven minutes to eight the prison's death bell began to toll to mark the start of the procession to the gallows. Palmer had a "jaunty stride" and even a smile on his face. The party included the Reverend H. Goodacre, who read the extracts from the burial service, the High Sheriff, the Under Sheriff Mr. T. D. Atkinson, the Chief Constable J. H. Hatton, the Governor and Deputy Governor, the Head Turnkey Mr. Chidley plus warders George Plimmer and George Roberts, as well as members of the press. Palmer, dressed in a prison suit, was paraded in front of the other prisoners as a warning to them. The party had to walk across the crescent yard past the prison hospital to the lodge (the prison gatehouse) and out into the road whilst all the time the "horrid twang" of the death bell sounded.

The *Staffordshire Advertiser* told that:

> *There were nearly 40 reporters and representatives of the Press present. So universal is the interest felt in the fate of Palmer that the press of London, Liverpool, Manchester, Birmingham, Nottingham, Huddersfield, Shrewsbury, and other places, as well as all the papers published in this county, had representatives present.*

For descriptions of the day I have drawn heavily on the reports published in the Second Edition of the *Staffordshire Advertiser* **14th June 1856 much of which was repeated in their next edition on 21st June 1856. All text in this Chapter in italics is taken directly from the** *Staffordshire Advertiser* **which was critical of the accuracy of reports appearing in some other newspapers.** They commented favourably upon the good behaviour of the crowd generally compared to some of the unruly behaviour seen at hangings in London:

> *The account of the execution of William Palmer was looked for, all over the country, with intense anxiety. The reporters who were at Stafford forwarded electric telegraphic despatches to London, Liverpool, Manchester, and the other towns from which they came, or proceeded by the first trains with their reports. In some few instances, we believe, the reports were sent the night before, subject to alterations. No wonder that some of the reports, prepared under such circumstances, were not very accurate. Those which represent the conduct of the spectators as having been very rude and disorderly was a gross misrepresentation; for it is admitted on all hands that nothing could be more orderly or becoming the scene than the behaviour of the immense concourse of the thirty-five thousand supposed to have been present on the occasion.*

In some other newspapers there were reports that there was much jostling to get a better view of the gallows with gangs of miners from local pits hell bent on trying to force their way to the front with no respect for anyone else.

Of the arrangements made to cope with the expected crowds the *Staffordshire Advertiser* wrote:-

> *The regulations of Mr. Hatton, chief constable, were admirable; and the men under his direction, many of whom were present the whole night, did much to prevent accidents and secure order on the occasion. We have stated, in the report elsewhere, how many persons visited Stafford from South Staffordshire. From Wolverhampton, Tipton, Sedgley, Gornal, and every part of that district, the numbers who came in vehicles of all*

141

descriptions were immense. All night long on the road between Penkridge and Stafford, the spring carts, omnibuses, and other carriages kept rolling along in uninterrupted succession, so that it really seemed as if the town would not hold this vast influx of carriages, with their living freights. On a very moderate computation, five thousand persons entered Stafford in carriages by that road only, whilst the number of pedestrians was very considerable. Similar vehicles drove into the town by the Stone road, from the Potteries and elsewhere, in great numbers; and every other road furnished its contribution of carriage loads of visitors. All the neighbouring towns and villages sent a portion of spectators. The railway, it may well be imagined, was extensively used for the purpose of conveyance to Stafford, both by the people of this and many adjoining counties. It is, indeed, incredible what numbers came from a considerable distance to witness the end of Palmer. On their return, Mr. Cartwright, the station master, adopted the precaution of sending two special trains off with about 5,000 passengers, in order to relieve the ordinary trains, and the pressure and inconvenience which such a multitude would have occasioned on the limited platform of the Stafford station. The great bulk of the people did not remain long in Stafford after the execution and Mr. Maurice Richards, the superintendent of the borough police, with his small Force was able to maintain good order in the town.

The clergy took the opportunity pretty generally on Sunday last of preaching sermons suitable to the occasion. At Rugeley Rev. T. Atkinson delivered an impressive admonitory discourse on the terrible consequences of betting and gambling especially in connection with other disreputable practices of "the turf"; and warning his hearers against taking the first steps in the path of crime.

The Rev. R. H. Goodacre, the chaplain of the County Prison delivered two most appropriate discourses, one before and the other after the execution.

In another column the *Staffordshire Advertiser* stated:

VISITORS BY RAILWAY. – *The railway authorities made all necessary arrangements to meet the increased demands upon them by the public. The unfavourable state of the weather must have deterred many hundreds from availing themselves of this mode of conveyance, as the number of passengers was not so great as the accommodation afforded. Many hundreds arrived by the different trains yesterday, intending to pass the night in the town. The early train from the north brought an accession of visitors, anxious to witness the end of the notorious poisoner. The train from Birmingham and the iron districts was well filled, and there was a large*

142

number from the Shropshire district. The two trains arriving about half-past seven, we suppose, brought eleven or twelve hundred passengers. They kept admirable time, and such were the arrangements of the railway company, assisted by a strong body of the county constabulary, that nothing like confusion prevailed. Shortly before eight a considerable number came in from the Potteries.

The Crowd Assembled for the Execution: In spite of heavy rain throughout the proceeding night the crowd was estimated to be between 30,000 and 35,000, the majority of which was made up of men. Many of them had walked the ten miles from Rugeley. By dawn hundreds had already taken their stand in the most favourable positions and in Stafford the heavy drizzle did not stop the atmosphere of anticipation and excitement. The public houses had stayed open all night as did many of the non-conformist chapels. In particular the Greyhound Inn in County Road opposite the prison did a roaring trade.

The Second Edition of the *Staffordshire Advertiser* 14th June 1856, under the heading of "THE TOWN AND THE SCENE AROUND THE DROP", stated:

A continuous drizzling rain fell through the night, and as the lamps were not lighted, the darkness was exceedingly dense. This served to drive a large portion of the visitors into the public-houses which accordingly became full, and were kept open all night. Whilst the demeanour of those assembled to witness the execution was by no means characterised by the solemnity which so awful a sight might be supposed to be calculated to inspire, there was, up to an early hour of the morning, a general absence of any outrageous coarseness. Here and there a party under the influence of liquor reeled out of a public-house, and shouted in drunken accents the refrain of a song, but the town was generally quiet until about three o'clock, when day gradually dawned, and groups began slowly to wend their way towards the prison, their pace constantly accelerating and their numbers increasing until the three approaches to the front gate of the gaol where the drop was placed, were filled for a considerable distance.

The New Connexion and Primitive Methodist Chapels were open, and religious service was being performed during the night. At its close numerous parties issued forth distributing tracts, composed with special reference to the terrible drama about to be enacted. Others carried large placards, bearing texts of Scripture of a solemn character, and proclaimed the consequences of indulging in sinful habits. One of the placards, containing texts of warning, encouragement, and hope was held at the barrier next the scaffold, towards which the wretched culprit would turn his last gaze.

Meanwhile an enormous influx of spectators commenced. Hundreds,

143

tired, foot sore, and travel-stained, had evidently tramped many weary miles to reach Stafford; and for five hours carriages of every kind, laden to the very extreme capacity of horses and vehicles, poured into the town in an unremitting stream, and their occupants gradually closed up the approaches to the entrance of the gaol. On the Wolverhampton road the scene was most remarkable. From twelve o'clock at night until six in the morning there was a complete procession of over-laden spring carts, omnibuses, many with four horses, and all descriptions of vehicles. From the Potteries the arrival of vehicles was also numerous, whilst all the neighbouring towns and villages contributed their quota of visitors.

The platforms near the prison were soon occupied, and looking at the crowds which assembled on them, the precautions taken by the Mayor and magistrates of Stafford appeared fully to be warranted. The hum of many voices gradually increased; here and there broke forth rude speeches and course wit, but the crowd did not present those revolting displays of brutality which often characterise their demeanour on such occasions.

The precautions of the police were excellent. People were gradually admitted within the barriers, and the rain helped to keep the crowd thinner than otherwise would have been the case. The representatives of the Press (with the exception of the select few accommodated within the gaol) were introduced by the police to the space near the drop at five o'clock, and had to remain in a drizzling rain, which at times increased to a very heavy shower, to await the period of the execution.

Precautions were taken by having ladders within the lower walls outside the gaol to remove any who might faint, and the necessity for this was soon evident, as instances of fainting presented themselves at an early hour.

The rain, which began to fall heavily at a little before six, did not cease until about seven, when the clouds began to break, and the sky brightened. The crowd gradually increased in density. The roofs of houses and every standing or clinging place from which a view of the drop could be obtained was occupied. There could not, towards the last, have been less than thirty or thirty-five thousand people standing within sight of the drop. Of those a very small proportion were women, none being admitted within the barriers; and of the spectators outside, and on the platforms, not more than one in twelve were female. The spectators appeared to be chiefly respectable working people and tradesmen, and not to any large extent "swells" and low blackguards. Their demeanour was highly decorous, and the patience with which they awaited the period fixed for the execution was really remarkable. So far as our observation went, no oath was uttered, and the hoarse murmur of voice never rose above the accumulated

144

hum of multitudes speaking in an ordinary tone. The placard above referred to, which was held by a strange-looking man, with long hair and a beard and without a hat, was removed some time before the execution took place. Perhaps nothing could more distinctly testify to the proper feeling which actuated the great body of the spectators than the fact that this man and his placard appeared to excite no ridicule. At seven minutes to eight the minute bell gave the first toll, announcing to the crowd the departure of the melancholy procession from the cell of the condemned convict, and at once the hoarse murmur of the crowd arose into a loud buzz of excited expectation, which the multitude of voices swelled into a roar. A cry of "hats off" was raised, but gradually, as this injunction was obeyed, the noise subsided, and a respectful, if not solemn, silence succeeded. Every face was eagerly upturned to catch the first glimpse of the wretched culprit. Here and there was a laugh, but popular feeling was against it, and at the rebukes of the more serious it ceased. The condemned man ascended the steps with a quick firm step, and placed himself on the centre of the drop with his face towards the gaol.

Other accounts claimed that the appearance of Palmer was greeted by cries of "Murderer" and "Poisoner" as he came out of the prison gates, and a *"powerful and indescribable sensation agitated the vast crowd"*. Palmer seemed to be the one least affected by the occasion. When he came out of the prison he was tripping along between the guards trying to avoid the puddles of water. Many people started to laugh at this because in only a few minutes time he would be in no condition to worry whether his shoes were dirty or not. The noise died down to be replaced by a breathless silence apart from some nervous laughter amongst the crowd.

I have seen suggestions that the cry of "hats off" at hangings was not necessarily a mark of respect for the solemn occasion, but more likely to be out of courtesy for other spectators whose view of the morbid scene would be enhanced by the removal of all hats.

The Gallows: The portable gallows (see picture on the page overleaf) had been erected in the street just outside the gates of the gaol at four o'clock in the morning and people took this as a sign that there was to be no last minute pardon. The scaffold was a huge affair, somewhat resembling an agricultural machine, and hung with black cloth. At least twenty platforms had been built near the prison to give good views of the execution, with people being charged up to a guinea for a good view and the area around the prison had been packed from 5 a.m. as the crowd jostled to get a good view. There were even some platforms erected on nearby roof-tops to give people, willing to pay, a good view of the hanging.

I have never seen a print or photograph of the scene at Palmer's hanging but the print above shows the sort of portable gallows which would have been used at the execution of William Palmer. It comes from a broadside sold at the execution of George Bentley on March 26th 1866. The print was also used on several other broadsides for other executions. The broadside is the property of the Staffordshire Arts and Museum Services.

The "Drop": The Staffordshire Advertiser 14th June 1856 wrote:-

The firmness with which the prisoner walked surprised every one who witnessed it. The senior officers of the gaol had never beheld a felon conduct himself with such coolness; and it may be truly said that he was the least affected of all that melancholy group. Even when
"*The dying knell toll'd for the living man,*"
And every other person trembled with emotion, he exhibited the same indomitable, or rather insensible demeanour which we have had so frequently the misfortune to remark. The prisoner ascended the steps leading to the drop with firmness and was immediately placed under the fatal noose.

In a moment the executioner adjusted the rope, and having shaken the hands of the prisoner, he quickly withdrew the bolt. The drop fell amidst the breathless silence of the immense crowd, and the criminal yielded up his life.

"*Those pinioned arms, those hands that ne'er*
Shall be lifted again – not even in prayer;
That heaving breast – enough; 'tis done;
The bolt has fallen; the spirit gone.
For weal or for woe is known but to One.
Oh! 'twas a fearsome sight - ah me!
A thing to shudder at, not to see."

The following week the *Staffordshire Advertiser* of 21st June 1856 gave additional details:

He wore prison dress – frieze jacket and trousers, and check shirt – and was bareheaded. He was ghastly pale, but preserved an unmoved expression of countenance, indicative of dogged resolution to meet his dreadful fate without flinching. A close observer might, however, detect a violent beating of the pulse in the neck, and his chest heaved quickly. His arms were pinioned, and he tightly compressed a handkerchief he held in his hand behind him. He never looked up or around him, but remained motionless as a statue during the few seconds occupied by the necessary preparations for the awful termination of his earthly career. He never flinched or shuddered as the executioner placed the rope around his neck and drew the white cap over his face. That done, the bolt was immediately withdrawn, and the drop fell. Being a stout heavy man he never struggled at all; a few convulsive twitchings of his arms and legs alone ensued, and after a few seconds his limbs hung motionless in death. The crowd did not shout or yell as do often such gatherings at the Old Bailey, but behaved with the utmost decorum, and in a few minutes after the drop fell began quietly to disperse. The body after hanging an hour, as prescribed by law, was cut down and removed. While the culprit stood on the scaffold there was intense silence, and when the drop fell there was a stifled scream, evidently of females, and a sense of the solemnity of the event appeared to be the prevalent feeling amongst the spectators. The small extent to which females mingled in the crowd had striking exceptions. Two in particular, perched in perilous positions, feasted their eyes with the scene, and one, while the rest of her sex were uttering a cry of horror, was coolly watching the contortions of the body through a glass.

The *Staffordshire Advertiser's* account differed from other accounts that had claimed the crowd was disappointed because Palmer did not make a "death speech", and also because he had not put up a struggle and it was all over very quickly, so quickly that many of the crowd felt that they had been cheated and cried out "Cheat!" or "Twister!"

The Rope: The rope used to hang Palmer was made by a man called Daniel Coates of 12, Friars Terrace, Stafford, and his workmates who worked as porters at Stafford Railway Station. They made the rope an extra 30 yards longer than was actually necessary and then, after the hanging, sold off two to three inch pieces of "the rope that hanged Palmer" for up to half a crown (two shillings and sixpence) each.

Philip Talbot told me a story told to him by his father. He claimed that, in the Barley Mow at Tividale, near Dudley, ten years after the execution the hangman,

George Smith, was still trying to sell bits of "the rope that hanged Palmer". This led to the following Black Country rhyme:-

E's a crafty *ode* charmer,   *{old}*
Is Smith, who 'anged Palmer,
An' the rope that *'e sode*,   *{he sold}*
Would stretch all the road,
From Dudley to regions much warmer.

I found the following additional verse to the rhyme in *A Memorable Medley of Great Black Country Characters* by Aristotle Tump, a 1986 Bugle Publication:-

He's a drunken *ode* wretch,   *{old}*
But a neck he *wull* stretch,   *{will}*
An' he *gozz* to the *gallus* a-singin'.   *{goes & gallows}*
He dances a jig an' he *dote* care a fig,   *{doesn't}*
For the felon who's chokin' an swingin'…..

Palmer's was <u>not</u> the last public hanging in England. That awful distinction goes to Michael Barrett hanged outside Newgate Prison, London on 26th May 1868 for his part in the Fenian bomb outrage on December 13th 1867, which killed twelve people outside Clerkenwell Prison. **Nor was Palmer's the last public hanging at Stafford.** George Smith was the hangman for the last public hanging outside Stafford Gaol, which was a rather bungled affair on July 5th 1866 when an eighteen year old, William Collier, was hanged for murder. The first attempt to hang Collier went wrong when the rope failed to remain tied to the beam and the poor young man had to go through the ordeal a second time. Executions at Stafford from then on were carried out within the prison up until 1914.

Milestones in Legislation in Regard to Hanging: Note that from 1832 the crime of shoplifting of goods to the value of five shillings or less no longer carried the death penalty. From 1841 hanging for the crime of rape was abolished with the death penalty only used for treason or murder. Gibbeting (where executed corpses were displayed publicly in cages), was abolished in 1843. In 1868 the practice of public execution was abolished. From 1908 they abolished the death sentence for children below the age of sixteen. In 1931 the execution of pregnant women was prohibited. In 1965 the Murder (Abolition of Death penalty) Act 1965 became law and the death penalty suspended for five years. The last executions in Britain were of two men on 13 August 1964. Peter Anthony Allen, aged 21, was hanged in Walton gaol, Liverpool and Gwynne Owen Evans, aged 24, was hanged in Strangeways, Manchester. They were convicted of the murder of John Alan West, a milkman, while robbing him in his house on 7 April 1964. In 1966 both Houses of Parliament agreed to abolish the death penalty for murder. When Britain abolished the death penalty for murder they became one of just 12 countries in the world that had fully abolished the death penalty. Another vote in 1969 finally made the abolition of the death penalty for murder "permanent" in Great Britain. A further vote in 1973 abolished it permanently in Northern Ireland. The UK Government introduced a late amendment to the Human Rights Bill in October 1998 that removed the death penalty as a possible punishment for military offences under the Armed Forces Acts.

148

Chapter 36: At the End
His final words and final resting place

William Palmer is often credited with having said, as he stepped upon the trap door on the scaffold, **"Are you sure this damn thing's safe?"** However, I could not find any reference to him having spoken these words in any of the contemporary accounts of his execution. In the Illustrated Life, Career, and Trial of William Palmer of Rugeley published in 1856 it stated that, -

> *After a brief prayer with the chaplain, he turned to the hangman, had the rope put round his neck, and the long cap drawn over his face. He then shook hands with his executioner, said, in a low voice, "**God bless you.**" and as the last word issued from his lips the bolt was withdrawn, the drop fell, and, after a slight convulsion of the limbs, he hung lifelessly from the gallows. So well had everything been managed by the hangman, so nicely had the fatal cord been adjusted, and so clear was the fall of the drop, that death was all but instantaneous.*

In Fletcher's book The Life & Career of Dr. William Palmer of Rugeley we were told that, -

> *On the morning of his execution, when the hangman came in to his cell, he was offered some wine before he was pinioned. When it was brought and poured out quickly, he blew off some bubbles and remarked "**They always give me indigestion next morning if I drink in a hurry.**" Within less than ten minutes he was dead.*

Before the execution party were due to start their walk to the gallows the Governor asked Palmer to agree that the sentence was just. Palmer replied, **"Cook did not die from strychnine".** The governor told Palmer, "This is not a time for quibbling. Did you, or did you not, kill Cook?" Palmer answered, **"The Lord Chief Justice summed up for poisoning by strychnine."** Much has been made of Palmer's words in the absence of a confession of guilt. Was he saying that the sentence was unjust and that he was innocent of poisoning Cook or was the implication that he had poisoned Cook but had not used strychnine?

His Final Resting Place
After the execution William Palmer was left hanging for one hour, in accordance with the sentence. Prison records tell us that the body was taken to the Death House (the prison mortuary). A death mask was made (see Chapter 37). No coffin was supplied; his body, "naked as it came into the World", was put in a sack and placed in a grave, which had first been lined with quicklime. It is

149

believed that he was the last culprit to be buried "without a shell" in any prison in this country. They used quicklime in a desire to destroy the physical remains as quickly as possible. However, it is now known that quicklime would, in fact, preserve a body for a longer period of time. He was buried in a grave beside the old prison chapel. A plan of prison graves is in the prison records but bodies were not buried in separate graves but were buried four or five to a grave to save space. He was one of 107 men and 4 women known to have been buried within the prison grounds.

The site of Palmer's burial (Photograph from around 1869 -1871)
The picture is from the Staffordshire Past Track
www.staffspasttrack.org.uk
The original is from the Staffordshire Arts & Museum Service.

In 1834 legislation had been introduced so that executed prisoners were to be buried within the prison grounds. The prison burial ground was located next to the old chapel. William Palmer's grave is under the window on the right (see above). In 2001 I was informed that the spot where Palmer was buried now lies beneath an artificial football pitch inside the prison although I now have it on good authority that this was never the case. The grave was actually sited in a shared plot that now lies between the new kitchen (built on the site of the old chapel shown in the photograph on previous page and the newly built chapel).

There is also a claim that an old Staffordshire drinking expression, "**What's your poison?**" asked when offering to buy someone a drink, is a legacy from Palmer. It is said that when there were rumours flying around about him having poisoned people he would use the phrase as a joke at his own expense. Some even say that Palmer first started using the expression in the Bell (now called the Pig and Bell), a public house that stands beside his house, after Mrs. Bradshaw had run in there claiming that he had poisoned yet another of his own children and that he also used the expression in the Shoulder of Mutton.

Unfortunately there is no way of knowing if this is true or whether this is yet another apocryphal tale that has sprung up from the Palmer story.

The *Staffordshire Advertiser* 14th June 1856, under the heading of "PALMER'S TRIAL – ANOTHER SPORTING VICTIM", carried the following report from the *Leeds Intelligencer*:-

Information was received in Wakefield on Thursday, that a person named Fisher, coachman to Colonel Smyth, M.P. for York, had committed suicide, in consequence of having lost a large sum of money betting on the probable acquittal of Palmer. He has left a wife and four children, who are living in this town.

Chapter 37: Miscellany – Palmer's Death Masks

Gruesome Artifacts

Palmer's Death Mask as it was in the County Records Office Photograph D. Lewis 1979

After the execution, as was the custom in those times when someone had been executed, a death mask was made, which was a plaster cast of the criminal's head. To make a mask they poured either hot wax or Plaster of Paris over the head to make a cast. A phrenologist is one who studies external bumps of the skull as an indication of supposed various intellectual and emotional faculties.

Mr. Bridges, a phrenologist from Liverpool, made one of the masks. I first saw this half death mask in the County Records Office at Stafford but now it is on display at Shugborough in the County Museum by kind permission of the owners, the Trustees of the William Salt Library.

Notice that Palmer had had his head shaved prior to his execution. It was claimed that he did this because the prison authorities had taken his comb and brush off him. This latter action would be taken as a precaution to stop Palmer attempting to use them to commit suicide. He gave his hair to his relatives as a remembrance of him

There was, however, a mystery as the mask in the Shugborough display is only half a head.

In George Fletcher's book *The Life & Career of Dr. William Palmer of Rugeley* published in 1925, there appears a photograph of a full cast *"made after W*ᴹ*. Palmer's execution"*. Efforts to find the whereabouts of this full cast, rather than the "Stafford half head", have initially proved unsuccessful.

Since I wrote the Palmer story web site, a third death mask by a different phrenologist, has come to light. Ross Turle, Curatorial Assistant at Winchester Museums Service contacted me with a picture of another Palmer death mask. It is a complete head but its base is different to the one in Fletcher's book.

Ross informed me that this death mask is

Palmer's Death Mask From Fletcher's 1925 book

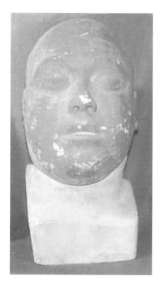

The Winchester Death Mask

believed to have been in their collection since the late nineteenth century when it was given to them by Winchester Prison, along with 28 other masks. Inscribed on the plinth of the Winchester death mask is the following:- *"The first cast of William Palmer taken by William Bally, Phrenologist of Manchester, the 14ᵗʰ June 1856 Stafford"*.

Unfortunately Winchester's collection of masks is not currently on display to the public and it is not known how or why the mask arrived in Winchester Prison. This picture was kindly sent to me by Ross Turle in May 2002.

Had I read the *Staffordshire Advertiser* 21ˢᵗ June 1856, I would have solved some of the mystery more quickly. The newspaper stated that:

Two casts were allowed to be taken of the head of Palmer after the execution on the Saturday morning.

The newspaper further stated:-

Mr. Bally, we understand, used a composition invented by himself, by which he is enabled to reproduce the texture of the skin; and secure that the plaster cast shall be precisely the size of the head. Mr. Bally was a pupil of Spurzheim; and he has taken casts of the heads of a very large number of condemned criminals in England and Ireland; but he has not in his collection, nor has he seen, a head so contracted in the sincipital region as that of Palmer's organisation:-

After a complicated phrenological description Mr Bally's summary was printed by the *Stafford Advertiser* quoting from the Manchester Guardian:-

Without saying that this is a type of head of what has been called the "poisoner class," Mr. Bally thus sketches the character he should predicate phrenologically:- A man who, as a rule, would be respectful, polite, and even charitable; but one who, for any preconceived object, would act most cunningly and secretly, perfectly indifferent to honour or truth; and who in such a case would be careless what became of the most intimate acquaintances or the nearest relative. Speaking generally, Palmer's head presents much the same conformation as that of Rush, but is less in size. Palmer's temperament was sanguine and lymphatic.

Mr. Bridges, practical phrenologist, of Liverpool, who also took a cast of the head, pointed out to those present at the time, *"the great deficiency of the moral region, and particularly the want of conscientiousness; the enormous base of the brain; the great preponderance of the selfish propensities which in such a head overruled all others.*

Mr. Bridges remarked that a man with phrenological developments like Palmer was *"capable of murdering to any extent by poison, but he was destitute of that determination which characterised men who, like Rush exercised great daring in carrying out their crimes. The head was altogether of the worst kind, and was inferior even to that of Rush, Gleeson, Wilson or Burke; it was of the type perculiss to the class who resort to poison."*

Are there other copies of the death masks that we have not yet discovered? What happened to the death mask in Fletcher's book?

Chapter 38: Miscellany - The Hangman

George "Topper" Smith the Dudley "Higgler"

The hangman who hanged Palmer was George Smith from Dudley. He had been a nailer (a nail-maker) but other accounts say that he was a hob-nailer (a shoe maker), before he became an apprentice hangman in 1840. He once was put in gaol for running naked through the streets of Wednesbury. Another time he was in Stafford Gaol for debt and failing to support his wife and family.

In 1840, at a time when George Smith was last a "guest" at Stafford Gaol, the regular hangman was a well-known hangman named William Calcraft. He charged the standard fee of £10 for hangings and he also performed the floggings. Calcraft was due to hang two of the men who had been found guilty of the Christina Collins murder (a crime committed on the canal near Rugeley and known as the "Bloody Steps" murder). His assistant then was a man called Mr. Cheshire nicknamed "Old Cheese". On his way to Stafford, Cheshire stopped at Rugeley to visit relatives, but they would have nothing to do with a hangman's

assistant. So instead he visited the Shoulder of Mutton where he became so drunk that he forgot the time and never arrived in Stafford to perform his assistant hangman duties.

Calcraft became more and more agitated waiting for his assistant to arrive. In desperation he approached the prison governor, Thomas Brutton, and asked if he knew of anyone who could assist him. The governor refused to let any of the turnkeys perform the task but suggested paying-off the debt of a prisoner in gaol for owing money, so that they could then assist him. So Calcraft paid Smith's debts and he was released in time to start a new career as an assistant hangman.

Smith went on to learn the trade from the famous Calcraft who was also from Dudley. Smith, as apprentice hangman, would have to wait below the trap door of the gallows through

A photograph of George Smith. It can be seen in the Palmer Display at the County Museum at Shugborough. Staffordshire Arts & Museum Services

which the condemned prisoner would drop. Sometimes the prisoner could take up to five minutes "dancing on the rope" before they finally choked to death. If they were taking too long to die Calcraft would stamp on the platform and Smith would have to speed up the process by jumping up and hanging on their legs.

It is widely believed that Calcraft was originally chosen to hang Palmer but George Smith offered to do the job for only £5 believing that by performing this hanging his reputation would be made for life.

A hangman in the nineteenth century was sometimes referred to as a "higgler". It was Smith's habit to wear a white smock with a top hat upon his head when he was "working" (see picture opposite). His nickname "Topper" might have referred to his habit of wearing a top hat or more likely because he "topped" people. He also had the nickname "Throttler" Smith.

In local public houses Smith was often bought his favourite drink by patrons eager to hear his stories of the men he had "sent to meet their maker" and as long as the drinks kept coming he would regale them with stories of his "infamous clients". George Smith himself died on Good Friday 1874.

If you wish to read more about the life of George Smith I would recommend that you read the first chapter of *A Memorable Medley of Great BLACK COUNTRY CHARACTES* by **Aristole Tump, a Bugle Publication.** The cover of the book (pictured left) bears an incredibly well preserved photograph of George Smith which is in far better condition than the picture on the previous page.

What of Palmer's Clothes? In the 1912 booklet "Palmer the Poisoner, Full and Authentic Account" I found the story that at 6 o'clock on the morning of his execution Palmer requested that he be brought a suit of prison clothes. The reason given in the booklet was that the clothes worn by a prisoner who is executed became the property of the executioner, however if the condemned person wore prison clothes the executioner could not claim them as they were government property. I find the next part of the booklet's story a little far fetched when it says that, when questioned, Palmer said:

"Am I within my rights in demanding the clothes?"

"Yes, I believe you are." replied the Governor.

"Then sir, my reason is that I do not want my clothes to fall into the hands of Madame Tussaud and be exhibited," was Palmer's surprising reply.

The Governor hesitated, and then ordered a suit of prison clothes to be brought. The first suit Palmer rejected, saying they were too worn, and when fresh ones had been procured he dressed himself with great nicety.

More than twenty years ago John Godwin gave me a copy of some verses about the hangman Smith which are reproduced below:

Smith's a toppin' fella,
With Calcraft he does work,
No matter what the contract,
He's never known to shirk.

He'll hang a pretty damsel,
Or a preacher old and grey,
And he's never late for duty
When it comes to Hanging Day

He swings upon the felon's legs,
When Calcraft springs the trap,
Then finds the nearest tavern,
To down his rightful "drop".

"Black Billy" is his tipple,   *("Black Billy" rum)*
Which he downs with certain glee,
A-drinkin' all the time to toast,
To Calcraft's Hanging Tree.

Source unknown

John Godwin also gleefully told me some more gruesome details concerning the hangman's craft. He stated that Calcraft had favoured "the short-drop" method which often resulted in a felon taking up to five minutes to finally choke to death. If the victims death struggles continued for too long Calcraft would stamp three times on the platform and it was George Smith's unpleasant duty to jump up, grab and swing on their legs until their death struggles ceased. He claimed that necks could be stretched by up to almost a foot (30 centimetres). He told me of one occasion when he claimed that, with Smith being such a hefty fellow, the victim's neck stretched and eventually tore away from the head causing Smith to crash to the floor holding a headless twitching body. The head alone remained attached to the noose. Fortunately for Palmer, George Smith did not employ "the short-drop" method.

Chapter 39: Miscellany - Rugeley's Name

Famous for the wrong reasons

There is another lovely tale, unfortunately apocryphal, that is associated with the Palmer case. A story was started, and passed down from generation to generation, suggesting that the inhabitants of Rugeley were absolutely horrified by the adverse publicity that Rugeley received before and during Palmer's Trial. The newspapers had a field day with several articles a day devoted to the case many being very disparaging about Rugeley. The Rugeley townsfolk believed that Rugeley's name had acquired worldwide notoriety and would be forever linked to the murderous actions of the by then infamous Dr. William Palmer. So outraged were Rugeley's inhabitants that it was decided to send a deputation down to London to petition Parliament to have the name of their town changed.

The story continued that, after listening to their complaints, the Prime Minister smiled and agreed instantly saying, "Of course! Why not name it after me?" Unfortunately the then Prime Minister was called Lord Palmerston and the last name that Rugeley would wish to be called was Palmerstown!

A lovely story; but that is what it is, only a story not based upon fact!

There is evidence from the World War I, that even then, more than fifty years after the trial, Rugeley had retained its notoriety. Troops stationed on Cannock Chase arriving at Rugeley's railway station commented upon this being the home of "The Poisoner".

The card on the right carries the inscription from the tombstone that was placed upon Cook's grave some years after his death. It is a memorial card for John Parsons Cook (typical of black edged memorial cards given out in Victorian times to relatives and friends of the deceased). Thought to have been sold as a postcard in Rugeley up until about 1905.

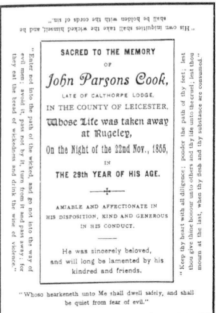

The inscription on the card and his tomb are incorrect as Cook died at about 1.00 a.m. on 21st November 1855 <u>not</u> 22nd November 1855. An example of this card can be seen on display at The Palmer Display at the County Museum at Shugborough Hall.

Chapter 40: Miscellany - His Demeanour

His demeanour: The calm prisoner. "His soft hands"

Neighbours regarded Palmer as a religious man; he noted down in his diary his attendance at the local parish church and often who delivered the sermon. He made notes in the margins of the family bible. Many, in the early part of his life as a doctor, considered him a generous man ready, without charge, to give help and advice to the poor and needy.

In the *Times Report of the Trial of William Palmer for Poisoning John Parsons Cook* printed in 1856 they said the following of Palmer on the first day of the trial:-

The prisoner is described in the Calendar as "William Palmer, 31, surgeon, of superior degree of instruction." In appearance Palmer is much older, and although there are no marks of care about his face, there are the set expression and rounded frame which belong to the man of forty or forty-five. His countenance is clear and open, the forehead high, the complexion ruddy, and the general impression which one would form from his appearance would be rather favourable than otherwise, although features are of a common and somewhat mean cast. There is certainly nothing to indicate to the ordinary observer the presence either of ferocity or cunning, and one would expect to find in him more of the boon companion than the subtle adversary.

His manner was remarkably calm and collected throughout of the whole of the day. It was altogether devoid of bravado, but was respectful and attentive, and was calculated to create a favourable impression. He frequently conversed with Mr. Smith his professional adviser, and remained standing until the close of the speech for the prosecution, when at his request his counsel asked that he might be permitted to sit - an application which was at once acceded to by Lord Campbell.

It might seem very strange but in 1856 there was a great deal of comment surrounding Palmer's hands. In the *Rugeley Number of the Illustrated Times* 2nd February 1856 Page 91, under the heading of "PALMER'S HAND" the following account appeared:

Wherever we went we heard people talk of Palmer's hand. In the coffee-room of the Talbot Arms three commercial gentlemen were chatting together about this terrible hand so white and soft. At the Bell, we are told that Palmer used to hold the wrist of the patient and feel the pulse in such a manner that his delicate hand might be seen to the best advantage.

There is something extremely horrible in the idea, that the hand which drops poison into the cup, and tenders it to the victim, should be round, white, and dimpled - such an one as you could not suspect of doing any injury.

Palmer, we were told by a gentleman who was his intimate friend, had very "pretty" hands, and he was very fond of and careful of them. He would rub them to keep them white, and when talking would sit still picking or trimming his nails, and looking at his fingers. The hand was small, and almost womanly. It was round, plump, and dimpled, and he had a great objection to touching anything which could in any way soil or stain them. He did not wear a ring, or show much of his shirt-cuff; but he was constantly washing his hands, and whenever he did, occupied much time in thoroughly drying them."

Robert Graves in his 1956 book, *They Hanged My Saintly Billy,* said this of Palmer at his trial:

William Palmer certainly looks at least ten years more than his thirty-one, with which he is credited on the indictment. He is solidly built, very broad-shouldered and bull-necked, though not above the average height. His complexion is florid, his forehead high, his features somewhat mean, yet respectable enough. He has thin, lightish-brown hair; brushed back over an almost bald head, and whiskers inclining to red. Nothing in his appearance suggests either ferocity or cunning; and his manner is exceedingly calm and collected, without a trace of bravado, guilt or remorse. Shrewd observers, however, will notice a remarkable discrepancy between the ruddy coarseness of his face and the extreme prettiness of his hands - which are white, small, and dimpled, almost womanly in their appearance, and which he spends a deal of time admiring as he sits in the box, sometimes picking at his nails for lack of a penknife to trim them neatly. He is no longer allowed to wear wash-leather gloves as a protection for those hands against the sun, but little sunlight penetrated into the County Gaol and House of correction at Stafford this last winter, and their colour seems to afford him great satisfaction.

His Characteristics:
Neat and tidy:
He was always an extremely neat dresser and one of his friends described him as, "The neatest man about the house I know".

The Good Host:
He gave very good dinner parties and the food and drink were always of a good quality.

Sober:

Unlike many of his friends and associates he did not drink heavily and was not seen drunk above once. Often his guests were seen to leave his house less than sober but he drank in moderation.

Well-mannered:

People spoke of his good manners and general politeness always pleasant and affable and never lost his temper.

Kind:

People regarded him as "a decent sort of a fellow". He was known to be generous and he treated the former workers at his father's wood-yard well. As a doctor he did not always charge his less well-off patients for their treatment. He was also very affectionate to his family especially towards his mother.

Afraid of sleeping alone:

It was said that after his wife's death he was afraid of sleeping on his own. When he was away at the races he would often share a room with one of his racing colleagues.

Calm and Composed:

In a criminal broadside Published 1856 in Bristol we found the following passage describing Palmer as Lord Chief Justice Campbell delivered the sentence:

During the whole of his Lordship's address, the prisoner retained the same composure which he had evinced throughout the whole proceedings, and did not seem, in the slightest degree, moved. At the conclusion of the sentence,he gave a glance at the bench which was occupied by several nobility, and then walked down the steps leading into the prison with a firm step.

The Globe states as a fact, that as Palmer was stepping out of the dock, on the adjournment of the court, previous to the conclusion of Lord Campbell's summing up , he dropped a note into the hands of Mr. Smith, his solicitor, stating that he felt perfectly certain of an acquittal.

Palmer and Charles Dickens:

Charles Dickens, the famous author of such books as *Great Expectations*, *David Copperfield*, *Oliver Twist* and many other classics, is known to have been fascinated by the Palmer Case, just as he had been interested in another famous poisoner Thomas Wainewright. In 1837 Wainewright was transported to Hobart Town, Van Dieman's Land, not hung for his crimes as Palmer was. On November 13th 1849 Dickens was present at the hanging of another famous poisoner Frederick Manning and his wife Maria for the murder and robbery of Patrick O'Connor. Dickens was known to be an opponent of capital punishment.

In 1856 Charles Dickens wrote an article about Palmer's Trial for *Household Words* a London weekly journal. In the article Dickens showed his fascination for Palmer's demeanour, which was always calm and controlled, and when the verdict of guilty was delivered he commented that Palmer had seemed interested but unmoved apart from his compulsive toying with his gloves. Dickens wrote:

THE DEMEANOUR OF MURDERERS

The recent trial of the greatest villain that ever stood in the Old Bailey dock, has produced the usual descriptions inseparable from such occasions. The public has read from day to day of the murderer's complete self-possession, of his constant coolness, of his profound composure of his perfect equanimity. Some describers have gone as far as to represent him, occasionally rather amused than otherwise by the proceedings; and all the accounts that we have seen, concur in more or less suggesting that there is something admirable, and difficult to reconcile with guilt, in the bearing so elaborately set forth.

As whatever tends however undesignedly to insinuate this uneasy sense of incongruity into any mind, and to invest so abhorrent a ruffian with the slightest tinge of heroism, must be prejudicial to the general welfare, we revive the detestable subject with the hope of showing that there is nothing at all singular in such deportment, but that it is always to be looked for and counted on, in the case of a very wicked murderer. The blacker the guilt, the stronger the probability of its being thus carried out.

Later in the article Dickens wrote:

Can any one, reflecting on the matter for five minutes, suppose it possible – we do not say probable, but possible – that in the breast of this Poisoner there were surviving, in the days of his trial, any lingering traces of sensibility, or any wrecked fragment of the quality which we call sentiment? Can the profoundest or the simplest man alive, believe that in such a heart there could have been left, by that time, any touch of Pity?

*An objection to die, and a special objection to be killed, no doubt he had: and with that objection very strong within him for divers very weighty reasons, he was – not quite composed. Distinctly **not** quite composed, but, on the contrary, very restless. At one time, he was incessantly pulling off his glove; at another time, his hand was constantly passing over his face; and the thing most instanced in proof of his composure, the perpetual writing and scattering of little notes, which, as the verdict drew nearer and nearer, thickened from a sprinkling to a heavy shower, is in itself a proof of miserable restlessness.*

In 1859 Dickens wrote a short story for the *New York Ledger*, which was printed in three parts called *Hunted Down*, reprinted in *All the Year Round* in

1860. The narrator is a Chief Manager of a Life Assurance Office. Another of the characters Beckwith reminds me of Palmer's brother Walter, but unlike Walter, Beckwith did not drink all the alcohol supplied by the would-be murderer but pretended to do so to trap him. Another character, the murderer Julius Slinkton, is said to have been modelled on another murderer Wainewright, but I feel he also had more than a little of Palmer in his calm manner. In *The Mysteries of Edwin Drood* a Dicken's character John Jasper shows a calm innocent face with his anxiety only shown, like Palmer, by the agitation of his hands.

A likeness of Dr. William Palmer from a drawing by Joseph Simpson, said to have been drawn from Palmer's death mask. From *Trial of William Palmer* (Part of the *Notable English Trials Series*) Second Edition published in 1923 revised by Eric R. Watson. (Original edited by George H. Knott published in 1912)

Chapter 41: Miscellany - Palmer Blackmailed

Blackmail (the infamous "Jane Letters"):

In the William Salt Library, Stafford there is an extraordinary collection of thirty four letters known as the "Jane Letters" written by Palmer to a secret lover called Jane. These letters were not discovered at the time of Palmer's trial or used at that time to discredit Palmer.

In this chapter are images taken by D. Lewis of a folded note which is the most unpleasant and shocking of the letters and is reproduced by kind permission of the owners of the letters the William Salt Library. In the letter Palmer is trying to persuade Jane to visit "the best dentist in Stafford". The "dentist" was actually an abortionist and was named Cooke. It is thought that this was James Cook of Forebridge Street, Stafford, who was advertising his services as a chemist and druggist in the 1850's.

Page 4

P.S. You see I am
not afraid 'to write
as I speak' because
I am sure that you
will burn this as
you have burnt the
others.
                    W.P.

The William Salt Library Reference
Number. D(W)1545/7/25

Page 1
Burn this
My dear Jane,
    Ascot tomorrow
so I must repeat
by letter what I said
to you on Sunday
because I wish
you very much to
do it - it wont hurt
you worth mentioning
and as I said you
have had toothache

164

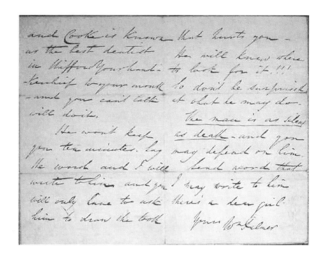

Page 2	Page 3
and Cooke is known	*that hurts you.*
as the best dentist	*He will know where*
in Stafford. Your hand-	*to look for it!!!*
-kerchief to your mouth	*So don't be surprised*
- and you can't talk	*at what he may do.*
will do it.	*The man is as silent*
He won't keep	*as death and you*
you ten minutes. Say	*may depend on him.*
the word and I will	*Send word that*
write to him and you	*I may write to him*
will only have to ask	*there's a dear girl.*
him to draw the tooth	*Yours, Wm Palmer*

We do not know for certain exactly who Jane was, with three possible surnames suggested, Burgess, Bergen and Bergin. The reason we cannot be certain of the true identity of Jane is that none of the accounts of Palmer's life mentioned his love affair with a Stafford girl called Jane until 1912. In that year G. M. Knott who was editing the *Notable English Trials* books, was the first to publish any mention of the letters, which had then been loaned to George Fletcher. Knott stated that a young woman called Jane Burgess left the letters at her Stafford lodgings. Dudley Barker in his 1935 book *Palmer the Rugeley Poisoner* also referred to her as Jane Burgess.

George Fletcher, in his book *The Life & Career of Dr. William Palmer of Rugeley* published in 1925, says this of the "Jane Letters":-

.... *thirty four letters written by Palmer to Jane Bergen, in the early months of 1855 up to the time of Cook's death. I have had the original letters submitted to a great expert in handwriting, and he says that they are undoubtedly all in Palmer's writing. They consist of thirty-four letters written to a Miss Jane Bergen, in a most lascivious, degrading style. They are not mentioned in any account of Palmer's life, except in the introduction to the trial in 'Notable Trials'. They show unmistakably the nature of the illicit intercourse existing between them both, and Palmer gives the name and address of a doctor in Stafford, who, he says, would be "silent as death," and who performed an illegal operation successfully on her.*

She kept all the letters - much to his surprise - and when he was unable to help her with much (or any) money she threatened to show these letters all round, unless he sent her £50 (after asking for £100). He sent £40 the very day he and Cook returned from Shrewsbury races.

I need scarcely say the letters are not fit for publication. But they are well written and clear, showing a man of education, though of a most disgusting nature.

It appears that in around 1902 George Fletcher had heard from a contact in Stafford that a tobacconist W. S. Wile possessed a collection of letters said to have been written by Palmer. Fletcher tried unsuccessfully to buy the letters but did manage to loan them, had them authenticated and it was he who showed them to G. H. Knott.

Historian John Godwin in his booklet *Pocket Palmer*, like Robert Graves in his 1957 book *They Hanged My Saintly Billy*, suggested her name was Jane Bergen and that when she suspected she was pregnant she had blackmailed Palmer by threatening to tell her father Daniel Scully Bergen who was the Chief Constable of the Stafford Rural Constabulary. Anne Kettle argued that there is no evidence that the mysterious Jane was Jane the daughter of Daniel Scully Bergen.

Following her research Anne Kettle concluded that the most likely Jane appears in the 1851 Census as a Jane Bergin, aged 22, a milliner living with her father Francis Burgin, a clerk of the land commissioners. The Bergin Family lived at 13, Martin Street, next to the Independent Chapel. In the *1851 White's Directory of Staffordshire*, Francis Bergin was listed as a dealer in hides and his daughter Jane as a milliner and dressmaker. There is no trace of the family in local directories after 1854 when Francis Bergin's wife, Sarah, advertised her services as a milliner. My own guess would also favour Bergin as being the surname of Palmer's lover.

Robert Graves, in *They Hanged My Saintly Billy*, was wrong when he said, "*Unfortunately, the thirty-four lascivious letters written by Dr. Palmer to Jane Bergen have disappeared since 1933, when Dr. Fletcher's collection of 'Palmeriana' was dispersed at his death.*" However Dudley Barker stated that in 1933 the letters became the property of Mr. Bernard Woollaston of Stafford, the great-grand-nephew of Superintendent Woollaston who had been responsible for Palmer's safe custody during his trial at the Old Bailey.

The "Jane Letters" are now kept at, and are the property of, the William Salt Library (Ref No. D.1548) and the information below is reproduced by kind permission of the Trustees of the Library. I am also indebted to a copy of work done on the letters by Ann J. Kettle but I have slightly changed the order of the letters.

The story contained in the 34 letters from Palmer to Jane is fairly easy to follow. In 1855 Dr. Palmer, by now a widower, wooed Jane and the letters make it obvious that Jane and Palmer were having a secret love affair. She became worried that she might be pregnant and Palmer encouraged her "to visit the dentist" (code for a visit to an abortionist). Jane did not burn his letters but used them to blackmail Palmer.

· **Letter 1: Planning an "accidental" meeting -**

My dear Miss Jane,
    I shall not be able to meet you at the Station but if you come straight to the back of the Grand Stand I will meet you <u>accidentally</u> and will take care that you have a pleasant day.

        Yours faithfully,

            Wm. Palmer
Rugeley, Tuesday morning

· **Letter 2: Wooing Jane with poetry -**

My dear Jane,
    How are you this morning? I shall see you this afternoon and then –
"As soon as night shall fix her seal upon the eyes and lips of men, oh dearest! I shall panting steal to nestle in thine arms again."

        Yours,

            Wm. Palmer

167

Letter 3: Meeting re-arranged -

My dear Jane,
    I cannot possibly be with you on Tuesday but you may expect me on Wednesday evening. Will that do for you?
        Yours,

          Wm. Palmer

Letter 4: Secrecy and innuendo -

My dear Jane,
    Break your journey on Saturday - book - to Rugeley – come to my surgery with your handkerchief to your face - no one will be in but <u>myself</u>. I will perform an <u>operation</u> on you and you can have a snack and go on by the next train.

        Yours,

          Wm. Palmer

Letter 5: With gifts – 'the food of love' -

My dear Jane,
    Send the enclosed note to Frantz by an errand lad, he will bring back a lobster, etc. I am coming tonight to help you to eat it.
        Yours,
          W. Palmer

Letter 6: More secrecy:

My dear Jane,
    If Mrs. K. calls on you or sends anybody poking into your affairs you will know what to do.

Mum's the word.

        Yours,
          W. P.

Letter 7: Concern for her health:

My dear Jane,
   I can't today, will try tomorrow.
   Is your cold better?

           Yours,
               Wm. Palmer

Letter 8: A missed meeting:

My dear Jane,
   I missed you - were you there?
   I shall be at Shrewsbury on Friday.
   Drop me a line.
           Yours,
               W.P.

Letter 9: Disappointment -

My dear Jane,
   No note for me at Shrewsbury. I hope you are well.
   I shall call on Monday,
           Yours,
               Wm. Palmer

Letter 10: His "supper" -

My dear Jane,
   Will you send the enclosed note to Frantz and give me my supper tonight.

           Yours,
               W. P.

Letter 11: Arranging to meet:

My dear Jane,
    I meant to have called before leaving the town to ask you to meet me at Lichfield next week. Will you?
    Write by return.
        Yours,
            W. P.

Letter 12: More meetings -

My dear Jane,
    You are the right sort. Be near the west door of the Cathedral at 11 o'clock on Wednesday - and leave the rest to me.

        Yours,
            W. P.

Letter 13: innuendo? -

My dear Jane,
    How do you feel today? Hope you slept well last night.

        Yours,
            W. P.

Thursday morning

Letter 14: Waddell = Dr. Cornelius Waddell of Tipping Street, Stafford. Was Palmer trying to insure Jane's life?

My dear Jane,
    Don't see Waddell until I have seen you which will be in the course of a few days.

        Yours,
            W. P.

Letter 15: Palmer tries to reassure Jane when she fears that she is expecting, it is the first time he gives the instruction "Burn this". -

My dear Jane,   Burn this

Don't trouble yourself - we can wait for a couple of months and see. All can be   made right easily. And I can drop in at any time?

I shall be over on Saturday.

      Yours,
          W. P.

Letter 16: More secrecy -

My dear Jane,
    I ran against Mrs. W. and Mrs. T. just now - they said they were going to call on you and had I seen you lately? Yes - I had been to ask you for slips of your pansies for my mother.

You will get this before they arrive – hadn't you better tell them where I passed the night?

      Yours,
          Wm. Palmer

Letter 17: Was medical opinion being sought before a possible insurance? Again the order to "Burn this" -

My dear Jane ,   Burn this
    I knew Waddell would find you all right. Of course he did not discover anything. Did he ask for a kiss? Or did he take one without asking?

      Yours,
          W. P.
Sunday morning

Letter 18: Worried about a proposed insurance?

My dear Jane, <u>Burn this</u>
I think the Devil is in it. Waddell says you had better not propose - that means that he will report unfavourably - so there will be a difficulty raising the needful for you as intended – though I am pressed you shall not suffer.

Yours,
W. P.

Letter 19: Compliments and innuendo:

My dear Jane ,
A lady asked me just now how I liked last night's concert. I said very well but I preferred a duet which followed.
So I did - rather - did you?

Yours,
W. P.

Letter 20: Palmer had upset Jane:

My dear Jane,
I do not know what to make of your last letter – "What do I intend?" Well I think it would be better to see and tell you. Shall I come on Sat. evening?

Yours,
W. P.

Letter 21: Playing hard to get?

My dear Jane,
I think you are rather out of temper. You would not let me come on Saturday - and you do not say when I may. I wish you would fix a time.
Any day but Thursday next week will do for me.

Yours,
Wm. Palmer

172

Letter 22: Palmer's letter when Jane suspects that she is pregnant?

My dear Jane,
I can't make you out - of course I am sorry that you are unwell. Perhaps the face ache is caused by that. I shall be over tomorrow.

Yours,
Wm. Palmer

Letter 23: A most sinister letter Palmer uses the 'dentist' as a euphemism for an abortionist -

My dear Jane ,   Burn this

Ascot tomorrow so I must repeat by letter what I said to you on Sunday because I wish you very much to do it - it wont hurt you worth mentioning and as I said you have had toothache and Cooke is known as the best dentist in Stafford. Your handkerchief to your mouth - and you can't talk will do it.
He won't keep you ten minutes. Say the word and I will write to him and you will only have to ask him to draw the tooth that hurts you. He will know where to look for it!!!
So don't be surprised at what he may do.
The man is as silent as death and you may depend on him. Send word that I may write to him there's a dear girl.

Yours,
Wm. Palmer

P.S. You see I am not afraid "to write as I speak" because I am sure that you will burn this as you have burnt the others.

W.P.

Letter 24: The abortion has been arranged. Cooke probably James Cook a chemist/druggist from Foregate Street, Stafford -

My dear Jane,   <u>Burn this</u>
    You are a good plucked one. I have written to Cooke - do just as he tells you - send me word how you get on.

        Yours,
            W.P.

Letter 25: Jane has had the abortion, Palmer sends two £5 notes cut in half -

My dear Jane,   <u>Burn this</u>

    All's well that ends well. I am glad that you were so little hurt - in a week or two you will be all right again. I enclose halves of two £5 notes. Say you have got them and I will send the others.

        Yours,
            W.P.

Letter 26: A Cautious Palmer sends the other two halves of the £5 notes -

My dear Jane,   <u>Burn this</u>
    I am deucedly sorry to hear that you are so unwell - but you have got rid of the <u>cause</u> and now as old Tylecote would say the effects will cease.
    Remaining halves enclosed - send me word you have them and that you are better.

        Yours,
            W.P.

Letter 27:   More money "to silence Jane":

My dear Jane,
I enclose halves of four £5 notes. Acknowledge receipt and I will forward the others - they can't be traced.

Yours,
W.P

Letter 28:   £20 given to Jane -

My dear Jane,

Enclosed are the remaining halves - drop me a line by return to York to say they are all right.

Yours,
Wm. Palmer

Letter 29: Note that Palmer's drunken brother Walter died on 16th, buried 20th August 1855:

My dear Jane,
Walter's funeral went off very well.
I caught sight of you at the window - when shall I call?
Hope you are all right now?

Yours,
Wm. Palmer

Letter 30: Palmer and Jane aware of gossip? -

My dear Jane,

Your letter is hard to understand. What queer things are people saying? Some damned chatterboxes can't mind their own business and are looking after mine, are they? You can't say I have used you ill. Let us speak of a man as we find him is my motto.

Please write and say why you think I "had better not call for a few weeks".

> Yours,
> Wm. Palmer

Letter 31: More poetry as he haggles over the amount of blackmail to be paid. Written on the same day as Cook's horse Polestar won at Shrewsbury and Cook was taken ill -

My dear Jane,   Rugeley, Nov. 13th 1855

It's <u>damned hard</u> for a fellow to find his friends turning against him and I was surprised to learn that you have never burned one of my letters - I cannot do what you ask

- <u>I should not mind giving £30 for the whole</u> of them though I am hard up at present. If you agree you shall have the money in the course of a week or ten days.

I enclose the only letter of yours I can find.

I shall always think with pleasure of our intimacy and can say with Moore:

We've had some happy hours together
But joy must often change its wing
And Spring would be but gloomy weather
If we had nothing else but Spring

Oblige me with an early reply and believe me, Dear Jane,
> Yours truly,
> Wm. Palmer

Letter 32: Blackmail - A compromise sum agreed (£40).

My dear Jane,

I am agreeable to split the difference and will send you £40 in notes tomorrow or the day after and shall expect you - <u>honour bright</u> - to let me have the letters on return of Bearer.

> Yours,
> Wm. Palmer

Letter 33: Part of the blackmail paid -

My dear Jane,

Enclosed you have halves of eight fivers. Please acknowledge receipt and I will send remainders.

In great haste.
> Yours,
> Wm. Palmer

Letter 34: Blackmail paid in full - Note that John Parsons Cook, for whose murder Palmer was hanged, died 1.00 a.m. on Nov. 21st 1855 :

My dear Jane,   Nov. 24th 1855

Remaining halves of notes enclosed.
Please keep letters for me until I send for them.

> Yours,
> Wm. Palmer

P.S. You have no reason to be unfriendly to me, remember. W.P.

The letters were not made public at the time of the trial and their affair was not general knowledge. The letters, however, do little to enhance the reputation of Palmer or Jane.

Background dates:

Palmer's wife Anne died September 29th 1854. On June 26th 1855, Palmer's housemaid Eliza Tharm gave birth to a son who later died on December 13th 1855. Jane must have had her abortion sometime around the beginning of August 1855. Cook died 21st November 1855.

Chapter 43: Miscellany – Criminal Broadsides

Carrying the news

Criminal broadsides were large single sided papers often crudely printed and usually having woodcut block prints as illustrations. These were sold for a penny or half-penny at the time of hangings by hawkers or 'chapmen'. They were important sources of reading material for the general public, most of whom could not afford to buy books.

The one on the left is the one that I first came across and is the property of the William Salt Library, a copy is on display at the County Museum at Shugborough. It was printed on the day of the execution by Hill & Haden, Printers, Stafford. It bore the title: "LIFE, TRIAL, AND, EXECUTION OF WILLIAM PALMER, FOR THE WILFUL MURDER OF JOHN PARSONS COOK, AT RUGELEY Nov. 20th 1855.

(*Note that Cook actually died in the early hours of the 21st November*)

The second broadside I found was found via a search on the Internet. The broadside was on the web site of Kent State University in Ohio, America. Originally printed in 1856 by John Chapman, 10 Lamb Street, Saint Judes', Bristol, England, it was donated to the university by Albert I. and Helen O. Borowitz, as part of the Borowitz True Crime Collection, catalogue *No. 79 Life, trial and execution of William Palmer*. It is particularly interesting because it took the unusual step of naming most of the jury.

A photocopy of their broadside

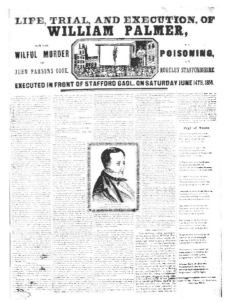

was kindly sent to me by the university's Special Collections & Archives Department. The verses found in its right hand column are reproduced in Chapter 44.

I went in to the William Salt Library to donate a photocopy of the criminal broadside that I had received from Kent State University. Mr. Randle Knight overheard my conversation and later e-mailed me to say that he had got yet another broadside.

He stated in his e-mail-

It is in poor condition with some small parts missing. It is headed 'TRIAL AND EXECUTION OF WM. PALMER, For poisoning at Rugeley, MR. JOHN PARSONS COOK', and includes two pictures, one of Palmer in his cell with a priest and two officials, and the other of him hanging on the scaffold.

It concludes with some verses, which are reproduced in the Chapter 44. Part of the printer's name is missing, with the rest reading: "PRINT . . . ERS AND EDWARDS STEAM PRESS, CANNON ST . . . .". (I been unable to discovered in which city it was printed)

Mr. Knight kindly allowed me to photocopy the broadside. A Dr. Edward Knight was one of Annie Thornton's guardians before she married William Palmer. Dr. Knight was the son of the Reverend John Knight who had been the vicar of Milwich and our Mr. Knight is a descendant of the vicar's brother. Randle bought the broadside at an antique shop in Market Drayton.

It is interesting to note that the last broadsheet is particularly inaccurate in that one block print shows a man confessing his sins and another a hanging on top of a prison gatehouse. In fact Palmer never ever confessed to murdering Cook and the execution was on a portable gallows in front of the prison gatehouse. Prints depicting a hanging were often reused for several different executions.

✦ ✦ ✦ ✦

I know of the existence of one other broadside published in London, but I suspect that there would have been other broadsides produced in other cities at the time of Palmer's execution. It is my hope that others will be tracked down.

Chapter 42: Madame Tussaud's, London

In the Chamber of Horrors

It is thought that Dr. William Palmer is the only inhabitant of Rugeley to have had a wax image in Madame Tussaud's Waxworks in London. For over a hundred years, from 1857 up until 1979 a waxwork figure of Palmer stood in their famous Chamber of Horrors. The modeller from Madame Tussaud's is said to have been present at court during Palmer's trial.

Madame Tussaud's kindly sent this picture of Palmer's wax effigy to me in 1979.

Palmer's effigy that stood in Madame Tussaud's until 1979.

In the museum's souvenir programme he shared a page with the likes of the murderers Burke and Hare. Of Palmer they merely wrote "Palmer poisoned his wife, brother and friend for £20,000".

Chapter 44: Miscellany -
Palmer Poetry/Ballads from 1856

Words "inspired" by Palmer's Story

From the sixteenth century onwards broadside ballads, popular songs, were printed on one side of a single sheet of paper and sold to the public by street sellers for a penny or halfpenny. These ballads provided cheap lyrics, which could be sung to popular tunes. The sheets usually had one or two 'woodcut' prints and verses printed on them. In the Eighteenth Century a common theme for ballads was the execution of criminals. Some broadsides also contained verses.

Up until September 2002 I had traced two broadsides with 'Palmer' verses and three individual ballads dating from 1856 which are dedicated to William Palmer, although I am certain that there would have been more than this. On the broadsheet which was originally printed in Bristol, that I tracked via the Internet to an America university library, were verses which are reproduced below:

A Copy of Verses: From part of a criminal broadside published in 1856 by John Chapman, 10 Lamb Street, Saint Judes', Bristol. The property of Kent State University in Ohio, America, donated to the university by Albert I. and Helen O. Borowitz, part of the Borowitz True Crime Collection; catalogue No. 79 Life, Trial and Execution of William Palmer.

Come christian people pray attend,
Unto those lines that here are penn'd,
Now I ascend the gallows high,
That I may be prepared to die.

Oh! What an awful sight to see,
A murderer on the gallows tree,
Young Men be warned by Palmer's fate,
Repent before it is too late.

In Rugeley town where he did dwell,
For many years respected well,
And E'er that he had reached his prime,
His hands are stained in blood and crime.

Oh! God of mercy hear the prayer,
And of thy pardon give a share,
When the dread moment it shall come,
Accept one through thy own dear son.

Young men be honest through your lives,
Husbands be kind unto your wives.
Refrain from gambling in your youth,
And tread the path of grace and truth.

Dear friends dry up the briny tear,
Kind heaven protect my mother dear,
My brothers and relations too,
Who came to take a last adieu.

She's praying for her wretched son,
That his poor soul be not undone,
And you who set a mother's part
Will strive to heal the broken heart.

Be warned by me both young and old,
And shun the love of cursed gold,
It may lead to murder in the end,
And sacrifice your dearest friend.

What gathering crowds around I see,
Young people all be warned by me,
Bad company and drinking shun,
And gambling or you'll be undone.

Relations, friends, all efforts tried,
But justice would not be denied,
Let's hope we all may meet in heaven,
Forgive as you would be forgiven.

Another Poem from 1856: Verses which were part of the criminal broadside, published to coincide with Palmer's execution, entitled TRIAL & EXECUTION OF WM. PALMER. For Poisoning at Rugeley, MR. JOHN PARSONS COOK. (Taken from a copy of the broadside which was the property of Mr. Knight, detailed in the previous chapter). Unfortunately the right hand side of the verses are damaged and also a small patch in the middle of the second verse. I have put question marks where some of the text is missing. In brackets and in italics are the suggestions of

A broadside –
The property of Mr. R. Knight

Mr. Knight as to what the missing words might be:-

You feeling Christians give attention, young and old of each ?? *{degree}*
A tale of sorrow I will mention, who will sympathise with ??   *{me}*
The fate of that unhappy culprit, William Palmer was his ??   *{name}*
And for the crime of dreadful murder, died a death of pub??   *{lic shame}*

All on the fourteenth day of June, was the day the wretch ??   *{would die}*
In woe and wail at Stafford gaol, before the public he did ??   *{??}*
In health and vigour, in you ??   *{th}* and bloom, upon the fatal g??   *{??}*
Compelled to fill a murderer's tomb - it was a shocking sig??   *{ht}*

When William Palmer did appear, upon the drop at Stafford Gaol,
It would extract a briny tear, or make the strongest man grow pale;
Christians all, a while consider, think what must his feelings be,
All for the crime of wilful murder, launched into eternity.

To see this wretched man to tremble, on his execution day,
Tens of thousands did assemble, for to hear what he should say,
The dreadful murder he related, mounted on the gallows high,
He seemed as if he had repented, fully reconciled to die.

The rope on him was soon adjusted, and the fatal bolt was ??   *{drawn}*
How sad to say, the light of day, before his eyes had o??   *{??}*
To see the wretched man suspended, struggling in t??   *{he throws of death}*
Until the spark of life was ended, thus he did resi??   *{gn his breath}*

Oh, Christians who have heard my story, mark you ??   *{well to what I say}*
Pray unto the Lord of Glory, to protect you night an??   *{d day}*
Only think on William Palmer, oh, that ever he????   *{??}*
Little did his kindred think, that he should die i ????   *{n such a way}*

A Broadside Ballad sold at the time of the execution: I found this via
Rugeley Library entitled "Life and Trial of Palmer" by David D. Cooper (sold at
Palmer's execution).   From the book 'The Lessons of the Scaffold' page 111 -
Allen Lane 1874.

Oh listen unto William Palmer
Who does in anguish sore bewail
Now guilty they at last have found me
And sent me back to Stafford Jail.
Every one appears against me.
Every person does me hate,
What excitement is impending
On guilty William Palmer's fate,

184

CHORUS
My trial causes great excitement,
In town and country everywhere.
Now guilty found is William Palmer,
Of Rugeley town in Staffordshire

Many years I was a sportsman,
Many wondrous deeds I've done
Many a race I have attended
Many thousands lost and won.
They say I poisoned my wife's mother
And took away her precious life
And dear poor Cook and my own brother,
And poisoned my own lawful wife.

Everything looks black against me
That I really must confess
The very thought that does oppress me
Causes me pain and distress,
Now the jury did convict me
And prove I did commit the deed
And sentence passed on William Palmer
To Stafford I was sent with speed

In Rugely I was once respected   (Rugeley mispelt on original)
A gentleman lived at my ease
With noblemen I was connected
And sporting men of all degrees
Although a doctor no one knew me
To do anything amiss
Now everyone strives to undo me
I never thought I'd come to this.

My poor old mother now at Rugeley
My awful end must now bewail
To know her son must die with scorn
a felon's death in Stafford Jail
Every charge alleged against me
I have strongly it denied
Twelve long days my trial lasted
and now I am condemned to die.

Dreadful is my situation.
Before the awful bar I stand

185

I might have filled a noble station
Unfortunate unhappy man
Infants yet unborn will mention
When to manhood they appear
The name of Doctor William Palmer
Of Rugeley town in Staffordshire.

Will no one sympathise with Palmer
Who every charge did strong deny
You are all aware I am found guilty
For by jury I've been tried
My situation makes me tremble
I am borne down with grief and care.
All conversation is of Palmer
Of Rugeley town in Staffordshire.

Ballad No 2: from the Bodliean Library, University of Oxford, entitled
"Lamentation and Confession of Palmer" Rial, Printer Monmouth-court, 7 Dials.
(This is A. Rial and Co. Printers, London)

In Rugeley town I was born and reared,
All in the County of Staffordshire,
Where I must die full of youth and bloom,
At Stafford, on the fourteenth of June.
Tens of thousands approached to see,
William Palmer die on the dismal tree.

From Stafford town they did me convey,
To the Gaol of Newgate without delay.
Where twelve long days did my trial last,
At length the sentence on me was passed.

They summoned witnesses from far and near
The evidence against me was clear,
And they was determined I well could see,
That I should die on the fatal tree.

When tried and sentenced they sent me down
A malefactor to Stafford town;
I caused my family much grief and pain,
They sent petitions but t'was all in vain.

They was determined my days should end,
They swore I poisoned my only friend,

186

They said I murdered John Parsons Cook,
Then stole his wealth and his betting book.

Farewell my mother, oh! A last adieu,
Oh what disgrace I have brought on you,
My own kind brother and sisters dear,
And all relations in Staffordshire.

Good bye my dearest, my lovely boy,
Did a wicked father your hopes destroy?
None shall upbraid you for what I've done,
My ever sweet little orphan son.

You have no father or mother now,
My conscience smites me I can't tell how,
Oh God forgive me for what I've done,
And be a father to my darling son.

Where is my father? the child did say,
From his little boy he's gone away,
He little thought sweet and tender lamb,
His father died on the scaffold stand.

This is the morning, the awful time,
When I must die, aged twenty nine,
And while my bones in the grave do rot,
The name of Palmer will ne'er be forgot.

My friends strove hard, but could not save,
I see the hangman, I view my grave.
In the prime of life, vigour, health and bloom,
They have hurried Palmer to his silent tomb.

My time is come, I am doomed to go,
My glass is run from this earth below,
My guilty soul speedily takes it flight,
Here's the end of Palmer, what a dreadful sight.

Under the title of Lamentation & Confession of Palmer it gives the tune as AIR – The Nightingale.

Before the words of the ballad there is the following text:

On the Thursday morning before execution, Palmer was particularly dejected. Mr. Goodacre, the chaplain, gave him the best advice he could, showing the distinction between private sins and public crimes, and pointed out, the latter demanded a confession before man. Palmer replied, "If it is necessary for my soul to confess this murder, I ought also to confess the others," adding, after a short pause, "I mean my wife and brother." He then threw himself on the pallet in his cell, and buried his face in the clothes. He shortly after said, he had neither denied nor admitted his guilt.

I cannot find any other report of this conversation in any other writings from 1856 and have to doubt the authenticity of the claims made by this broadside.

Ballad No 3: I first came across this ballad in 1980. It can also be found on the Bodliean Library web site. It is entitled "Palmer's Farewell to the Turf"

Farewell ye sporting young men,
Who spend your money free,
Give over all your gambling,
And a warning take by me.

Farewell to every race course,
In England's happy land,
On you I've spent my happy days,
Among the sporting band.

For now into this prison strong,
In fetters I do lie,
Confined into a dungeon dark,
By men condemned to die.

My sisters and my brothers all,
I must bid you adieu,
For this it is the last time
That ever I'll see you.

I wish that my burial day,
My birthday it had been,
And wrapt into my winding sheet,
And ne'er this grief had seen.

Farewell my darling Mother,
My heart will break in two,
When I think on the great disgrace,
That I have brought on you.

I have brought your grey hairs,
To the grave in sorrow and shame,
But pray for mercy unto me
Through that all sacred name.

Farewell my dear and only boy
I must leave you all alone,
May Heaven be your protection
When I am dead and gone,

And cruel men upbraid you
With my murders and my crimes
I hope we'll meet in yonder world
In happy blissful climes.

Your mother dear lies in her grave
It makes my heart to bleed,
When I think on her gentle spirit,
And on the murderous deed.

I loved her dear, yet for the sake,

Of thirteen thousand pound,
To pay my debts of honour,
I laid her in the ground.

And Walter, too, my brother dear,
And Cook my faithful friend,
Which has brought me to this fatal day
And this untimely end.

Farewell world - friends - and foes,
No more of you I'll see,
For now I'm sentenced to be hung
Upon the gallows tree,

Farewell to Rugeley's pleasant town,
You will tell in future time,
Of crimes of William Palmer
Who poisoned by strychnine.

I have always suspected that there would have been other broadsides produced at the time of Palmer's execution and hoped that others would be tracked down so I was delighted in January 2003 to receive the following e-mail:

Hello Dave

I see from your website that you are interested in William Palmer the Rugeley Poisoner. You may be interested to know that at our sale of autographs, historical documents and ephemera we are selling what appears to be a completely new contemporary broadside (actually about quarto size) called 'Copy of Verses on the Execution of William Palmer who underwent the extreme penalty of the law at Stafford on Saturday June 14 1856'. There then follows a set of verses as though Palmer has written them himself "My solemn hour at last is come, and thousands flock to see, a wretched culprit end his days, upon the fatal tree etc etc etc."

It is slightly creased but complete and in otherwise good condition, considering that it is printed (by W Pratt of Birmingham) on typical flimsy paper.

We are selling it by auction on Thursday March 14th in Ludlow, Shropshire. Further details on the sale nearer the time. If you would like any further information about the sale, please contact me via reverse email or you can call me.

Regards
Richard Westwood-Brookes
Mullock-Madeley

COPY OF VERSES ON THE
EXECUTION OF WILLIAM PALMER

Who underwent the extreme penalty of the law

AT STAFFORD.

On Saturday, June 14, 1856.

My solemn hour at last is come,
And thousands flock to see,
A wretched culprit end his days,
Upon the fatal tree.
To die a death of sad disgrace,
Exposed to public scorn,
It would have been a happy day,
If I had not been born.

Alas! William Palmer is my name,
Awful my death bell sounds,
The grave lies open—I must go—
Lord, have mercy on my soul.
Poor Cook I murdered—
How awful to relate,
And in the prime of youth & bloom
I meet my wretched fate.

In Rugeley town I did reside,
All with my friends so dear,
Who often times advised me,
To alter my career.
My wicked course I still did run,
My folly now I see,
Alas, William Palmer is my name,
I must die on the gallows tree.

In a dark and dismal cell,
My silent hours I spend,
Thinking of my only child,
And of my awful end:
My aged mother little thought,
When she was nursing me,
That I should die a public show,
Upon the fatal tree.

In dungeons dark, in irons bound,
I bitterly do weep,

The midnight bell and thoughts of
death,
Deprived me of my sleep:
Poor Cook appears to me,
His agonies he displays.
No rest, no peace can I get
He's with me night and day.

Lord, have mercy on my soul,
Have mercy, Lord, I cry,
Oh, claim my spirit as thy own,
Before the day I die:
My blessed Saviour, I know Thou
died,
Upon a shameful tree,
For sinners spilt Thy precious blood
Upon Mount Calvary.

Farewell, my child, farewell,
My troubles will soon be o'er,
I hope I soon shall meet with you,
On Canaan's peaceful shore;
Dear mother and brothers, dry up
those tears,
For me I pray don't fret.
I am going a little time before,
To pay this worldly debt

Adieu, vain world, adieu,
Likewise my mother dear,
I pray you think upon my child,
When I am no longer here:
A warning take by my sad fate,
All who come to see my end,
And when my spirit takes its flight,
May it to heaven ascend.

W. Pratt, Printer, 82, Digbeth, Birmingham,

A broadside published in 1856 by W. Pratt Printer 82, Digbeth Birmingham. Note that the original was crudely printed and not straight on the page. Reproduced by kind permission of its new owner Mr. Randle Knight. © RWK.

A week after the auction I was delighted to be contacted by Mr. Randle Knight to inform me that he had purchased the broadside and that I could photocopy the original for use on the Palmer web site and in this book (see previous page).

✦ ✦ ✦ ✦

A Counterfeiting Problem in 1856

In the *Staffordshire Advertiser* 7th June 1856 under the heading of "A COUNTERFEIT INDEED" I found the following paragraph:

With reference to the portraits of Palmer a correspondent of the Newcastle Guardian says:- "There are, as you will suppose, none of them of very great accuracy; but the most atrocious of all is one which, some 12 or 13 years ago, when the CORN law agitation was at its height, did duty for a portrait of Mr. Cobden. Some scoundrel of a printseller, it seems, has got hold of the plate, has hammered out the name of Cobden, and inserted that of Palmer and in that condition the rude cheat is selling about the streets at a penny."

Please note that, to the best of my knowledge, all items included in this book are genuine.

Chapter 45: Miscellany – Memorabilia

Other items of interest associated with the case

It was inevitable that a case as notorious as Palmer's was bound to generate many items of memorabilia. In view of the fact that, sometime after Palmer was arrested, all his possessions were seized and sold to pay his debts there must be a great many more items of memorabilia than I have unearthed so far.

Robert Graves in his book, *They Hanged My Saintly Billy*, reported that numerous bills to the value of £10,400 "fell due" after Palmer's arrest and that Palmer couldn't, and his mother wouldn't, pay. Mr. Wright a solicitor from Birmingham was refused entry to Palmer's house by Mr. Bergen a Rural Superintendent who had been given the job of safeguarding the contents of the house which included papers, drugs, other household items, furniture and 222 gallons of Palmer's home brewed ale, 67 dozen bottles of port and 43 gallons of other spirits. Mr. Wright however, got in by breaking the glass in the scullery window then opening the latch. He then made arrangements for a public auction of the Doctor's effects. The sale drew enormous crowds to view Palmer's belongings although there were more sightseers than buyers. Several items were stolen as souvenirs and most items were sold for less than their true value by an auctioneer who wanted to finish his business quickly. In the end he sold everything in ten hours.

When his property was seized it is thought that his faithful maid-servant Eliza Tharme managed to save his instrument case but all other items were sold. It is assumed that the instrument case is the one that is now the property of the Trustees of the William Salt Library currently (Year 2003) on show at The County Museum, Shugborough.

*Palmer's instrument case
Photographed by Andy Holt.
(April 2001)*

A Manchester photographer, Mr. C. Allen was keen to make money from the notoriety gained by the Palmer case so he hired "Palmer's House" for a day to take peoples photographs. A copy of his tradesman's card was reproduced in *They Hanged My Saintly Billy* by Robert Grave.

The County Museum at Shugborough Hall, which stands between Stafford and Rugeley, has a small Palmer Display containing a number of items.

The Items in the display which are the property of The County Museum are

as follows:-
- A memorial card for John Parsons Cook (*a typical black edged memorial card given out in Victorian times to relatives and friends of the deceased*).
- A print of Palmer's House (thought to have been published by the then owners of the house).
- A prescription issued to Dr. Palmer dated Tuesday 20th November 1855.

The Items in the display which are the property of the Trustees of the William Salt Library currently (Year 2001) on show at The County Museum are as follows:-
- A death mask - a half mask. (See Chapter 37).
- Palmer's own medical instruments case.
- A commemorative jug dated 1861 given to Inspector Ellis Crisp a Rugeley superintendent at the time of Palmer's trial.
- A photocopy of a 'criminal broadside' that was published in 1856.
- A copy of a photograph of George Smith the hangman taken in 1874. (See Chapter 38)
- A picture of Palmer drawn from the death mask.

In the autumn of 2002 Phyllis Higginson of the Tamworth Civic Society e-mailed me to say that Tamworth Castle had appointed a new Collections Officer, with a brief to audit and assess the collections of artefacts that the museum had stored in various places. In the early stages of this audit she discovered a wooden cabinet that was reputed to have belonged at one time to William Palmer. The contents of the cabinet are as follows:

In the top compartment - baby feeder, metal miniature balance (metal rusted), 3 glass bottles with glass stopper, Grey Power, James' Powder, Dover's Powder, large glass jar with metal top Epsom salts, SOD Salts with glass stopper, unidentifiable glass bottle with glass stopper (this one has a leak and is stuck), Bicarbonate of Potash, a metal measure and a glass measure 10-60 ml

In the front opening door - 5 Glass bottles with glass stoppers, 1 label illegible, Mindererus' spirit, Tincture of Myre, 1 unidentified with contents degraded into layers of varying colours, and 1 empty bottle with pepper coloured residue,

In the 4 drawers – Drawer 1: Brass measuring spoon, small glass bottle with cork, white substance (label illegible), small glass bottle cork broken off inside, cream substance (label illegible). Drawer 2: Drawer with loose powder under sliding lids labelled "Callcined Magnesia" and "Fine Turkey Rhubarb". Drawer 3: Drawer with two lead interiors, no labels, contents not identifiable. Drawer 4: Drawer with miniature glass mortar and pestle.

The cabinet is thought to have been part of a large collection donated to Tamworth Castle in 1952 by a former Mayor of Tamworth, Councillor Frederick

These pictures are the copyright of Tamworth Castle Museum and are reproduced here with their kind permission.

Pictures taken in December 2002

Alfred Addison Allsop, an avid collector of curios. Allsop died in September 1959 in Tamworth Hospital aged 75 years. It is thought that Allsop got the cabinet from a friend of his William Macgregor who was a "philanthropic gentleman" who came to Tamworth from Liverpool and was a vicar in Tamworth.

The murder, being in Staffordshire, gave local back-street Stoke-on-Trent potters the chance, in 1856, to produce 'souvenirs' of a pottery house and a figurine of Palmer. At a meeting of the Landor Society, the local history group in Rugeley, I saw a remarkable collection of four Palmer pottery houses which were brought along by Mr. and Mrs. Pope (see picture below). Each house had been individually coloured in enamel and each one was quite differently coloured to any other house. The houses are based upon a print from the Illustrated London News 24th May 1856. The Pope's latest acquisition is a Palmer figurine (see picture) bought through a contact I had made. Examples of these two pottery pieces can also be seen in the Potteries Museum and Art Gallery in Hanley, Stoke-on-Trent.

1856 Palmer Figurine from the back street potters of Stoke-on-Trent, in enamel colours with a gold title.

There are other items of memorabilia in private hands: A booklet entitled *Palmer the Rugeley Poisoner, Full and Authentic Account* by Reginald B. Jones was written in 1912 and published by the Daisy Bank Printing and Publishing

Company, Wellington Street, Gorton, Manchester, priced 3 old pence. I was loaned a copy by Mr. John Godwin. It was given to John by Glen Chandler who wrote the two part series for Yorkshire Television entitled *The Life and Crimes of William Palmer*, a 180 minute two part series, directed by Alan Dosser, filmed in 1998 and starring Keith Allen, Jayne Ashbourne and Chloe Newsome.

The booklet (see picture below) gives a somewhat sensational account of the Palmer story. It starts:

Doctor William Palmer, poisoner, forger, and robber, who cast a slur on the fair name of Rugeley which can never be effaced whilst memory endures. Even to-day, 56 years after Palmer's terrible crime, as the mail trains go rushing through the peaceful little Staffordshire town on their journey from the north to London, all eyes peer through the carriage windows, and passengers point out to each other the town "where Palmer the Poisoner lived."

Other places larger than Rugeley have had their disgraces but have lived them down, time having mercifully cast oblivion over their ill-fame.

Not so Rugeley, for the crime that Palmer committed was so outrageous and revolting that even when another generation has come and two reigns have closed since the fell deed was perpetrated, still is the murderer's wickedness kept green, and his accursed name passed on from one sire to son as the height of human wickedness. The town for over half a century has groaned under her shame, and efforts have been made to change the name, but without avail. It seems as if Palmer's name will for ever overshadow and blight the town.

John Godwin also owned an embroidered napkin (pictured right by A. Holt) from Palmers wedding day on 7th October 1847. It was given to him by Mr. E. Toye who was a Rugeley historian.

The following is embroidered on the napkin:-

18
William Palmer
47

The watercolour (see next page) was photographed in March 2001, by Dave

Lewis, in its protective plastic cover. It is the property of the William Salt Library. It might be strange to see a little boy in a dress but that was not uncommon in the early part of the Nineteenth Century. Even at four or five years of age it appears that William Palmer had a love of horses and is seen pulling a toy horse. In the 1935 book *Palmer the Rugeley Poisoner* by Dudley Barker it is stated that two years before his book was written this unsigned watercolour was inherited by Mr. Bernard Woollaston, of Stafford. He was the great-grand-nephew of Superintendent Woollaston who was

responsible for Palmer's safe custody during his trial at the Old Bailey. Woollaston also inherited the Jane Letters and Palmer's death mask.

In the William Salt Library there are a number of pamphlets and sermons relating to Palmer dating from the 1856; but probably their most scandalous items of memorabilia are the collection of love letters written, in 1855, by Palmer to a lady known only as Jane. (For further details see Chapter 42).

Following an article in a local newspaper about the launch of our Palmer web site, I was contacted by a Rugeley pensioner, Mr. Thomas Cooper, who had a pocket inkwell (pictured below). When I visited him he told me about his late wife Florence (nee Williscroft). After Palmer had been arrested Florence's great-great-grandfather, Mr. Williscroft, and his wife had been given the job of cleaning Palmer's house before new tenants moved in. Whilst clearing out the cellar Mr. Williscroft, who lived at Colton, had found a pocket inkwell that he assumed had once belonged to Palmer, a fair assumption given Palmer's love of writing notes. The inkwell had been kept in his wife's family ever since.

Pocket inkwell found in the cellar of Palmer's House. The property of Mr. T. Cooper

Mr. Cooper also told me another story surrounding the Palmer case that had been handed down through his wife's family. After the first post-mortem on John Parsons Cook, Professor Taylor had requested that he be provided with extra samples for analysis. An uncle of Mrs. Cooper's great-great-grandfather, Mr. Williscroft, was a self-employed drayman. (A drayman was a haulier who had a dray, which was a horse-drawn cart, and could be hired to transport goods)

The uncle had been given the job of carrying the samples, taken at the second post-mortem, to Rugeley's Trent Valley Railway Station ready to be taken by train to Professor Taylor. As the cart slowed to cross over the narrow canal bridge several "ruffians", whom the family assume were employed by Palmer, dashed out from their hiding place behind the bridge parapet and bushes. In the struggle that followed the attackers failed to get their hands on the samples but succeeded in knocking the uncle unconscious. The horses, startled by the attack, bolted, not stopping until they had carried the unconscious uncle all the way back to the stable yard at Colton.

When I was giving a talk about Palmer to pupils at Churchfield Junior School in Rugeley I met young Michael Cass who told me of Mrs. Davidson, his great grandmother, who was eighty four years old. She told me that, before World War II, when she was about eighteen years old, she had worked at the Shrewsbury Arms Hotel, working from seven in the morning to often as late as midnight if they were busy. She talked of Room 10 where Cook had died in agony. She told me with a chuckle that they cruelly put young married couples in Room 10. One morning honeymooners came down and asked her if she had knocked on their door as they had been woken in the early hours and they remarked that the floor was very peculiar, very uneven and they had also heard people walking about and talking in the room.

Mrs. Davidson had heard tales of ghostly sightings and stated that it was "a very creepy and a very spooky room". She remembered one particular gentleman who came to stay at the hotel and always requested Room 10. One year the room was already taken by a young couple but when they retired to their room they were horrified to find the gentleman in question lying in their bed. They reported this to Mrs. Davidson who along with the hotel owner, Mr. Ward, ran upstairs to confront the man. Mr. Ward was standing no nonsense and ordered the man to go to his own room or he would call the police.

Mrs. Davidson was also related to the Williscroft family mentioned previously in this chapter. Her version is different from Mr. Cooper's, saying that her great, great, great grandfather used to work for Palmer. He used to drive a horse and cart and would fetch hay from Colton where he lived for Palmers horses. One day he stopped at the Palmer's House where he was approached by Palmer who suggested, "Let me give you a drink whilst I fetch the money I owe you." Palmer gave him a drink and departed, however, the drink was poisoned and Williscroft fell backwards in to the cart with a thud which caused the horses to bolt. The horses ran all the way back to the farm at Colton, where it was discovered that Mr. Williscroft was dead.

In September 2002 I received an e-mail from Mr. John Tribe:

Dear Mr Lewis

I read with interest your web site about William Palmer.

In 1998, I sold via Christies 3 letters written by William Palmer the transcript of them is below. If you would be interested in seeing scans of the originals, I will organise for you to see them;

Letter 1: 23rd March 1851

Dear Sir , you can do what you like with my horse to send him back in the market so that I can get my money on at a little better price than he is now, but however I must be on at some price and shall leave myself entirely in your hands but if you look after Josh Royle and his friend you will find that they will lay against him freely for I have written to him by this post to say that the horse is coughing be sure to have his and his friends money. I saw the horse gallop yesterday and no horse in the world can be doing better, in fact he is fit to run for a man's life you must put me £300 on him but try if you can't get a better price than 3/1 and I shall find you plenty of commissions to execute. and now mind you if the public are all on before me I will take and scratch him.

Please let me hear from you by return of post. I shall leave here on Tuesday night for Northampton and shall stay at the Angel Hotel. Come and see me when you get in and I am dear sir.

Yours faithfully
Wm Palmer, Rugeley March 23rd 1851.

Letter 2: December 11th 1851

My dear Sir,

I know you are in always open to do anything that will make you a little money and to your advantage and I want you to lend me £1200 for 2 or 3 months (of course I shall be glad to pay you for the accommodation) and for your security I will either give you a bill or some deeds of some freehold land of my own or will make over all my horses to you in number about 15 or 16 or will give you such authority that you can either run them or not for the Chester Cup if the money be not returned to you-you must do this as I want the money to complete a purchase which will be of essential service to you and I. and I will come to town for the money - write to me by return and I am my dear sir

Yours faithfully,
Wm. Palmer, Rugeley, Dec 11th 1851.

Letter 3: April 25th 1852

Dear Sir,
I am very sorry that you should write such an angry letter - if I should
come to Newmarket I will find you money if I do not come you shall have
it before the races commence at Chester as regards "Quick Step" I have
taken as you know from Mr. Mounds 75/5000 which you can have to
cover what you have laid and as to the horse let me beg of you not to
hedge the money at present in fact not till you get to Chester and if it be
not hedged before the time of starting I will give you the money; so that in
that case you'll stand harmless. I ask this of you as a most particular
favour and by doing it when we meet at Chester I will tell you of a something
that you can win £500 by forget the past and I feel certain when we do
meet and I have explained to you how I have been treated by certain
parties you will be sorry for me I think one of my horses will be very near
winning and pray let me beg and entreat of you to come to an amicable
arrangement without the interference of Capt. Rees as I am certain it will
do you no good bear in mind that whatever you wish me to do with regard
to the money that you have laid out I shall do it on anything else I can and
I am dear sir

Yours truly,
Wm. Palmer, Rugeley, April 25th 1852

If I should not come please drop me a friendly line.

The pencil writing on the envelope containing the letters reads:

A knife has been driven through these letters by Wm Palmer trying to
murder Mr Swindell the letters were in his pocket and saved him. Given
to me by Mrs. Peter Saunders. 23.4.34 A.F. Somerset.

I hope that they are of some interest
P.S. A. F. Somerset was my Grandfather

John Tribe

John Tribe then sent me the following information concerning the letters:-
The story is as follows: My grandfather Raglan Somerset was recorder

of Gloucester in the late fifties and kept them in a walnut bureau which was sold in 1990. As a child I was fascinated by the fact that the pencil writing on the envelope containing the 3 letters, stated that a knife had been driven through the letters whilst they were in Mr. Swindell's top pocket. I suspect my Grandfather had kept them as memorabilia concerning a criminal legend. When the walnut bureau was sold in 1990, my mother suggested that I keep the letters and so they remained in my possession until 1998 when I saw that they were doing a drama about William Palmer, bells rung and I dug the letters out. With the help of a friend who deals in antiquities in London, I scanned the letters and we painfully deciphered them. I at the time needed to purchase a computer to continue my web designing. I approached Madam Tussaud's and the Staffordshire museum department both institutions suggested that they might be able to take them off my hands for a few quid, but were very off hand. The discovery appeared in the London Evening Standard. My friend then advised me to go to Christies who then auctioned them for me and I was told that they were purchased by the descendant of a woman who almost married the infamous Palmer. I looked out for announcements and publication of the letters but nothing appeared anywhere on the web apart from 1 site which mentioned that a man from Gwent had found Palmer letters in an attic and that they had been sold. There was no mention of their content. The other night I saw the letter scans in a directory on my computer, found your website via Google (an Internet search engine*) and emailed you.*

The letters certainly would confirm that Palmer was having financial difficulties as early as 1851, it would also imply from the note written on the envelope that he was trying to murder Mr Swindell.

I have heard a rumour that Palmer's table is now owned by someone living in Norfolk and that Palmer's desk was, at one time, in a doctor's surgery in Kent although so far I haven't been able to track either item of furniture. However it my hope that a lot more of Palmer's memorabilia can be tracked down.

Chapter 46: Miscellany – Views Now & Then

Evidence of the past

The Palmer family Vault from the *Illustrated Times* of February 2nd 1856. By then Joseph William's father, his wife Ann, his brother Walter and 4 of William's 5 children were buried in the vault.

This photograph of the Palmer Family vault was taken by D. Lewis in 1980. The house in the background on the right is where Palmer was raised.

Palmer Family Vault – Picture by D. Lewis January 2001.
It is thought that the vault was vandalised. The top now lies flat with the end side supports strewn on the ground to the right.

Palmer's House as it looked
in 1856
*The Illustrated London
News* May 24th 1856.

In Fletcher's 1925 book, this
was said to be photographed in
1855 and that the lady in the
doorway was his maid Eliza
Tharme. However, I feel that it
is far more likely to be a
postcard from about 1900.

Palmer's house later became a
post office and then an
ironmongers shop.
John Godwin's 1979
photograph.

"Palmer's House" much
changed in this picture taken
by Dave Lewis in March
2003.

The Talbot Arms where, in Room 10, John Parsons Cook died in 1855. Picture appeared in the *Illustrated London News* May 24th 1856. (Also see the picture on page 6)

Ex Talbot Arms – later called the Shrewsbury Arms - and The Shrew as it was called in 2001. Photograph taken by D. Lewis.

Chapter 47: Author's Final Thoughts
The book is finished, many questions still remain.

I first became interested in Dr. William Palmer in 1979 when I was the deputy headteacher at Etching Hill Primary School in Rugeley. I have always loved stories from local history and, whilst searching for local stories for my pupils, I stumbled upon the Palmer story. I became fascinated and spent months researching the case. I ended up writing a musical for our school's annual play, which was performed at the end of Spring Term 1980. With my pupils we produced a large display in the school's entrance hall but afterwards all the work was packed into a box and left in my loft to gather dust.

I have since moved house twice but still live and work in Staffordshire. Each time I moved, the box was transferred to our new loft. Twenty years later just before Christmas 2000 I went up in to the loft to get down the Christmas decorations and rediscovered the box. I thought about the hours of work that had gone in to tracing the story and the probability that, if I were to die, my wife or my children would probably throw the box in to the dustbin. By 2000 I was interested in computers and, when considering the best way to preserve the study, I decided to try and make a Palmer web site so that other teachers and pupils could use the information that I had gathered.

When the project was well under way I approached the school's history advisor for Staffordshire, to see if this work was of interest to the Education Department. She in turn passed me on to Andy Holt the Education Department's Web Manager. Andy was responsible for managing the Staffordshire Learning Net and especially for developing the Staffordshire Multimedia Archive. The SMA was a site containing hundreds of historical photographs and historical resources. He wanted my Palmer work for an exhibition site on the SMA.

The SMA used the Macromedia 'Dreamweaver' software package, so he put me in touch with a great local web designer, Jim Wheeler. Over the next five months I researched and wrote the text whilst Jim tirelessly worked on the visual impact and design of the site. In continuing my research this time round I had the benefit of using the Internet to aid me. From a few web pages the site just grew and grew until, after five months of hard work, the site resembled a mini-encyclopedia on Palmer. The launch of the web site was in June 2001, timed to coincide with the 145th anniversary of Palmer's hanging. The SMA has been replaced by the Staffordshire Past Track site (the Palmer web address is now **www.staffspasttrack.org.uk/exhibit/palmer**).

Since the site was launched I have received many e-mails sending me additional information, I have even had an e-mail from one of Palmer's direct descendants living in Australia, who had read my web site. I the spring of 2003 Jim and I worked together again to produce a new Palmer web site to bring together all the resources from the Palmer story **www.williampalmer.co.uk**. On this web site we highlight the places from the Palmer story that can still be seen today. I have worked with Kevin Smith the landlord of the Surgery Café Bar and Lounge, Crabbery Street, Stafford, to produce a permanent Palmer display. One of the murals created by Mark White is a large picture of Palmers head (see below). Some of the local drinkers swear that his eyes follow you as you move around the room, although I suspect that this might have something to do with the alcohol they consume. It is hoped to have a display in the Shrew, Rugeley.

Wall mural by Mark White at the Surgery Bar in Stafford.
Based upon a likeness drawn from his death mask
From the Trial of William Palmer
(part of the Notable English Trials Series)
Second Edition published in 1923 revised by EricR. Watson.
(Original edited by George H. Knott published in 1912).

I had been challenged to change my Palmer web site knowledge into book form so that Palmer's fascinating story could reach a different audience and at last, in the year 2003, the result of the challenge is this book.

Many people still ask my opinion about Palmer's guilt or innocence -
I <u>still</u> say – Read all the rumours, the gossip and the evidence
<u>and then make up your own mind -</u>

Just how many, if any, did Dr. William Palmer poison?

Appendix I:
Items not included elsewhere

In 2001 Andy Holt, Web Development Manager for the Staffordshire L.E.A., created the likeness (below) of Dr. William Palmer. He took a photograph of the Stafford half-head death mask and then used modern software technology to add skin tones, eye-colouring, eyebrows and hair. The hair should perhaps be a little thinner and redder and the sideburns wider and shaped down towards the mouth, but it still is a very fascinating effort.

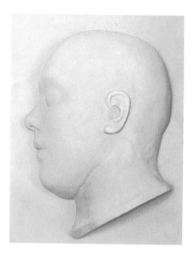 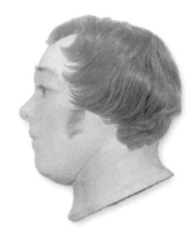

Acknowledgments: In the writing of this book I have been fortunate to receive a great deal of help and cooperation from many individuals. I would particularly like to thank the following persons: Andy Holt, Web Development Manager for the local Education Authority in Staffordshire for his IT technical knowledge and enthusiasm; Jim Wheeler web designer and computer "whizz-kid"; the late John Godwin, author of *Pocket Palmer*, who gave me tremendous assistance over many years; Kath Smith for her dissertation claiming Palmer's innocence; Tony Stanley for his knowledge of the history of Stafford Prison; Mrs. Thea Randall Head of Archive Services, William Salt Library; Roy Lewis retired history advisor for his extra historical knowledge and proof reading; Mr. Randle Knight owner of two Palmer broadsides); Glenda Chard, Linda Robinson and my son Adam (for proof reading and encouragement); Chris Copp curator at the County Museum Shugborough; Ross Turle, Curatorial Assistant at Winchester Museums Service; Sarah Williams at Tamworth Castle, Glenn Chandler writer of the two part Yorkshire Television series "The Life and Crimes of William

Palmer"; Fiona Pirrie Press Assistant, Madame Tussaud's; Mr. & Mrs. Pope allowing me to photograph their Palmer pottery; Philip Talbot, Mr. Cooper and Mrs. Davidson for their Palmer stories. I would also wish to thank anyone else, who has helped me with this mammoth project, whom I have failed to mention individually.

Last, but not least, I would like to thank my long suffering wife Chris (I hope William Palmer is not mentioned in any future divorce case) and my daughter Katie, for putting up with me whilst I have been involved in this long, long project.

There is probably more of the story yet to be discovered. If anyone has further information then I can be contacted by e-mail at:
dave_lewis_gnosall@hotmail.com

Appendix II : Suspicious Deaths

SUSPICIOUS DEATHS – GOSSIPS ACCUSED DR. WILLIAM PALMER

Dr. William Palmer
Christened by the newspapers as
"The Rugeley Poisoner"
&
"The Prince of Poisoners"

Born in
Rugeley
October 24th
1824.

Hanged in
Stafford
June 14th
1856.

Hanged for the murder of
John Parson Cook,
who died in November 1855.

Abley – First Victim?
Died after drinking with Palmer
October 1846.

Leonard Bladen.
Died in Palmer's House
May 1850.

Bly from Beccles
Date of death unknown.
(Reported in the Norfolk Chronicle)

Cross Keys Mystery
A navvy went missing
Was there a murder?

Spurrier's ghost
A Manx Murder?
Died after a bet with Palmer

Other suspicious tales:
"Aunty's chickens"
Mr. Williscroft

4 of his 5 Children
died in infancy 1851 – 1854.
Palmer accused of poisoning.

Uncle Joseph
Died after drinking with Palmer
October 1852.

Other Children
Jane Mumford's child died.
Palmer accused of performing abortions

Palmer's Mother-in-law
died in Palmer's house January
January 1849.

Palmer's Lovely Wife Annie.
Died after Palmer paid only one
insurance premium in Sept. 1854.

Palmer's Brother Walter.
Drink or poison?
Died August 1855.

Eliza Tharm's Baby - Palmer's
illegitimate son died
November 1855 after visiting him.

The "Rugeley Tragedies"

Other suspicious deaths

208

Bibliography
Useful sources of further information and study

Books used in the research for this book:
- **Illustrated Life, Career, and Trial of William Palmer of Rugeley** Pub. 1856 Ward and Lock
- **Illustrated Life and Career of William Palmer of Rugeley** Pub. 1856 Ward and Lock
- The Illustrated and Unabridged Edition of **The Times Report of the Trial of William Palmer**, for Poisoning John Parsons Cook of Rugeley. Pub. 1856 Ward and Lock
- **The Life & Career of Dr. William Palmer of Rugeley,** George Fletcher M.D.(Cantab); Pub. T. Fisher Unwin Ltd. 1925
- **The Verbatim Report of the Trial of William Palmer**, published by J. Allen in 1856.
- **They Hanged My Saintly Billy, Robert Graves** (First published in 1957 by Cassell & Company) **Pub. Xanadu Books (paperback edition)** ISBN 1 85480 004 3 (Due for reprint?)
- **A Memorable Medley of Great Black Country Characters** by AristotleTump
  A Bugle Publication 1986 *(For more detail on the hangman George Smith)*
- **Lord High Executioner** (An Unashamed Look at hangmen, Headsmen, and their Kind) Howard Engel, Pub. Robson Books Ltd. ISBN 1 86105 096 8
- **Palmer the Rugeley Poisoner** (1912) Reginald B. Jones Published by Daisy Bank Printing and Publishing Company
- **Palmer The Rugeley Poisoner** (1935) **Dudley Barker** One of the Rogues Gallery Series, Published by Duckworth
- **Trial of William Palmer (Part of the Notable English Trials Series)** original edited by George H. Knott published by William Hodge and Company Limited in 1912, Second Edition revised by Eric R. Watson, published in 1923.
- **The Pocket Palmer** (1992) **John Godwin,** Published by Benhill Press Ltd.
- **A book of the William Palmer story** that I found in the William Salt Library, Stafford (WSL reference number B1 PAL), written in Greek and published in 1860.
- **A booklet - Stafford Prison, Sentenced to 200 Years,** booklet by A. J. Standley

- **Gaols Staffordshire Study Book 1**, booklet by Staffordshire Education Department edited by R. A. Lewis 1974.
- **Pugilistica** (The History of British Boxing) Henry Downes Miles, Pub. John Grant. Edinburgh, 1906.

Newspapers from 1856 used in the research:
- The **Rugeley Number of the Illustrated Times** February 2nd 1856.
- The **Illustrated London News** – various from 1856.
- The **Staffordshire Advertiser** – various from 1856.

Pamphlet (with an unbelievably long title) from 1856 used in the research:
- THE CRIES OF THE CONDEMNED OR PROOFS OF THE UNFAIR TRIAL AND (IF EXECUTED) THE LEGAL MURDER OF WILLIAM PALMER, LATELY SENTENCED TO DIE ON A CHARGE OF POISONING AND Reasons why he should not be HANGED, From circumstances that have since Transpired, unknown to the Public, and which were not mentioned at his trial. with suggestions as to WHAT SHOULD BE HIS PROPER FATE INSTEAD OF SUFFERING DEATH. Including a Strong Parallel Case of the Uncertainty of Circumstantial Evidence, the Weakness of Human Judgment and the Danger of Sacrificing Innocent Life. Published in 1856 by C. Elliot 2 and 3 Shoe Lane, Fleet Street. Supposedly written by coroner Mr. Thomas Wakley a copy held by the William Salt Library, Stafford.

Also worth reading:
- **Infamous Victorians** *Palmer and Lamson* Giles St. Aubyn Published by Constable 1971.
- Chapter "What's Your Poison?" from **Midland Murders & Mysteries** by Barrie Roberts, published by Quercus 1997.
- Palmer Chapter in the **Staffordshire Casebook**, by David Bell published by Countryside Books.